CW0082591O

The British in rural France

Manchester University Press

New
Ethnographies

Series editor
Alexander Thomas T. Smith

Already published

Devolution and the Scottish Conservatives:
Banal activism, electioneering and the politics of irrelevance
Alexander Thomas T. Smith

The British in rural France

Lifestyle migration and the ongoing quest for a better way of life

Michaela Benson

Manchester University Press
Manchester and New York

Distributed in the United States exclusively
by Palgrave Macmillan

Published by Manchester University Press
Oxford Road, Manchester M13 9NR, UK
and Room 400, 175 Fifth Avenue, New York, NY 10010, USA
www.manchesteruniversitypress.co.uk

Distributed in the United States exclusively by
Palgrave Macmillan, 175 Fifth Avenue, New York,
NY 10010, USA

Distributed in Canada exclusively by
UBC Press, University of British Columbia, 2029 West Mall,
Vancouver, BC, Canada V6T 1Z2

British Library Cataloguing-in-Publication Data
A catalogue record for this book is available from the British Library

Library of Congress Cataloging-in-Publication Data applied for

ISBN   978 0 7190 8249 8   *hardback*

First published 2011

Typeset in Minion with Futura display by
by Special Edition Pre-press Services, www.special-edition.co.uk

Printed in Great Britain
by CPI Antony Rowe Ltd, Chippenham, Wiltshire

Contents

List of illustrations

Series editor's foreword

At its best, ethnography has provided a valuable tool for apprehending a world in flux. A couple of years after the Second World War, Max Gluckman founded the Department of Social Anthropology at the University of Manchester. In the years that followed, he and his colleagues built a programme of ethnographic research that drew eclectically on the work of leading anthropologists, economists and sociologists to explore issues of conflict, reconciliation and social justice 'at home' and abroad. Often placing emphasis on detailed analysis of case studies drawn from small-scale societies and organisations, the famous 'Manchester School' in social anthropology built an enviable reputation for methodological innovation in its attempts to explore the pressing political questions of the second half of the twentieth century. Looking back, that era is often thought to constitute a 'gold standard' for how ethnographers might grapple with new challenges and issues in the contemporary world.

The *New Ethnographies* series aims to build on that ethnographic legacy at Manchester. It will publish the best new ethnographic monographs that promote interdisciplinary debate and methodological innovation in the qualitative social sciences. This includes the growing number of books that seek to apprehend the 'new' ethnographic objects of a seemingly brave new world, some recent examples of which have included auditing, democracy and elections, documents, financial markets, human rights, assisted reproductive technologies and political activism. Analysing such objects has often demanded new skills and techniques from the ethnographer. As a result, this series will give voice to those using ethnographic methods across disciplines to innovate, such as through the application of multi-sited fieldwork and the extended comparative case study method. Such innovations have often challenged more traditional ethnographic approaches. *New Ethnographies* therefore seeks to provide a platform for emerging scholars and their more established counterparts engaging with ethnographic methods in new and imaginative ways.

Alexander Thomas T. Smith

Acknowledgements

From my fieldwork to the writing of this book many people have inspired, encouraged and helped me along the way. Without them this book would not have been possible, and their contributions, no matter how small, are not forgotten.

In particular, I wish to thank my respondents in the Lot for taking part in my research and opening up their lives to me. Special thanks are due to Andrew Lord for introducing me to the Lot in the first place and showing me this beautiful place through his eyes and camera lens. I am also extremely grateful to Brian and Mary Lord, and Sue Baxter for their generosity, hospitality, kindness, and support during my fieldwork, and to Peter and Lesley Phillips for the laughter and friendship that they showed me. And how could I forget Monsieur Exposito who saved me from being housebound by lending me a car when mine (inexplicably) broke down.

Since my time in the Lot, I have had the privilege of working with many exceptional people. The analysis presented in this book was originally conceived during my PhD and benefited from the continuous support and encouragement of my peers at the University of Hull and my supervisors, Mark Johnson and Vassos Argyrou. I owe Mark a huge debt of gratitude for his tireless engagement with my work and for gently persuading me to think more critically about my research. To Vassos I also owe thanks for the meticulous reading of my drafts and the lessons he taught me in how to write clearly and concisely; his eye for social theory challenged me to really get to grips with my arguments. I am also very grateful to my friend Julia Scott, who from the start listened patiently to my ideas and helped me to think clearly, and to Dennis Low, who taught me that the art of writing a PhD thesis lies in producing one beautiful sentence every page!

My colleagues in the sociology department at the University of Bristol, where I held my first teaching post following my PhD, were influential in helping me to refine my ideas further. And in 2008, I received a post-doctoral fellowship from *The Sociological Review*, which provided me with the time and space to write this monograph. I am particularly grateful to Caroline Baggaley and Roland Munro for their support during this period. I am also grateful to Tony Mason, commissioning editor at Manchester University Press, and Alex Smith, editor

Acknowledgements

of *New Ethnographies*, for their enthusiasm about this book and encouragement throughout the publication process.

Over the years, my colleagues on the Lifestyle Migration Hub have provided a sense of community and support. Special thanks goes to Karen O'Reilly, my friend, colleague and mentor. Perhaps of all the people I acknowledge here, Karen has had the greatest impact. Through her enthusiastic engagement with my research and her willingness to discuss and develop ideas, she has undoubtedly inspired my professional development. Indeed, it was at Karen's initiative that we, together, developed the conceptual and theoretical framework for explaining lifestyle migration. This development in the field has inspired me to think through my research at a much deeper theoretical level and has been instrumental in the production of this monograph.

My family – my parents Carol and Trevor, John and Eddie, my grandmother Wazira, my aunt Bubbles, and my siblings Roger, Melissa and Madi – have been with me every step of the way. This book is the result of their constant and unwavering belief in my abilities, and investments in my professional development. Lastly, but by no means least, I thank my partner, Dimitrios Theodossopoulos, for providing a supportive environment for me to undertake my academic enquiries, but most of all, for encouraging me to believe in myself.

Michaela Benson
University of Bristol, June 2010

Introduction

Ask anyone on the streets of a British middle-class town or village why their compatriots move to rural France and the answer will be immediate: the beautiful landscape, the good food and wine, cheap property and a slower pace of life. These impressionistic and aestheticized accounts are mirrored in academic explanations of this decision to migrate; as Tombs and Tombs summarize, 'the relative cheapness of France has for centuries permitted a genteel lifestyle, with a pleasant climate, sparsely inhabited countryside, and gastronomic pleasure' (2007: 655). It seems as though the decision to migrate to rural France is a self-evident truth. But to what extent do these presentations match the experiences of the estimated 200,000 Britons (Sriskandarajah and Drew 2006) who actually live in France today?

This book uniquely explores the everyday lives of the British living in the Lot, a rural, inland department (administrative unit) in southwest France. This focus allows critical insights into the intersections of imaginings of these post-migration lives – understood as located within a particular cultural framework – with their embodied experiences. As I argue, it is this tension between imagining and experience, between structure and agency that results in the ambivalence that characterizes the migrants' lives in the Lot.

On the one hand, I present the cultural logic that makes migration 'thinkable, practicable, and desirable' (Ong 1999: 5), highlighting the significance of cultural (and classed) understandings of life in the Lot in prompting migration to this particular destination. In this manner, I demonstrate that the rural idyll – an image of rurality favoured by the British middle class (Williams 1973) – not only inspired the act of migration, as other authors have argued (Buller and Hoggart 1994a; Barou and Prado 1995), but also framed their post-migration lifestyle choices. On the other hand, through the ethnography presented in the pages of this book, it becomes clear that life following migration does not always conform to its imaginings. As the migrants experience life in the Lot on a day-to-day basis, they gradually refine their ideas about the lives on offer there, incorporating their own embodied knowledge of how to live into their understandings and practices.

Through this lens, a nuanced understanding of post-migration lives emerges. While migration had been presented as transformative, resulting in the better

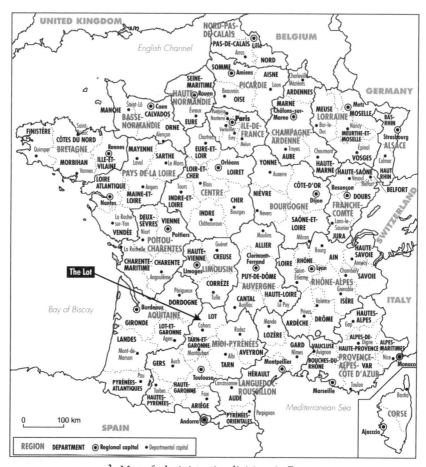

1 Map of administrative divisions in France

way of life that my respondents sought, through the examination of the lives led in the Lot, it emerges as just one step *en route* to a better way of life. The ethnography presented in this book thus explores the extent to which the migrants' lives remain characterized by the desire for distinction, marked by their rhetoric of authentic living, and questions what these ambitions and ideologies mean to and do for the migrants.

Setting the scene

The British migrants of today are the latest in a long line of Britons who have fallen for the charms of rural France. Documented accounts of British travel have extolled the virtues of an unspoiled and rustic France since the late nineteenth century (Tombs and Tombs 2007: 406). Early reports presented a voyeuristic view of rural France, and migrants of this era resembled their colonial compatriots, socializing exclusively with expatriates living locally (*ibid.*). But it was not until the late twentieth century that the number of Britons living in rural France reached significant levels (*ibid.* 2007: 654; see also Garriaud-Maylam 2004). As Garriaud-Maylam estimates, 'Britons … now own 3 percent of all 'rural space' in France, including vineyards, farms and forests' (2004: 271). These recent incomers differ from their predecessors; they do not only want to gaze on the social and physical landscape of rural France, they express a desire to be a part of it by becoming integrated into the local population (Tombs and Tombs 2007; Drake and Collard 2008; Benson 2010a), to live the quintessential rural French life, including the idea of returning to the land.

The Lot

Since the 1960s both nostalgic Parisians and north Europeans – predominantly British, but also increasing numbers of Dutch and other nationalities – have been snapping up property in the area. Initially, this meant holiday and retirement homes but nowadays there is a noticeable trend towards younger people coming to settle and work. (Dodd 2007: 396)

Lot has a relatively long history either as a Dordogne overspill, offering cheaper properties than Dordogne but in a largely similar landscape, or as an alternative to Dordogne for those seeking to escape the higher densities of British residents in that *département*. (Buller and Hoggart 1994c: 204)

The Lot, a rural, inland department in the Midi-Pyrénées region of southwest France (Figure 1), is a popular destination for both tourists and migrants from Great Britain. It is found within the former French province of Quercy, an area noted for its cuisine and wine. As Buller and Hoggart have argued, along with the Dordogne, in the Lot, 'the British percentage of their foreign populations is among the highest in France' (1994a: 56).

The most recent census data (2006) present a population of 169,531 in the Lot (INSEE n.d.). It covers 5,217 km², with the result that it has a low population density of 32.4/km²; to put this into some perspective, the average population density of the United Kingdom is 246/km².

With its sparse population, the Lot benefits from an incredibly picturesque appearance. Travelling along the river Lot, which traverses the south of the department, one witnesses the awesome limestone cliffs of the east (Figure 2) giving way to rolling farmland and vineyards in the west (Figure 3). On account of its inland location, the weather is generally dry and mild in the winter, while summer temperatures of around 28°C are interrupted only by the occasional thunderstorm.

Throughout the department, there is evidence of the local history and of the people who have occupied the land over the centuries. This evidence records that humans have lived in this part of the world since the time of Cro-Magnon man: the cave system that runs beneath the limestone cliffs is known for its prehistoric cave painting; dolmen (megalithic stone tombs) dating back to 7000 BC litter the

2 View over the river Lot and the limestone cliffs that characterize the landscape to the west of the department

3 View over the vineyards and countryside in the east of the Lot department

landscape; the Celts, migrating to the region around 700 BC, set up trade routes, towns and hilltop fortresses; and the Romans established the city of Divona Cadurcorum, where modern day Cahors, the prefecture of the department, is now located as the regional administrative centre, leaving behind ruins which are still being uncovered.

The history of the relationship between England and France is also etched on the landscape: landmarks such as Le Château des Anglais at Cabrerets remind the knowledgeable viewer that this land once belonged to the English throne, only to be lost during the Hundred Years' War. My respondents were aware of this history, stressing the Lot's credentials as 'a landscape steeped in history', thus informing their understandings of their new surroundings. As one of my respondents explained to me one morning as the mist rose off the fields outside his house, 'I can just see the cavemen running along the valley floor'. Others sought to connect themselves with this history. When Susan Sparrow's bank manager asked her why she moved to the Lot, she (jokingly) explained, 'we've come to reclaim the land that we lost during the Hundred Years' War'.

The recent history of the Lot perhaps helps to shed more general light on its present-day appearance. After the Second World War, France experienced rapid urbanization and industrialization. There were suddenly more jobs in the towns and cities, and the mechanization of agriculture meant that less manpower was required in this sector. Massive rural depopulation occurred. The Lot suffered during this period because much of the land in the area was unsuitable for the use of machinery; many of the local farms could not keep up with their mechanized competitors. The call of the towns and cities has continued to this day; young people leave the villages for school and later for university and job opportunities. In some of the more isolated hamlets there are no young families left because there are no schools nearby. As the older farmers die, there are few younger farmers to step into their shoes. Their abandoned old farmhouses have in recent years been bought and renovated by incomers to the Lot – mostly British, Dutch and Parisian – who are often in pursuit of a more rural life. Nevertheless, the economy of the Lot still relies upon agriculture, alongside a small amount of industry and tourism.

When I first visited the Lot in 2000, I could immediately understand why people would choose to live there. To the inexperienced eye, it offers a certain tranquil mystique, with its verdant green valleys and the Lot river, the back-drop of awesome limestone cliffs and its sense of emptiness. Modernity seems to have bypassed the Lot with the result that it has been described as 'the place that time forgot' (Neame 2004: 13). In reflection of this, life moves slowly in the Lot; the shops still close for two hours or more in the middle of the day, and on the winding roads that traverse the department there is rarely any traffic apart from the occasional tractor. Wild boar forage in vegetable gardens and startled deer dart across roads. The slow pace of life hypnotizes the senses, lulling the outsider into a state of restfulness.

Medieval villages perched on cliffs are yet another reminder of the colourful history of the Lot (Figure 4). In the summer months, these are crammed full of tourists purchasing souvenirs and local delicacies from the artisan shops that line the cobbled streets, sitting in the *cafés* drinking beer or eating ice cream, or jostling for a position on the viewpoint to photograph the view down to the valley floor. These tourists are also attracted to the tastes of the Lot, gorging themselves on its rich cuisine – locally produced *foie gras* (fattened duck and goose livers produced by gavage), truffles, duck breast and Quercy lamb, accompanied by the full-bodied *Appellation d'Origine Contrôlée* (AOC) red wine.

My respondents in the Lot consider themselves lucky to be able to experience these views and tastes all the year round. Indeed, at the height of the summer they avoid the tourist spots, complain about the increased traffic on the roads

4 Saint Cirq Lapopie, a medieval village overlooking the river
Lot

and the inflated prices in the supermarkets. They express their relief when life returns to normal in September, with the pace of life slowing even further when Christmas approaches. Life in the Lot, for my respondents and for other inhabit-ants, is seasonal. While the summer months are characterized by outdoor living – with many festivals and *al fresco* meals – in the winter, many of the residents retreat into the warmth of their houses.

The 2006 French census revealed that 3,017 (legally registered) foreigners had moved to the Lot since 2001 and that there were a total of 10,465 individuals who had been born outside of France currently residing in the department (INSEE n.d.). These data have not yet been broken down by nationality. However, the results of the 1999 census revealed that forty-five per cent of migrants living France were of European origin (INSEE 2005). Based on my own observations, I suggest that the percentage of European migrants in the Lot exceeds this figure; there has been a large influx of Spanish and Portuguese labour in the area. Indeed, it has also been demonstrated that, compared to many other departments with high non-European migrant populations, the migrant population of the Lot is mostly composed of Europeans (INSEE 2005). As Dodd has argued, rural de-population in the Lot and Dordogne 'has been partly offset by immigration, in this case by pieds noirs … and by north Europeans in search of the good life' (2007: 395). I would argue anecdotally that many of these recent incomers were British or Dutch, attracted to the characteristically French, localized and pro-vincial landscape offered by the Lot, an emblem of *La France profonde*. It is these qualities – intrinsic to the better way of life that they seek and translate into the framework of their middle-class values – that initially attracted my respondents to this part of France.

Describing the British residents of the Lot

British migration to the Lot can be understood as a form of lifestyle migration, the migration of relatively affluent individuals motivated by the promise of a more fulfilling way of life within the destination (Benson and O'Reilly 2009; O'Reilly and Benson 2009). In this respect, migration has a transformative potential; through relocation individual migrants imagine that they will be able to improve and take control of their lives (see also Oliver 2008). The act of migration is thus understood as part of the search for a better way of life; destinations are framed in culturally specific terms and are thus meaningful within the context of particular imaginaries; and while there are undoubtedly economic factors which contribute towards this migration trend (O'Reilly 2000), they need to be understood within the context of the other considerations which influence individual relocation. In order to explore this more complex understanding, it becomes necessary to outline the basic characteristics of this migration trend, to define my respondents and to describe the key features of their migration.

For my respondents in the Lot, migration was a move to relocate their lives to rural France. They had often had previous touristic experiences of rural France, even if not specifically the Lot, and claimed that these had inspired their decision to migrate. These Britons were permanent residents in France and were not peripatetic or seasonal migrants of the type identified in other destinations (see for example O'Reilly 2000; Gustafson 2001, 2002). There were some seasonal visitors, but I chose not to focus on them within my research, feeling that while their motivations for spending time in the Lot were similar to those of my respondents, their status as remaining fully resident in Britain, and only temporarily resident in France, gave a distinct flavour to their experiences.

All of my respondents had moved to the Lot within the last fifteen years; those who had been resident for the longest had therefore arrived in the late 1980s and early 1990s, but there were others who had arrived only six months prior to the research. Therefore, the timing of their migration could coincide with very different political, economic and social contexts in Britain. This is not to say that there had not been earlier migrants. There were several Britons who had arrived in the Lot between the 1950s and the 1980s, but they were difficult to track down. On the rare occasion that I managed to get into contact with them, they declined to participate in my research. Nevertheless, as I demonstrate later in this book, they were significant as role models to which the migrants aspired.

My respondents had taken the decision to migrate at different stages within their life-course, their ages at the time of migration ranging from the early forties (except for one young man in his thirties) to the seventies. Although there were a significant number of retirees (including many who took early retirement) among this population, there were also a number of families – parents migrating with their children – and those who made an active choice to leave Britain and their careers during their thirties and forties. While most people appeared to migrate in couples, there were a small number of single migrants as well. In this respect, the family circumstances of the migrants varied.

Furthermore, it became clear that, following migration, my respondents had different requirements in respect to their income. While many of the retirees relied on British pensions and the remaining capital from property investments back in Britain, younger migrants (and some retirees) also needed to generate an income once living in the Lot. In most cases, they ran small businesses that were somehow connected with the local tourism industry; many of them had a *gîte* (holiday home), which they rented out, one couple ran a *chambre d'hôte* (bed and breakfast) and one woman worked as a bilingual tour guide. Other migrant-run businesses included a hand-made greetings card company and IT services business. These enterprises were kept deliberately small in an effort to maintain the renewed work–life balance that many of my respondents desired. But for one couple, who set up a very successful website advertising *gîtes* around France, their working lives became more central to their existence following migration than they had imagined it would. As they explained, they were even considering moving back to Britain as their French dream had been destroyed by their own success in business.

There were further sociological characteristics of this migrant population that may be considered significant. They were a predominantly white population, and although all were of British origin, many were in fact English (as opposed to, say, Welsh or Scottish). Nevertheless, the majority of my respondents came from diverse locations around Britain, reflecting Buller and Hoggart's (1994a) finding that the British in the Lot had come predominantly from Britain. One couple, Robert and Justine Grange, had moved from Hong Kong, where they had spent their working lives, when they retired, and Hannah Blunden, a retiree, had been working in Norway immediately before migration.

Invariably they shared in common their middle-class status, demonstrated by their educational and professional qualifications. Despite this, it was common to find them stressing that, as a population, they came 'from all walks of life'. As I argue, this was a reflection on the individualized circumstances of their migration and a demonstration of their engagement in broader middle-class practices through which they sought to distinguish themselves from others, similar to the processes of distinction identified by Bourdieu (1984; see also Bennett *et al.* 2009). Once established in rural France, they continued to reflect this diversity in their lives, demonstrating the peculiarity of their individual lifestyle choices.

Nevertheless, it is clear that there were commonalities in the lifestyle choices made by my respondents. First, migration was perceived as transformative, a way in which they could improve their way of life; second, they presented a common narrative about the ills of life in contemporary Britain; and third, the better way of life that they sought through migration had the characteristics of the rural idyll (see also Buller and Hoggart 1994a; Barou and Prado 1995). In this respect, migration emerged as the consumption of particular imaginings of rural living, with life following migration projected as a way of (gradually) realizing this sense of rurality and becoming part of the local community.

The purchase of property in the Lot was the first step in making this possible; property ownership and the possibility of a particular way of living were therefore clearly linked. As Bell states, 'house-buyers are attracted by the whole experience of living in France. The phrase "quality of life" is much used, and in heartfelt tones' (2004: 246). In the Lot, these ambitions were realized partly as a result of rural depopulation. In the 1990s many properties stood empty, for sale at relatively low prices, and ownership of a rural French property was therefore easily achieved. Against this background, for all but a few of my respondents, migration coincided with moving into a home that they owned outright, having been able to pay in cash without taking out a mortgage or any other loans.

When I asked specifically about why they had chosen the Lot as a migration destination, the migrants presented their choice as self-evident. One of my respondents gestured to the landscape around him, exclaiming, 'Look around you! Who wouldn't want to live here?' However, I was uncomfortable with this reduction of the Lot to an emblem of rurality. While idealized descriptions of the area might outline certain attractive features, they did not give any real insight into individual decision-making processes and everyday lives as actually experienced following migration. Indeed, it emerged that the overly aestheticized, and often romantic, accounts of the life available in the French countryside masked the complexities of the decision to migrate; and life following migration was characterized by ambivalence as the migrants sought to reconcile their imaginings with their experiences.

Locating the British residents of the Lot

Another significant aspect of this migration trend was the dispersed nature of the migrants' settlement in the Lot. While colleagues working on the extensive British population in Spain (see for example O'Reilly 2000; Oliver 2008) have described how many of them live in urbanized communities and residential blocks built specifically for the development of residential tourism, in rural France this type of enclaved living had not been developed and so was not a possibility. Many of my respondents in the Lot lived in small villages and hamlets, where the majority of residents were French. It is clear that the different histories of tourism and different national cultures affect the manifestation of lifestyle migration within these two destinations.

The village that I lived in had a population of around 200, five of whom were British. While this is by no means intended to be representative for other villages in the department, it does gives some indication of the settlement patterns of those migrants who claimed that they had chosen the Lot because so few Britons lived there (unlike in the neighbouring Dordogne department). Furthermore, the amenities available varied according to the size of the population and the administrative standing of the location. In some cases, the migrants lived in the proximity of a small, well-served town. In these locations the density of British residents was higher, but they were never the majority of the population.

It is difficult to obtain an accurate estimate of their numbers (cf King and Patterson 1998; Casado-Díaz et al. 2004). Statistically, they are an invisible population as they no longer need to register their residence in France, and the French census data, until recently collected once every five years, have been criticized for their lack of accuracy in providing estimates of the size of migrant populations (Pan Ké Shon 2007). Nevertheless, the presence of these British incomers to the Lot is evident year-round. As you walk around the weekly markets in Cahors and many of the *Lotoise* villages, you can hear British voices. Old village houses which once stood empty have been renovated in a sympathetic manner that respects the local architectural styles; this is often an indicator that the owners are incomers to the area, as the local people tend not have the finances (and arguably the inclination) to carry out this work. A trawl through the English-language newspapers produced in France also reveals that some British residents in the Lot are offering services that include building work, gardening, computing, removals and much more. A visit to the local airport, which has had low-cost flights to and from the United Kingdom since 2003 (now scheduled daily), reveals a car park full of cars with British licence plates; their owners had not changed the plates despite the legal obligation to do so within six months of importing cars to France. While my respondents in the Lot were at times highly visible, at other times they and the rest of this substantial population quickly became invisible. As the market stalls were packed up, the shops closed for lunchtime, or the days became shorter, the British retreated into their private homes, as did the other residents of the Lot.

Where, then, can you find the British of the Lot? Peer into their back gardens and you may see them pottering around in their Wellington boots, watering flower beds, hoeing, planting, harvesting fruit and vegetables, or taking vegetable scraps to the compost heap. On a summer's evening, as the sun begins to set, you can find them sitting on their private terraces drinking *apéritif* (pre-dinner drinks). At this time of year, you may also find them working in the kitchen, making jams and chutneys, blanching vegetables ready for freezing, all in an attempt to preserve the fruits and vegetables grown in the garden. The long winter evenings invariably see the migrants sitting indoors in front of a roaring fire, watching British television channels; it is at this time of year that they 'hibernate', as their social lives wind down. But, come Wednesday morning, you might find them attending a language workshop organized in the centre of Cahors, timed conveniently to coincide with the weekly food market. Walking down the Boulevard Gambetta at around eleven o'clock in the morning, when the classes are over, you can hear the *cafés* resounding with British voices.

This simultaneous visibility and invisibility of the British residents of the Lot reflects their ambivalence about life in rural France. Those same people who flock to the *cafés* on Wednesday mornings to meet their compatriots may at other times claim that they do not really socialize with other Britons; that they did not come to France to be a part of the 'English circle'. Their lives in the Lot are characterized by such contradictions. Nevertheless, the narratives of these incomers indicate that they carefully negotiate the conflicting demands and desires that they place on themselves, demonstrating that they have the necessary flexibility and fluidity to come to terms with the challenges of their new lives in the French countryside.

From international counterurbanization
to lifestyle migration

The subject of British migration to France has, to date, received little critical academic attention, despite the magnitude of the phenomenon, its potential social impact on the host communities and the abundance of impressionistic and popular accounts of it (see for example Mayle 1989, 1990; Drinkwater 2001, 2003, 2004; Bailey 2002). While there is an established sub-field of anthropology interested in rural France (see for example Bourdieu 1962, 1977, 1980, 2002; Zonabend 1984; Segalen 1983, 1991; Rogers 1991; Reed-Danahay 1996), its traditional focus on peasant society often disregards the diversity of the rural population and ignores significant migration flows beyond those of the peasant community. Similarly, the extensive academic coverage of immigration to France with its lens focused on migration from outside the European Union pays little attention to relatively affluent migrants moving to France from within Europe. Indeed, contemporary studies of migration to France predominantly adopt a problem or policy-oriented approach to the study of immigrants (Fassin 2001), focusing their attention almost exclusively on African migration (Silverman 1992; Hargreaves 1995; Noiriel 1996). And while there has been extensive academic coverage of the British in Spain (for an overview see Casado-Diaz 2006), there has been relatively little written on the British in France.

In the early 1990s, the British geographers Henry Buller and Keith Hoggart, and the French anthropologists Jacques Barou and Patrick Prado, prepared the now seminal texts on British migration to rural France. Buller and Hoggart (1994a) argued that the existing model of counterurbanization, but on an international scale, could explain the appeal of the French countryside to British consumers. In this rendering, those who were disillusioned with urban life chose to live in the countryside instead. In an era when the cost of property in rural Britain had risen sharply, France provided a less expensive alternative. Barou and Prado (1995) instead stressed an underlying green ideology (*idéologie écologiste*) driving this migration trend. Furthermore, they promoted the idea that the resulting change in the rural population had brought about a fundamental transformation in the social landscape of the French countryside. Both pairs of authors therefore placed a particular emphasis on explaining the initial decision to migrate, with Barou and Prado tentatively theorizing about the potential outcomes for the receiving communities.

Subsequent research has similarly concentrated on the appeal of the French countryside to the British (see for example Gervais-Aguer 2004, 2006; Depierre and Guitard 2006). Drawing predominantly on quantitative data, these studies list the attractions of specific regions in France, focusing exclusively on the pull factors behind migration. It seems that, even in academic accounts, the attractions of the French countryside have remained stable, as descriptions still reflect the rustic charm identified in early travel writing. However, as Tombs and Tombs (2007: 657) highlight, there has recently been a significant change in the lifestyle that British migrants imagine is available to them in France: unlike their predecessors who had formed exclusive expatriate clubs, migrants today express a desire to be part of the local community. As recent research has demonstrated, migrants have experienced different levels of integration, based on a number of factors that include, but are not limited to, their inclination to integrate, their linguistic abilities, and also the willingness of the French community to incorporate them (Smallwood 2007; Drake and Collard 2008; Benson 2010a).

To date, studies of British migration to rural France have not accounted for the degree of correspondence between migration as it is imagined and migration as it is experienced in real life, particularly during the post-migration period. In contrast, the recent theoretical literature on lifestyle migration – the migration of 'relatively affluent individuals, moving either part-time or full-time, permanently or temporarily, to places which, for various reasons, signify for the migrants something loosely defined as quality of life' (Benson and O'Reilly 2009: 621) – proposes a more inclusive framework which shifts the focus from the initial act to the lifestyle choices that are inherent within the decision to migrate (Benson and O'Reilly 2009; O'Reilly and Benson 2009). Broadly understood, the lifestyle migration framework draws attention to the idea of migration as motivated primarily by the search for a more fulfilling way of life, articulated as an individualized lifestyle choice and indicative of the reflexive project of the self. In this rendering, the act of migration is integrally linked with the individual's self-identity. Indeed, Rapport and Dawson (1998) argue that it is precisely through movement that the individual understands their identity and the world around them. However, this is an ongoing process of self-revelation that continues after migration, as they make sense of and impose order on their new surroundings.

As a search for a better way of life, lifestyle migration is often presented as being predominantly culturally determined. While there are other factors (economic, for instance) that undeniably contribute to the decision to migrate, the cultural elements of lifestyle migration trends have been the starting point in analysis. For example, D'Andrea (2007), Bousiou (2008) and Korpela (2009a) describe how the destinations that they focus on in their research – Ibiza and Goa, Mykonos, and Varanasi, respectively – attract certain countercultural individuals. These locations provide a temporary sojourn for these hyper-mobile migrants, who seem through their travels to be searching for the existential meaning in their lives. These examples of bohemian lifestyle migrants (Benson and O'Reilly 2009; Korpela 2009a), global nomads or expressive expatriates (D'Andrea 2007) draw attention to pre-existing understandings of particular places, while also stressing the highly individualized nature of lifestyle migration. In this respect, it is evident that particular destinations are significant beyond the individual, already occupying a position within cultural imaginings and mythologized by the collective imagination. It is these kinds of culturally distinctive imaginings that are incorporated into the justificatory framing of lifestyle migration. Furthermore, the significance of a particular destination may often be reduced to its role in offering the possibility of a particular way of life. Against this background, it becomes clear that lifestyle migration should be understood in terms of the underlying cultural logic that makes those particular destinations and ways of life meaningful and that frames the experiences of life following migration.

Against the background of the lifestyle migration framework, the research presented in this book captures in intricate detail the experience of everyday life following migration. As Henry Buller has recently argued, there needs to be a shift in the study of the British in rural France, to focus 'on the ways in which migrants rework their life worlds and re-imagine social networks and identities', and 'research needs to recognise the varying outcomes of relocation' (2008: 64). This book is the first to attempt to analyse and conceptualize the post-migration lives of the British living in rural France. Through a micro-level approach focused on the everyday practices and experiences of the individual migrants, it provides a critical insight into the realities of the migrants' daily lives within their new social and physical environment. By locating migration within the context of the migrants' lives before and after migration (Benson 2010a), I argue that the decision to migrate and experiences of life in rural France should be understood within the context of the imaginings that drive migration and influence expectations for post-migration life. The book therefore focuses on the migrants' efforts to negotiate a more fulfilling lifestyle as they come to terms with life in rural France.

In this respect, my research uniquely explores the migrants' successes and the obstacles that they face *en route* to a better way of life. I argue that the recognition of the British middle-class imaginings which prompt the decision to migrate (Buller and Hoggart 1994a; Barou and Prado 1995) needs to be extended into discussions of life following migration. In this rendering, the middle-class beliefs and dispositions of my respondents mediate their post-migration experiences. The ethnography presented in the following pages therefore reveals unprecedented and detailed insights into the lives led by these migrants, which have been gained as the result of my long-term immersion in their daily lives. Among these insights, I not only reveal the particular characteristics of the lifestyle sought but also present the paradoxes and ambivalence that characterize the migrants' lives. Furthermore, I place this peculiar migration trend in a historical context, emphasizing the social and material conditions of its emergence.

Blurring the boundaries between tourism and migration

The framework that I adopt to explain this particular migration trend derives in part from the extensive literature on tourism; indeed, it is the literature on the search for authenticity within tourism that informs my extensive discussion on the search for a better way of life later in the book. In contrast, I found myself using very little of the literature on contemporary migration. While this can perhaps be ascribed to the problem and policy-oriented approaches that much of such research takes, it is rather the case that migration research does not often examine the intersections of culture and migration. As a result, there are no established frameworks and theoretical positions for dealing with the cultural mechanics of migration and the continued role of culture in post-migration lives. In contrast, studies of tourism pay close attention to the cultural dimensions of

the tourism encounter. This has resulted in a considerable literature theorizing tourism, which I believe can provide many insights into the contemporary
experience of mobility and could form the basis of a discussion about how to
theorize migration.

There are, however, an increasing number of people researching the intersections of tourism and migration (Bell and Ward 2000; Williams and Hall 2000,
2002; Benson and O'Reilly 2009). While these investigations started as an exercise in definition – determining who is a tourist and who is a migrant – there has
been a more recent move towards recognizing the shared motivations underlying
migration and tourism. Bell and Ward (2000), for example, argue that migration,
as in the case of tourism, is becoming increasingly consumption-oriented, while
Williams and Hall stress that 'the re-evaluation of valued living and working
environments' (2000: 10) has been responsible for a rise in both tourism and
migration. In other cases, discussions have centred on the relationship between
migration and tourism, demonstrating that in some cases tourism may give rise
to migration (Williams and Hall 2000; Rodríguez 2001); to a lesser degree, it is
also worth noting that migration may result in new forms of tourism (Williams
and Hall 2000).

There has also been a focus on the various practices – second-home ownership, lifestyle migration – that, because of their nature, can be considered to be
somewhere between tourism and migration (see for example Williams and Hall
2000; Müller 2002). For example, as Williams and Hall (2000) describe, lifestyle
migration is linked to tourism because of its initial reliance on the tourism experience in the choice of destination; moreover, the amenity-seeking nature
of this form of migration often leads many people to choose places with well-
developed tourism infrastructures.

What is overwhelmingly absent from these presentations of the relationship between tourism and migration is the discussion of the transferability of
theories developed within the context of tourism in explaining migration. What
I present in this book is one possible way that certain studies in the literature
about tourism can be used to explain the everyday lives of my respondents.
While I do not claim that this is an approach that could more widely be applied
to discussions of migration, the quest for a better way of life and the desire for
self-improvement that lie at the core of lifestyle migration and tourism may in
many ways resonate with the contemporary migrant experience. Similarly, the
discussion of the role played by the imagination within migration, framing the
initial migration and shaping post-migration lives, has implications for understanding migration more broadly. As I argue, it is time to examine the interface
between tourism and migration, both as it manifests itself in the world around us
and within our theoretical enquiries.

Everyday life: from imagination to lived experience

As the ethnography in this book demonstrates, it is clear that through migration
my respondents in the Lot aimed for an improved lifestyle and an opportunity

for self-realization. The migration of the British to rural France is symptomatic of an individual lifestyle choice, part of the wider trend of lifestyle migration. In this rendering, migration is just one point on the journey towards a better way of life, an intrinsic aspect of the lifestyle trajectory of individuals and a part of their self-making projects. As the daily lives of my respondents unfold in the pages of this book, we witness their continual engagements in the reflexive project of the self (see Giddens 1991). It therefore emerges that the quest for a better way of life, itself analogous to the migrants' own self-realization, is a never-ending process.

Within this process, it became clear that there were certain aspects of the migrants' lives before migration that they could not shake off. A middle-class aesthetic for rural French living that prompted their migration (Buller and Hoggart 1994a; Barou and Prado 1995), similarly influenced practices in life following migration, and it is apparent that my respondents in the Lot remained thoroughly entangled in the subtle processes of distinction of the British middle classes (see Savage *et al.* 1992; Bennett *et al.* 2009) in their particular consumption practices and more broadly in their everyday lives. On the one hand, as Oliver and O'Reilly (2010) argued in the case of their respondents on the Spanish Costa del Sol, it was clear that these persistent class structures dictated the criteria for successful living within the destination. On the other hand, the continuity between life before and after migration highlighted by the recognition of such processes of distinction reveals that migration can be characterized as part of the pursuit of distinctiveness (Benson 2009).

From an early stage in this book, it is clear that the lives of the British in rural France were not, as at first sight, easily explained; they were as diverse and complex as the lives that these individuals had led before migration. Once living in the Lot, the migrants found themselves in a new and challenging social environment. There were the local *Lotoise* French, the people whom, in their imaginings of life in the Lot, the migrants had wanted to emulate and create sustainable relationships with. But they also found that there were a number of other incomers who shared their dreams and motivations. They readily stumbled upon not only their compatriots but also other incomers, such as the Dutch and Parisian migrants who had settled in the area. Finally, there was a transnational element to their social relations, as the migrants often maintained links with friends and family back in Britain. A model of insiders and outsiders that recognizes that the criteria for belonging to each of these categories are contingent on the particular social situation (see for example Waldren 1996) can broadly explain the dynamics of my respondents' encounters. However, such an approach still contains a normative assumption that insider status is denoted by belonging to the local community, when in fact individuals may be insiders to a variety of different groups at the same time.

The ethnography presented in this book demonstrates that the migrants performed and expressed multiple identities in their daily lives as they negotiated their way through the complex, new social environment that they inhabited. They strived to become ultimately indistinguishable from the local community, but this was a difficult goal to achieve. It required not just effort from the migrants themselves but also the willingness of the local population (Smallwood 2007; Drake and Collard 2008; Benson 2010a). Along the way, the migrants found comfort in the familiarity of their compatriots and other incomers (Scott 2004, 2006; Benson 2010a), while their continued relationships with their friends and families provided them with a captive audience for their stories about life in the Lot. Nevertheless, the migrants made efforts to distance themselves ideologically from their compatriots and other incomers living locally, as well as from their friends and family back in Britain. They emphasized that they were closer to a better way of life than these others, with their comparative claims neglecting the subjective character of the better way of life sought.

While uncertainty and dissatisfaction with life in Britain had prompted migration, it seems that the Lot did not provide the ready remedy that the migrants had expected. As their narratives reveal, they found themselves in an ambivalent position, caught between their initial desires and their lived experiences of life in rural France. The complexity of their social relationships was but one indicator of their ambiguous status. As I argue, this was why the quest for a better way of life was so important to the migrants: it gave them some hope that they would eventually escape their uncertain standing and find a place for themselves in the world.

How the migrants' lives unfolded following migration therefore indicated their progress on their personal quest for a better way of life. The migrants' experiences of life in rural France caused them to constantly re-evaluate their expectations and aspirations for life in the Lot; the better way of life that they sought remained elusive. This book, therefore, presents an ethnography of the social change and process that characterized the lives of these Britons. It recognizes that this particular type of migration was but one step *en route* to a better way of life. The migrants' Holy Grail, the gold at the end of the rainbow, was yet to be fully discovered and realized.

Researching the familiar in an unfamiliar setting

In December 2003, I packed my belongings into the back of the car and began the long drive to the Lot, the start of twelve months of ethnographic research among its British residents. On my previous visits to the Lot, I had found a British family who were prepared to share their daily lives with me, and now, after the fourteen-hour journey, I arrived on their doorstep to be greeted with a glass of red wine and a hot dinner. This family acted as my initial gatekeepers. They readily introduced me to their friends and acquaintances in the Lot, organized for me to accompany them when they had invitations for dinner, and on a couple of occasions, on hearing other Britons talking in restaurants and *cafés*, approached them to ask if they would be interested in taking part in my research.

Their help at these early stages of my fieldwork proved to be invaluable; although I had additionally advertised in shop windows and emailed and telephoned people who had classified advertisements in *The French News*, an English language newspaper, I had only received two positive responses. Serendipitous encounters were rare, and it would have taken me a long time to build up a reasonable number of people to take part in the research without help. I soon discovered the reason for this: there were very few public places where the British in the Lot regularly congregated. Over time, my initial participants would introduce me to their friends or recommend other people I could approach. In this manner, I established myself within a wide network of Britons living in the Lot.

My decision to focus on the worldview of my respondents shaped the research. This was an epistemological choice, focused on understanding the British of the Lot and their everyday lives in their own terms. It is against this background that, within the following chapters, local French actors and transnational relationships are present in as much as they were meaningful to my respondents. By shifting the focus of the research from the migrants' everyday lives to the relationships between the native French population and such incomers, or to an examination of a transnational community, different studies could have been produced. Furthermore, this epistemological choice influenced the methodology of the research, as I traced their networks and followed in their footsteps as they went about their daily lives in the Lot; in this respect, the migrants' actions determined the direction that the research subsequently took. I had never imagined that I would end up driving distances of up to 150 km in a day as my respondents suggested that I visit them in their homes, which were dispersed around the department.

The ethnographic fieldwork comprised extensive participant observation, a series of unstructured interviews, the collection of life and migration histories and documents (both pictorial and written) relating to the field. I regularly attended events alongside my respondents, and we often walked together, but I was also welcomed into their houses and in this respect gained unprecedented insights into their home lives. I volunteered to help with some mundane elements of their lives, helping one family to change their swimming pool lining and preparing marketing material for their holiday home, booking tickets for one couple's holiday on the Internet and providing transport for one of my elderly respondents so that she could do her weekly shopping in Cahors. From the start of my research, the data I collected were detailed and presented a seemingly coherent picture of the lives that these migrants' led in the Lot; they presented the match between their expectations and life following migration. But as I spent more time with my respondents, I realized that their accounts were full of contradictions.

During the early stages of my research, and to facilitate my relationships with members of the research population, I conducted unstructured interviews with forty-nine participants. I often interviewed these individuals more than once, circumstances allowing, to construct a more detailed account of their lives in the Lot. The interviews ranged in length from one to four hours and were recorded so that I could revisit the interviews at a later date. Most of my interviewees invited me to their houses to conduct these interviews, which gave me an insight into how and where they lived, in terms of how their homes were located in relation to other houses and local amenities. The rapport I built up during these interviews resulted in opportunities to carry out further participant observation.

My decision to collect life and migration histories emerged somewhat organically from the research. To break the ice with my respondents, I would ask them about the decision to migrate. This produced rich retrospective accounts of their migration choices, including details of the timing and circumstances of their migration. The centrality of imagination to this migration flow was clearly illustrated in these histories. As Ken Plummer argues of life histories,

> They help establish collective memories and imagined communities; and they tell of the concerns of their time and place … Indeed, the stories we construct of our lives may well become the 'stories we live by'. What matters to people keeps getting told in their stories of their life. Listening carefully to these stories may well be one of the cornerstones of ethnographic enquiry. (2007: 395)

In this respect, I was able to get an insight into the common imaginings that had prompted migration, as well as an understanding of how these were articulated in individual lives. These really enhanced the ethnography collected (Aull Davies 1999), providing crucial background to the decision to migrate and making sense of their post-migration actions and practices. In this respect, the life and migration histories of my respondents were a resource that helped me to comprehend their daily lives and which provided unique insights into how they understood the world.

In addition to the vivid and descriptive accounts of everyday lives, the migrants' narratives also gave some insight into their subjectivities, demonstrating the ongoing process by which the self is reflexively (re)constructed (Giddens 1991; Polkinghorne 1991; Rosenwald 1992; Maines 1993; Ochs and Capp 2001; Jackson 2002). The performance of narrative is central to this self-making project, constructing a sense of continuity in an increasingly flexible and fragmented world (Giddens 1991; Bauman 1995; Sennett 1998; Burkitt 2005). The migrants' accounts mirrored this transformative process. While to begin with they presented rational and coherent life histories, over time, their stories exposed the contradictions intrinsic to this project of the self, the actual lack of coherence of their lives (cf Giddens 1991; Polkinghorne 1991; Rosenwald 1992; Maines 1993; Ochs and Capp 2001; Jackson 2002).

In many respects, my own personal journey during my time in the Lot resembled the early experiences of my respondents. Just as they had done, I had to learn about how to live in the Lot. Indeed, I often used my own experiences to instigate discussion on a particular topic during interviews or on social occasions. I shared with my respondents a particular national and class status, aspects of my identity which would certainly locate me as a native anthropologist (cf Bakalaki 1997; Greverus and Römhild 2000); I was familiar to them, as they were familiar to me, on account of our shared membership of the British middle classes. As a result, I found that it was easy to build a rapport with the migrants and to gain their trust; I also had the sense that they were relaxed both when they were being interviewed and during participant observation, as they could easily classify me. In many ways, my fieldwork was reminiscent of carrying out fieldwork 'at home'.

I find myself asking, however, whether ethnography of the British living in rural France, when conducted by a British researcher, counts as ethnography at home. Certainly, by focusing on the research subjects and the subject position of the ethnographer there is an undeniable familiarity between the researcher and the researched, but in a non-home setting. Where on the continuum between anthropology at home and anthropology abroad would we locate this ethnography of the familiar within an unfamiliar setting?

As ethnographers, we experience different levels of familiarity with our surroundings and with the subjects of our research. Undoubtedly, we need to maintain a sense of distance between our respondents and ourselves if we are to conduct effective analysis, but this is a social and intellectual distance (Hammersley and Atkinson 1995). Paradoxically, it is precisely this distance that ethnographers reflexively try to dissolve as they gradually enter the 'culturally intimate' (Herzfeld 1997) worlds of their respondents. The benefit of anthropology closer to home, as Jackson argued, is that it allows us to question 'the "taken-for-granted" acceptance of things in small communities' (1987: 11) and to achieve a greater understanding of ourselves as well as others (*ibid.*). Fundamentally, the assumption underlying the privileging of fieldwork abroad is that there is little to learn about our own societies. However, I concur with Okely (1996) that we may, in fact, know very little about the cultures within our 'home'. Indeed, 'some of the inhabitants of one's own village may remain as elusive as cannibals' (*ibid.*: 4). Within this rendering, it becomes increasingly difficult to describe what can be counted as anthropology at home (Coleman and Collins 2006; Hannerz 2006).

By participating in the daily lives of the British in the Lot over twelve months, I can now present a nuanced and insightful account of their lives in rural France. I recognize the continuity of their lives before and after migration. And alongside the migrants, I experienced the challenges and intricacies of coming to terms with life in an unfamiliar setting. My own re-evaluation of that which I had previously taken for granted about the British in rural France mirrors the experiences of my participants as they come to terms with a new social, political and economic environment. When I packed my car back in December 2003, I had no idea what the journey that lay ahead would hold. The research process was one of discovery; and as the researcher, I found myself encountering new configurations of the familiar at every step of my way through an unfamiliar landscape.

Chapter summaries

The progress of the migrants' lives unravels through the chapters of this book. I trace their individual quests for a better way of life from the initial decision to migrate, through to their daily experiences of life following migration. The ethnography presented in the following pages demonstrates the way in which the migrants' aspirations and ideals continually change in response to their embodied experiences of life in the Lot, with the act of migration emerging as only one step in the lifelong project of self-realization.

The book is divided into two parts. Part 1 explores the intersections of imagination, migration and post-migration lives. It recognizes the project of self-realization that lies at the core of the migrants' quest for a better way of life needs to be understood within the context of their lives before migration and how they explain their migration. Chapter 1 provides this context. On the one hand, it introduces my respondents in the Lot, highlighting their common origins as members of the British middle class and the various contexts that brought about their migration. On the other hand it sets the scene for the remainder of the book, explaining migration, both as presented by the migrants and in the terms of the ethnographic analyst. It traces how the migrants recounted the decision to migrate, highlighting the potential for self-realization; in the process, the chapter stresses that migration was viewed as significant because of what the migrants believed it would do for them.

Chapter 1 also critically assesses the explanations presented in the now seminal texts on British migration to rural France and builds upon them to draw attention to the cultural determinants that drive this form of migration. In particular, the chapter focuses on the British middle-class idealization of the French countryside, using this as an example to argue that this form of lifestyle migration needs to be interpreted through a framework that is sensitive to structural and material prerogatives; economic, social and political contexts; culturally significant imaginings; as well as more individualized circumstances prompting migration. The recognition of the persistent role of class in the migrants' lives sets the stage for the rest of the book, presenting initial insights into how the migrants unwittingly reproduce the British middle class(es) in rural France. As I argue, they regularly engage in processes of social distinction, their migration to France emerging as a way of improving their social status through the accumulation of cultural capital.

A recurring theme in Part 1 is the interrelationships between imagination – here understood, following Appadurai (1996) as a social practice – and lived experience. Whereas Chapter 1 provides some insights into the role of imagination in motivating migration, Chapter 2 explores how the migrants' imaginings of community life and local belonging – intrinsic elements of the rural idyll – shape and influence their social relationships within their new surroundings. In particular, it examines the migrants' efforts to become part of the local community and demonstrates that success in this area of their lives is by no means predictable.

As I argue, becoming part of the local community, being socially integrated, is predicated unequally upon diverse factors that include linguistic capability, common interests, possibilities for social interaction and the reception of the local community. Furthermore, Chapter 2 presents insights into what relationships with local social actors do for the migrants. In this respect it draws attention not only to the identity claims that these relationships enable but also to the realization of their difference and the recognition that self-realization remains in process. In this respect, their relationships with local French actors served as measures of the migrants' success at developing a distinctly local subjectivity, an effort that, as I argue later in the book, was inherent to their claims to a distinctive way of life. Building on the theme of imagination, Chapter 3 further explores tensions between how the migrants had imagined their post-migration lives and their lived experiences. While the distance between imagination and experience is a story that often emerges from lifestyle migration research, attributed to the migrants' occupation of a liminal phase, I question the applicability of the concept of liminality, arguing instead that ambivalence is a more useful analytical concept for understanding the lives of my respondents. By recognizing the persistence of ambivalence in both pre- and post-migration lives – aligned to the wider sense of ambivalence experienced by all modern social actors – migration emerges as an attempt to overcome the uncertainty and indeterminacy of the migrants' lives in Britain. Through the examination of various sources of ambivalence in the migrants' lives – their position between one lifestyle and another, their status as intra-European migrants and their social relationships – the chapter demonstrates that migration is just one of a number of creative ways in which these people strived to resolve their feelings of ambivalence and take greater control over their lives.

Chapter 4 concludes the discussion of imagination laid out in Part 1, examining further the interface between imagination and experience and presenting an explanation for the way in which the migrants understand their post-migration lives. This lays the foundations for the migrants' identity-making practices as discussed in Part 2. Through an examination of the varying ways in which my respondents relate to the landscape, the chapter reflects on the process of getting to know the landscape through experience, stressing that while imagination plays a central role in their expectations for post-migration lives and shapes their experiences, it can also be challenged and subtly transformed through experience.

In this respect, imagination and experience are intrinsically interrelated, and this relationship is central to understanding how the migrants relate to their new surroundings. Against this background, I argue that Bourdieu's concept of practice is useful for understanding the migrants' everyday lives in the Lot, allowing a role for their embodied experiences and individual biographies as well as the cultural logic that lay at the root of migration. In this interpretation, my respondents' perceptions of the landscape and their practices emerge as a site for the negotiation of structure and agency.

Part 2 of the book is concerned with the intersections of processes of distinction, identity and the quest for a better way of life. Chapter 5 explores how the migrants understood their homes and what the migrants' home-making practices revealed about their identities and their lifestyle ambitions. It moves on from the wider discussion of property selection that has characterized previous research on the British in rural France, to reveal the role of individual biographies, histories and desires in shaping the home. In particular, it opens the door on three different households, putting the material culture of these home on public display. Through the examination of these different properties, it became clear that the migrants related to their homes in different ways and used them to different ends.

The various examples presented in the chapter demonstrate that while the home could be the site of new identities and ways of living, it could also be used as continuation of their lives before migration, allowing the migrants to retreat into the comfort and familiarity of their home in what remain unfamiliar social and physical environments. As I argue, it becomes clear that the migrants' personal ambitions for their post-migration lives, both in respect to the relationships within the household and with the outside world, are reflected in their choices about how to furnish and decorate their home.

The final two ethnographic chapters examine the various ways that my respondents in the Lot distinguished themselves from their compatriots and how this was connected to their ongoing quest for a better way of life. Chapter 6 discusses the mechanisms by which the migrants distinguished themselves from others – their compatriots in Spain and the Dordogne and tourists – through these processes laying claim to particular identities and ways of living. As I argue, through the recourse to stereotypes, the migrants revealed more about themselves than these others, drawing boundaries of inclusion and exclusion around an imagined community of others like them – the British of the Lot – who held in common the desire for a way of life that was uniquely available in the Lot.

Furthermore, their discussions of these others focused attention on their unique understandings of a better way of life, highlighting once more the process of self-realization that lay at the core of their pursuit of this goal. The use of stereotypes, in this rendering, has a self-evaluating and self-defining potential. Finally, I argue that, by using stereotypes, the migrants continue to engage in processes of social distinction, which highlighted the continued influence of their middle-class culture on their everyday practices.

Chapter 7, the final ethnographic chapter of the book, explores the relationship between social distinction, migrant subjectivities and the quest for a better way of life. Authenticity acts as a lens through which to examine this relationship. On the one hand it becomes clear that the migrants' ideologies about life in the Lot are characterized by their desire for a more authentic way of living; migration had offered them self-realization precisely because of the promise that this would be available in the Lot. However, as my account of the migrants' lives in the Lot demonstrates, migration is not as transformative as originally imagined, with the result that the quest for authentic living continues until long after migration. As I argue, this is particularly telling, revealing the interrelationship between status discrimination and the quest for a better way of life.

In this interpretation, the quest emerges as one aimed at achieving a distinctive life; the migrants thus measure their progress against that of their compatriots living locally, openly laying claim to more or less authentic lives. As the ethnography presented in this chapter demonstrates, there is also a self-referential element to these judgements, as the migrants reflect on the ways that their practices have changed over time. Importantly, it emerges that processes of social distinction and the quest for a better way of life are mutually reinforcing. By working towards the goals, the migrants strive for distinction. At the same time, distinction is achieved through their commitment to achieving authentic lives. The migrants may appear to be moving closer to a better way of life, but there is no end in sight.

The conclusion draws together the various themes discussed in the book, exploring the intersections between distinction, ambivalence and authenticity. On the one hand, the analysis argues that particular ideologies for living in the Lot underwrite migration and the search for a better way of life. On the other hand, it becomes clear that lifestyle migration has at its core a focus on processes of self-realization. In this respect, it becomes clear that a persistent tension in the migrants' lives originates in the opposing roles played by individual agency and the structural determinants in shaping their migration and experiences of life in the Lot. Somewhat ironically, it emerges that the desire for self-realization emerges from a particular cultural framework.

Finally, the conclusion analyses the persistence of the quest for a better way of life. As the ethnography presented throughout the book demonstrates, the migrants' ideologies for living are regularly put to the test and authenticated as they engaged in processes of social distinction. Understood through the lens of authenticity, these processes of distinction highlight the degree to which the migrants' quest is a comparative endeavour through which to lay claim to cultural capital.

It seems that, as many actors in the contemporary world, the migrants remain in a constant state of movement and change; they perform a variety of identities on a daily basis, their tastes change and adapt, and they build new relationships while maintaining old ones. The ethnography presented in this book demonstrates the complexity of the lives they lead following migration. While they had understood their move to France as heralding a new way of life, the examination of post-migration lives presented here demonstrates that, instead, the migrants had taken just one small step in realizing their imaginings.

1

Imagination, migration and post-migration lives

1

Explaining migration

This chapter introduces the migrants, broadly outlining their sociological characteristics, and providing some initial insights into their individualized migration stories. In this manner, I draw attention to the migrants' accounts of their lives before migration, to demonstrate the diverse contexts that motivated relocation and to reveal their different circumstances (familial, economic, age) at the time of migration. What was particularly striking was the homogeneous class background of my respondents in the Lot, who originated exclusively from the British middle classes. In this respect, their emphasis on the diversity of the British population in the Lot can be understood as an effort to claim their individual migrations as being distinctive – prompted by their own subjective circumstances – rather than as an accurate statement about the diversity of the population. Indeed, this focus on distinctiveness is also evident in their claims to the exclusivity of the Lot as a destination.

The manner in which the initial decision to migrate was conceptualized was revealing of the lives that my respondents envisaged leading following migration. In particular, this chapter draws attention to the cultural determinants of this migration trend, a feature of migration that has been overlooked and under-theorized in migration research more generally due to its policy-oriented and problem-focused nature. In particular, it is clear that culturally significant renderings of rural living prompted migration (Buller and Hoggart 1994a; Barou and Prado 1995). However, as I demonstrate, they intersected with individualized motivations and wider material, historical and structural conditions. Fabricant (1998) emphasizes that the motivations behind migration should be understood as diverse and multiple; intersecting with one another, they become internalized by the individual. Following this argument, I call for a more nuanced understanding of British migration to rural France that incorporates structural and material prerogatives; economic, social and political contexts; culturally significant imaginings; as well as more individualized circumstances prompting migration. Against this background, it becomes possible to understand that British migration to rural France is a largely individualized action, which nevertheless remains influenced by wider structural concerns, conditions and constraints (see Benson and O'Reilly 2009; O'Reilly and Benson 2009).

For my respondents in the Lot, migration was presented as a way in which they had been able to overcome their uncertainties about the future and their general dissatisfaction with the life on offer to them in modern Britain. Their retrospective accounts of the decision to migrate thus presented migration as a transformative action allowing for self-realization (Benson and O'Reilly 2009; O'Reilly and Benson 2009). The changes in their lives that led to migration provoked them to examine their lives in more detail; as Bourdieu (2000) has argued, it is understandable for people unsettled by these transformations to reassess the way in which they understand the world. This reassessment was clearly highlighted in their narratives when they stressed the risk and adventure of migration and explicitly drew attention to their own efforts in regaining control of their lives. Against this background I argue that lifestyle migration can be understood as part of the broader pursuit of happiness that Bauman (2008) stresses is part of the liquid modern condition. In this respect, the act of migration emerges as just one element of the quest for a better way of life, a life project that characterized the migrants' lives before migration and after migration and that was intrinsically linked to the reflexive project of the self (Giddens 1991).

Describing British migrants in rural France

To understand this particular migration phenomenon requires some background information on the individuals who chose to undertake it. I argue that migration made sense within the context of their lives and can be explained broadly in relation to their sociological characteristics, particularly their common middle-class culture. Furthermore, the different expectations and experiences that this trend encompassed were the result of the diversity of this migrant population: the timing of their migration, their position on their life course and their family circumstances.

A peculiarly middle-class migration

By far the most striking sociological characteristic that my respondents in the Lot held in common was their membership of the British middle classes.[1] This was an emic category that was reflected in the consumption practices of my respondents. The middle-class status of Britons living in rural France has been documented by other scholars, who claim that migration reflects the ecological and hedonistic aspirations of the middle classes (Barou and Prado 1995) and wider middle-class longings for rurality (Buller and Hoggart 1994a). These explanations both highlight an understanding of the middle classes as oriented toward consumption and the pursuit of particular lifestyle choices rather than around working practices, as reflected in the refashioning of class analysis in recent years (see Scott 2002; Bottero 2004).

The middle-class backgrounds of my respondents were significant, demonstrating the relatively high levels of cultural capital that these individuals possessed and belying their affluence. In most cases, migrants had been university-educated and had worked in such professions as teaching, held jobs in the civil service or been managers. Although some of my respondents were not affluent in material and financial terms, the high levels of cultural capital that they had accrued through education and occupation did, in part, facilitate their migration (see also Amit 2007). It therefore becomes clear that the migrants had extensive cultural assets at their disposal. As Savage *et al.* (1992) have argued, these assets, alongside those from property and organization, consolidated their position as middle-class actors. In part, the cultural assets that the migrants accrued had been converted from their property assets: in most cases, my respondents in the Lot owned their own houses.

> French rural property ownership is becoming incorporated into the cultural experience of middle class British nationals. Even for those who do not own a French home, contemporary fiction, television and store catalogues increasingly allude to living in France. (Buller and Hoggart 1994a: 127)

> Owning a corner of France and making it a second or even first home, came to embody the Arcadian dream close to British hearts, but unobtainable at home at a reasonable cost. (Tombs and Tombs 2004: 657)

It is evident that owning a house in France has symbolic value in the British middle-class imagination, with acquisition marking improved social status. Furthermore, I argue that living in rural France has been similarly valorized, and can thus be converted into a cultural asset. Property ownership and a commitment to living in France were therefore sources of symbolic and cultural capital for my respondents, through which they reinforced their position within the British middle classes. This resonates with Ong's (1999) discussion of the way that the transnational Chinese have combined migration strategies with capital accumulation within the transnational arena. My respondents in the Lot had carefully chosen to articulate and manifest their quest for a better way of life by using cultural referents that would be significant to their compatriots; in the process they sought to enhance their social status.

The homogeneous class culture of my respondents stands in contrast to life-style migrant populations elsewhere, which attract migrants from a wider range of class backgrounds. For example, both O'Reilly (2000) and Oliver (2008) highlight that their Spanish field sites attracted migrants from both the working and the middle classes. It seems that class has been inscribed on rural France in a way not paralleled in other destinations. At least in the British perception, rural France has a particularly classed significance, which is undoubtedly influenced by the historical relationship of the British to the French countryside. As Tombs and Tombs argue, 'Rural France was the recipient of a unique devotion going well beyond considerations of price, convenience and weather, and which … dates back to the nineteenth century' (2007: 656–657).

The question remains as to what these representations of rural France and the lives on offer there reveal about the migrants. In this respect, I consider the extent to which these representations are emblematic of the migrants' ambitions for their own lives rather than reflecting the objective reality of the lives available in the Lot. Aldridge (1995) argued that *A Year in Provence*, the autobiographical account of Peter Mayle's life in Provence, could be understood to be more about the English than about the French people portrayed in the pages of the book. Indeed, this can equally be seen in the way that my respondents in the Lot refer to the landscape and people within their new environment. Their representations of the *Lotoise* landscape draw heavily on the conceptualization of the countryside as the rural idyll, which, as Williams (1973) describes, emerges out of a particular opposition to the city. This is a romantic conceptualization that influences how they understand the social and family relationships within it – as based on mechanical solidarity (Rapport 1993) – and incorporates their back-to-the-land fantasies. Such renderings of the countryside are specific to the British middle classes.

In the case of my respondents in the Lot, these moralized presentations of the countryside provide justification for their migration. However, they are also significant in the migrants' understandings of their post-migration lives. They strive to emulate the social relationships that they imagine the local French have with one another, aiming for integration and privileging a sense of local community. I argue, however, that the claimed desire for integration and ever-present discussion about their abilities at speaking and learning French are in part influenced by their belief that, as good migrants, they should strive to be integrated. This, as in the case of the rural idyll, can be considered as a moral position that frames the migrants' actions and discourses about their lives in France.

From all walks of life

The diversity of the British population was something that many of the migrants emphasized. They claimed that this was evident in the different lives that people had led back in Britain and the individualized circumstances behind migration. Susan Sparrow explained that her compatriots living locally 'came from all walks of life', while Robert Grange stressed, 'Everyone comes down here for different reasons'. These reflections on diversity were representative of how my respondents understood the British population of the Lot. Jon Morris was keen to point out how this diversity translated into different styles of post-migration life:

> There are the ones that want to come over because they've got English friends in the area and they know they'll mix, and the circle will be within the English group. And then you'll have the others. I mean, we know English people who are on the edge, and you touch that group as well. And then you'll have people who will move to a very rural part of France where it's literally French.

This typology of British people living in the Lot focuses predominantly on themes of social integration and the establishment and maintenance of social networks (Benson 2010a; see also Scott 2006). It is significant in the extent to which it mirrors the account of one of Buller and Hoggart's respondents in the Lot:

Crudely speaking there are: [1] retired or early retired who tend to integrate much more slowly and are often more jaundiced about the French, living in France not for the French, etc., etc. An extraordinary Somerset Maugham mixture of folk; [2] the mid life refugees like ourselves who make a lot of how well they have adjusted; except those who cannot manage a conversation in French and generally behave like superior beings; [3] driftwood of the UK recession – younger and much poorer than previous groups. (1994a: 115)

While I reserve further discussion of social integration for the next chapter, I draw attention to this quotation here to demonstrate the pervasiveness of distinction within the migrants' lives. Buller and Hoggart (1994a) argue that age did not appear to have a significant impact on the extent to which and with whom individual migrants socialized with; nor was this evident on the level of occupational groups. Rather, what this quotation demonstrates is the perception of diversity within the British population, which, when understood in the context of their middle-class origins, came to represent the basic distinctions that the migrants adopted to describe and evaluate the lives of their compatriots. It is therefore the case that these distinctions are significant, not so much in what they tell us about the people referred to but in terms of the work they do to (re)produce the identities of the people using them (see Chapters 6 and 7).

The perceived diversity of the British population influenced the migrants' experiences of life in rural France. Despite their efforts to underplay this aspect of their social lives, they regularly mixed with their compatriots. Within the social arena they were therefore able to gauge the diversity within the population. As Martin Johnstone stressed, 'you tend to mix with people you might not necessarily have chosen to be friends with in England'; the heterogeneity of the British population thus led to friendships. Equally, discussions of diversity also highlighted that people often did not have anything much in common beyond their British citizenship – which in Ron Stampton's opinion, was 'not enough to hold people together' – or their desire for a different life, which was equally no guarantee that they would get along with one another. Although I too recognized diversity within the British population, I also recognized the extent to which this was limited, and not just in terms of class. This was an exclusively white population. Given the displacement of the desire for the British countryside onto rural France that this migration trend has been claimed to represent (Buller and Hoggart 1994a), it is possible that this reflects a racialized desire for the countryside, consolidated in the first place by the recognizable whiteness of the British countryside (see for example Agyeman and Spooner 1997; Neal 2002; Cloke 2006).

A typology of British migration to the Lot

My respondents in the Lot can be categorized by the timing of their migration, their family circumstances at this point, and their position in the life course (Benson 2010a). While many of my respondents were of retirement age or older, a number had relocated to the Lot at an earlier age. There was also an increasing population of much younger migrants, aged between thirty and forty-five, who had left their jobs in Britain and moved to the Lot to start a new life. The population also included children who had grown up in rural France. Members of each group held in common their reasons for leaving Britain – located within specific social, economic and political contexts – and their aspirations for life following migration. The British residents of the Lot can therefore be categorized as: families who migrated between the late 1980s and early 1990s; retirees, migrating from around 1996 onwards; and mid-life migrants, relocating to the Lot from 2000 onwards. This model therefore draws initial attention to the diverse motivations influencing this migration trend, as these were particular to my respondents' position in their life course at the time of migration. These categories are intended as a conceptual tool to identify the similarities and differences in the migrants' experiences of life before and after migration. Understood within this conceptual framework, it becomes clear that the lives that my respondents had led in Britain and the events and circumstances that influenced their migration continued to impact on their post-migration lives.

During the late 1980s and early 1990s, many of the Britons migrating to the Lot came as families, with middle-aged parents and children of school age.[2] As they explained, the benefits they derived from migration included healthier and safer lives for their children, a better education, and 'quality time' to spend together as a family. James Harvey-Browne, who had moved to the Lot with his wife and children in the early 1990s, aptly captured the context and drive behind such family migration, 'We came to France for quality of life, or perceived quality of life should I say ... cheap property prices and redundancy in England ... not necessarily in that order'. It was often the case that life in Britain had taken a turn for the worst; for many of these families migration had coincided with redundancy. It is against this background that their desires for an improved 'quality of life' became meaningful. Although the initial motivations behind migration had been articulated around a better future for their children, over time, it became clear that priorities had changed. At the time of the research many of the children who had arrived in this wave had left home. They discovered that they could no longer remain in the Lot as there was very little work. Several of them returned to Britain, while others, alongside their French peers, moved to the big towns and cities in the vicinity. For their parents, aspirations for life changed, and they became more concerned with their status as ageing individuals.

A large proportion of the British living in the Lot at the time of my research had chosen to migrate when they retired. This reflected a more general trend in international retirement migration (IRM) from Britain to southern European countries (see for example King, Warnes and Williams 2000; Oliver 2007), and included a number of individuals who had taken early retirement. In this respect, the population of retirees varied in terms of age, health and experiences of life following migration and therefore should not be considered as a homogeneous population. Of my respondents, the majority of retirees had arrived in the Lot post-1996. Migration and retirement were thoroughly intertwined, as they stepped down from their working lives and into the more laid-back life available in the Lot. Susan Sparrow, who had moved to the Lot with her husband Trevor when they retired and was now aged seventy, explained, 'there reaches a time when old horses should be put out to graze'. There was an additional perception that the virtues of the French countryside included a greater respect and value for the elderly. As they approached old age, they felt that in this context they would be more valued by society than if they had stayed in Britain. Following Oliver (2008), it becomes clear that retirement migration was presented as a way of achieving positive ageing.

For the mid-life migrants – often young, childless couples – migration co-incided with the decision to leave behind their well-paid and respected jobs in Britain. Mirroring the accounts of both family and retired migrants, these mid-life migrants listed the decline of British society and the detrimental effects of stress and pollution on their health as reasons for leaving Britain in search of a better, more relaxed and healthier lifestyle. They unanimously believed that there was more to life than sitting in an office all day long. They stressed that through migration they had been able to transform their working lives dynamically as they set up their own businesses within the destination. This desire to be self-employed was an aspiration that was intrinsically linked to their migration choices. This was an aspiration that was facilitated by the low cost of property and land in the Lot (see also Drake and Collard 2008). Setting up a business and running it on a day-to-day basis took a lot of hard work, but my respondents explained that this was undoubtedly preferable to the lives that they had led before migration as they had now achieved a better work–life balance.

To consider the migrants in the terms laid out by this typology helps us to recognize the diversity of population (Benson 2010a; see also Buller 2008), but this kind of rigid framework cannot adequately be used to represent the diverse experiences and lives led following migration. The model is therefore limited in the extent to which it can explain the post-migration lives of my respondents. In particular, it becomes clear that while the migrants' imaginings and aspirations had often influenced their experiences, when it came to social relationships, there were other parties involved whose actions and behaviours needed to be accounted for. Equally, the nuances of individual migrations continued to influence certain aspects of life in the Lot, such as choices about where and how to live and efforts to become socially integrated into the local population. British migration to the Lot is a social phenomenon that must therefore be understood in terms of broader historical contexts, while also questioning the individual circumstances that led to migration.

It is evident that the Lot attracts white British middle-class lifestyle migrants. Nevertheless, by their own admission they are a diverse population, reflecting the fragmentation of the British middle classes. As will be seen throughout this book, the migrants continually drew attention to the diversity in the local British population, particularly highlighting the way in which their lives were different from those of their compatriots (Benson 2009). Processes of distinction were a central feature of their lives, and as I argue below, particularly revealing of their original class origins, from which they had not yet fully escaped.

Contextualizing migration

It's the quality of life. I wish I could have done it much earlier than I did. But then, having said that, I did enjoy every minute of my working life. (Ron Stampton)

To move to France had always been my husband's dream … he really wanted France … At that time [the French] were more concerned with how they lived than what they had … It felt so much like coming home … it was just so different to England. (Samantha Harris)

So you come away from it and you find a different life, and people are living longer in the Lot. (Susan Sparrow)

The fact that it is a more relaxed way of life is good … the way of life was so frenetic there, so you'd just collapse in the holidays. (William and Victoria Cardew)

The property in the Lake District was very expensive. And the season up there is so short and you get good weather about five days a year, and that wasn't very suitable after having spent a long time in Hong Kong. I find Britain … a very aggressive place. I'm amazed at the aggression on the radio, on TV, on advertising, everywhere, everywhere … and so, we kind of couldn't quite face going back to England. (Robert and Justine Grange, who had lived in Hong Kong for thirty years)

I'd made the break, so going back, I'd been living in the Savoie (department in the French Alps), been skiing. I couldn't go back to work in an office after that. We'd just moved office buildings to this smoked-glass, air-conditioned, no-opening-windows building. You couldn't see whether it was sunny, or whatever, outside. That was it. I went back and, I think it was six months or so, and that was it really. (Jon Morris)

Southern French culture, it's like stepping back into an England that you do remember as a child; it's very much like 50s/60s England, our social and cultural norms … there's more respect for the elderly built into the children's culture … Children are more respectful, and possibly because of the environment, the elderly are more active … France represents something we've lost. (Simon Glass)

This selection of extracts from the migration narratives of some of my respondents demonstrates the various motivations behind migration and reveal the constituent parts of the better way of life that they seek. These include quality of life, migration to rural France as a long-held dream, the rural idyll, migration as an escape from the rat race, lower cost of property, climate, a healthier environment and nostalgia for French culture. While it is seen that rural France had a particular cultural significance for my respondents, there are also indications that they took into consideration other more pragmatic concerns, financial and health among others (cf King, Warnes and Williams 2000; O'Reilly 2000). These brief extracts give an initial insight into the complexity of the decision to migrate, representing views common to other narratives. Broadly, a tale of dissatisfaction with life in Britain emerges, whereby rural France offers salvation and the possibility of self-realization.

Nevertheless, generic explanations of the decision to migrate, which contrast the decline of society in Britain with the perceived life on offer in the Lot, are limited. On one level, they can help us to understand the migration of people to and from the same places. However, they cannot account for flows of migration taking place at different points in time and under different circumstances. Indeed, with the migration of my respondents taking place over a period of twenty years, the timing of migration could correspond to very different social, economic and political contexts (Buller 2008; Benson 2010a). Similarly, reducing the decision to migrate to its cultural dimensions does not allow for the point of view of the individual to emerge or for the presence of individual agency within migration choices (Ong 1999). While my respondents all presented a similar over-arching rhetoric about the decision to migrate, further inquiries reveal that these were articulated to account for often very different individual circumstances. To account for these nuances in this section I present a more detailed examination of British migration to the Lot.

Historical contexts and individualized migration stories

The circumstances of life before migration could, to a degree, be read in the timing of migration and how this related to wider social, political and economic events. As my respondents were lifestyle migrants, their migration was broadly facilitated by relative economic privilege and ease of movement (Benson and O'Reilly 2009; O'Reilly and Benson 2009). On the one hand, the latter is a result of globalization; our place in the world is different under the conditions of time-space compression (Giddens 1990) and a sense of the world as a single place (Robertson 1992). Indeed, this migration trend, which has been growing in recent years, reflects the increasing levels of travel within the world (Faist 2000; Papastergiadis 2000; Castles and Miller 2003; Urry 2007). On the other hand, this ease of movement was specific to my respondents' position as European Union citizens who are entitled to freedom of movement within Europe. Given the timing of their migration and the specific context of the Lot, unlike contemporary tourism and labour migration flows which have been positively affected by low-cost air-travel (Williams and Baláž 2009), this particular migration had not, as yet, been facilitated by low-cost air travel.[3] While these broad structural conditions can facilitate migration, there are time- and space-specific contexts that need to be recognized.

For my respondents in the Lot, it was evident that subjective experiences of life in Britain influenced migration. In this respect, the decision to migrate needs to be understood within an individualized context of pre-migration life. For example, the migrants regularly drew on their disillusionment with life in Britain on a political level, stressing how this had influenced their migration. For those who had migrated in the 1980s and early 1990s, this was directed towards the Conservative government; these migrants had felt the effects of the economic recession of the late 1980s and early 1990s, which had resulted in wide-scale redundancy. Indeed, several of my respondents had been made redundant. Turning disadvantage to advantage, they had sold their British properties, cashed in their savings and relocated to the Lot. Property ownership was a central element of this migration trend, and even against the backdrop of a poor economic situation in Britain, the pound was still strong against the French franc and the differential in property prices remained in the favour of British incomers. In this political and economic climate, many Britons found that they could purchase their new homes without mortgages and relocate.[4]

Such disillusionment with the system was also evident for those migrating from the mid-1990s onwards, with those migrating from 1997 onwards expressing their dissatisfaction with the then Labour government, to which they attributed broader changes in British society. Ironically, the structural conditions at this time facilitated their migration. The more favourable economic climate of the mid-1990s, as Britain moved out of the recession, resulted in wide-scale retirement migration to rural France, and also in the migration of younger professionals, aged in their thirties and forties, trading in their working lives in the cities of Britain for simpler lives in the French countryside. Despite the inflation that had hit property prices in France at that time, the relative disparity in property prices meant that they were still able to buy property with cash. Following migration, while most of the retirees had enough capital retained alongside their pension payments to live comfortably, for the younger migrants life was significantly different. Their strategy had been more risky as they needed to establish a continuous source of income once they lived in the Lot.

The subjective experiences of such structural and material conditions were integral to the context of migration. As Harold Jones explained to me, he had been unhappy with the transformations to his working life that he had experienced in the late 1980s; he had been encouraged to work towards promotion and threatened with penalization if he did not comply. He openly admitted that he had had no desire for promotion and that the opportunity to take voluntary severance in 1990 had been a blessing. Such a watershed event often coincided with migration, and the migrants commonly cited such events as retirement, bereavement, redundancy and even marriage. In this rendering, relocation was presented as a turning point (O'Reilly 2000; Hoey 2005, 2006).

By spending time with my respondents I often uncovered migration stories that they did not tell so readily; tales of family difficulties, second marriages and affairs that had caused outrage among friends and family, and of the events leading up to redundancy and retirement. For example, one couple initially explained that their move had been prompted by redundancy. However, as I became closer to them, I discovered a long-term family disapproval of their relationship. They had first met when married to other people, and their respective families had never quite come to terms with the circumstances of their relationship. The painful histories that sometimes lay hidden behind positive depictions of migration demonstrated that while lifestyle migration was often reduced to a particular cultural logic, for my respondents the act of migration was prompted by individualized circumstances.

Rurality as remedy

Previous research on the British living in rural France uniformly argues that this migration is spurred by the desire for an idealized and romanticized form of rural life that is no longer available back in Britain (Buller and Hoggart 1994a; Barou and Prado 1995; Gervais-Aguer 2004, 2006; Depierre and Guitard 2006). In this rendering, rural France

> represents an idealized rural form that has no effective counterpart in Britain ... the principal components of which appear to be the maintenance of traditional values, the existence of viable and genuinely welcoming rural communities, a slower 'pace of life', and an enhanced 'quality of life'. (Buller and Hoggart 1994a: 128)

It is the search for this particular mode of rural living, viewed through rose-tinted spectacles, that distinguishes such lifestyle migrants from labour migrants and refugees (Buller and Hoggart 1994a; Benson and O'Reilly 2009; O'Reilly and Benson 2009). Migration is therefore primarily grounded in middle class-aesthetic and ecological considerations, claimed as a form of counterurbanization (Buller and Hoggart 1994a; Buller 2008).

My respondents reflected these counterurban longings in their presentations of the Lot as the quintessential rural idyll, characterized by its community spirit, intimate relationships with the landscape, and a life of slow pace and good quality. Their responses closely echoed those of Buller and Hoggart's (1994a) respondents ten years earlier. The features that my respondents ascribed to rural France were projections of the idealized lifestyles that they hope to lead following migration. While rural Britain could no longer offer the opportunity for them to realize these ambitions – owing not only to the high cost of living in the British countryside but also the fear that it had been irreparably ruined by (sub)urbanization (at least in the minds of the migrants) – the sparsely populated French countryside, itself a result of industrialization, agricultural modernization and rural depopulation (Buller and Hoggart 1994a; Barou and Prado 1995; Ardagh 2000; Tombs and Tombs 2007), with its bocage-style landscaping (Buller and Hoggart 1994a) and the continuing agricultural system (Barou and Prado 1995), offered a welcome alternative. In response to the migrants' desire for the rural idyll, the bucolic French landscape became an apt location to appropriate as my respondents searched for a better way of life.

For Barou and Prado (1995), this phenomenon also reflected the hedonistic aspirations of middle-class individuals from the developed world, a feature of this lifestyle migration that has otherwise been overlooked. Similarly, my respondents in the Lot sought a better way of life that was more than just rural living and that contained elements of the migrants' own modest hedonistic desires. They found pleasure in 'the more laid-back life' and slower rhythms of the Lot as well as in the locally produced food and wine. Indeed, as one migrant succinctly explained, 'life here is a pleasure'. Relaxation was associated with the slow pace of life, as was local produce with the fruits of local labour; and the sociality embedded in eating and drinking was emblematic of conviviality and community spirit. In this rendering, some of their more hedonistic desires were concealed by the virtues of rural living. Yet, there were other qualities of their lives in the Lot that were not so easily encompassed. At times, the motifs of hedonism and rurality sat alongside one another. The migrants built swimming pools alongside orchards of fruit trees or looking out onto a beautiful view, took their evening *apéritif* on terraces that overlooked vegetable gardens and played golf on beautifully manicured courses bordered by the untamed *Lotoise* landscape.

Individual circumstances also influenced my respondents' imaginings of life in rural France. For families with children, rural France was considered to offer a safer, better and healthier life for their children, reflecting a wider notion that life in the countryside was better for children (Halfacree 1994; Müller 2002; Schmied 2005). Those for whom migration had coincided with retirement stressed that in the Lot they could experience the more leisurely lives that they desired, while also escaping such structural constraints on their movements and actions that they felt would have been imposed on them if they had stayed in Britain – a concern characteristic of retirement migrants more broadly (King, Warnes, and Williams 2000; Oliver 2008). In contrast, many of the younger migrants needed to generate an income following migration. The employment choices these migrants made often reflected the economic rationale behind buying a home in France. As Buller and Hoggart stressed,

> In reality many of these jobs are part-time or seasonal, but the purported ability to survive on uncertain or low incomes is undoubtedly influenced by the initial security migrants have from buying a relatively inexpensive French home which left them with significant capital after selling a home in Britain at a time of high prices. (1994c: 207)

However, it also became clear that the decisions my respondents made about earning an income were reflected in their project to change their lives. Many of them stressed that relocation to rural France had given them the opportunity to become their own boss, to have control over their working lives, and thus to re-evaluate their work–life balance. While it was premised that their work was supporting their new lifestyles, it was also clear in some cases that being able to be self-employed or taking on a dream job – for example, Pat and Jean Porter had dreamed of running and owning a vineyard for several years prior to their migration – was part of the rationalization for living in France (see also Williams and Hall 2000; Stone and Stubbs 2007; Drake and Collard 2008).

Irrespective of age and family situation, it seems that all my respondents sought to change their lives through migration. This desire for transformation was further consolidated in their cynical and fatalistic representations of life before migration, a common theme in lifestyle migrant narratives (see for example Waldren 1996; O'Reilly 2000; Oliver 2008). On the one hand, the migrants presented a general sense of decline, stressing that life in Britain was not what it had been. Themes within these narratives of discontent included high crime rates; the threatening behaviour of young people; poor health care and their own poor health, the latter often presented as the embodiment of the stress of life in Britain; difficult and competitive working conditions; a general absence of community; and a bad environment in which to raise children. On the other hand, they stressed the impact that these problems of life in Britain had had on them personally.

Vivian St. John, a retiree, explained to me that she had been afraid to venture out into the streets at night and that her property had been vandalized on several occasions; Vic and Anne Wilson, also retired, told me that their house in Britain had been burgled three times. James and Sian Harvey-Browne explained: 'one of our sons suffers from asthma very badly and we found that every time we went out shopping he'd suffer from the pollution in the towns'. William and Victoria Cardew felt 'like we'd worked a life sentence', and Simon Glass described the negative effects that working non-stop had had on his health. In this respect, while the common feeling of disillusionment with life in Britain was based on the migrants' subjective experiences, it also informed their fears for their projected future lives. Migration was viewed and presented as a remedy for an unsatisfying present and an unpromising, uncertain future.

While it is evident that the quality of life that my respondents sought was influenced by their culturally specific imaginings of rural living, reflecting a wider enchantment of the British middle classes with rurality (Williams 1973), at the same time the quality of life that they desired represented a re-evaluation of their lives. It became clear that although the decision to migrate was often articulated in broad cultural terms, it was much more complex. As I have demonstrated here, migration results from the intersection of certain structural and material conditions with more individualized circumstances. It is against the background of this more nuanced understanding of migration that my respondents in the Lot imagined and experienced their post-migration lives.

Telling migration stories

The migrants' reflections on the decision to migrate were, necessarily, retrospective; over time they had had opportunities to rework and refine their migration stories. The understanding that through the performance of narrative the individual is able to regain or augment their sense of agency (Becker 1997; Ochs and Capp 2001; Frank 2002; Jackson 2002) reveals that by narrating their progress *en route* to a better way of life, the migrants enhanced their sense of achievement. Giddens (1991) has argued that people tell stories to displace uncertainty and make sense of the world, and that the content of these stories reflects how the individual overcomes discomfort. Through narrative a sense of continuity and coherence emerges that is otherwise unattainable in an increasingly flexible and fragmented world (Giddens 1991; Bauman 1995; Sennett 1998; Burkitt 2005). In this respect, the performance of narrative is central to the way in which individuals understand themselves and their position within the social world (Bruner 1990; Gergen and Gergen 1988, Langellier & Peterson 2004). As I demonstrate below, the contents of my respondents' narratives, when examined, reveal the sense that they have transformed their lives through migration, overcoming the perceived constraints of life in Britain, to reclaim control.

The unique appeal of the Lot and the adventure of migration

In their accounts the migrants express the sense that they have increased control over their lives by presenting the act of migration as adventurous and somehow risky, while also stressing the distinctiveness of the Lot as a migration destination.

> There is one thing we do say here; normal people do not come to France. (Martin Johnstone)

> It was quite a risk at the time. Some of our friends thought we were absolutely bonkers ... because it was just moving out of that line that everybody takes. You work, you have kids, you get your own house, then you retire. (Jon and Kay Morris)

> It's surprising how many people don't know about the Lot. We've had two or three sets of people come here who have spent time on holiday in France – but either in Brittany, the Loire or Provence – that didn't know this bit. (Robert and Justine Grange)

In this rendering, both the act of migration and the destination were presented as distinctive, as something out of the ordinary. It seemed that my respondents were keen to present their choice of the Lot as original, as though they had stumbled across some long-buried treasure, an uncharted territory. They would, for example, stress that 'there were not many other Britons living here when we first arrived', in this manner drawing attention to the distinctiveness of their own migration. Within the context of migration as eliciting self-realization, this rhetoric of discovery revealed more about the migrants than it did about the Lot. Correspondingly, migration emerged as a risky act through which the migrants were able to augment their individual agency. In this manner, the migrants' perceptions and representations of their new surroundings were revealing, not only in terms of what they convey about the Lot but also because they allow insights into the value that the migrants placed on migration.

The migrants' self-presentations as 'pioneers' and 'trailblazers' similarly reflected this representation, and they stressed the exclusivity of their destination. Recalling the decision to migrate, my respondents were keen to emphasize that, by taking the risk of moving to the Lot, they were demonstrating their courage to think beyond their otherwise normal life-trajectories. When I spoke to the children who had been brought to the Lot when their parents chose to migrate, they explained that they had been excited about the prospect of living elsewhere and had seen the whole process as an adventure; undoubtedly, this was an 'adventure' sold to them by their parents. But many of the other migrants similarly spoke in terms of an adventure or of a certain 'pioneering spirit' and of the sense of 'get-up-and-go' required to make the move. As Bruillon (2007) found in the case of British migrants in the Lot, my respondents' accounts too revealed an underlying rhetoric of migration as an, albeit risky, adventure.

These self-presentations were further reinforced by the focus on the emotional criteria driving migration; as Jack Stone explained, he had moved to the Lot after 'falling in love' with the surroundings while visiting a yoga retreat. Simon Glass, who worked as a relocation specialist in the Lot, explained to me that he had been surprised by the extent to which such emotional criteria dominated the decision to migrate, to the extent that migrants were often ill prepared for the realities of life in the Lot. Indeed, Sally Stampton, who had moved to the Lot with her son Ollie (aged eleven at the time of the research) explained, 'I didn't research it at all when I brought Ollie; if I had I probably wouldn't have come. I'm glad I didn't'. It was the unknown that had facilitated her migration; she felt that if she had had a greater degree of knowledge, particularly about the French education system, she might never have taken the decision to migrate.

In relation to their relatively predictable lives were they to stay in Britain, life in France was more unknown. Arguably, the migrants believed that they had known what they were moving to, but there was always a chance that life would not work out in the way that they had hoped. Indeed, several of the migrants were keen to point out the high numbers of Britons who returned to Britain.[5] In this respect, migration to rural France was an undeniable risk. But, as Giddens (1991) has explained, in the era of late modernity, people often take risks in order to grasp the opportunities available to them.

Nudrali and O'Reilly (2009) have argued that lifestyle migration acts as a mark of social distinction. I build on this argument, stressing that it is precisely because it was risky and with an unknown outcome that this lifestyle decision distinguished my respondents in the Lot from their compatriots who dwell in the safety of their 'normal' lives back in Britain. However, the decision to migrate was further revealing on the level of the individual; when placed within the context of reprieve and escape, these stories demonstrated that through migration the migrants had gained a greater sense of being in control of their own lives. Migration to the Lot may have been a risky adventure for them, but the migrants remained hopeful that it would bring better consequences than if they had stayed in Britain.

Lifestyle migration as the pursuit of happiness

By presenting migration as an action through which they had been able to transform their lives, my respondents demonstrated the possibility of improving their lives. Lifestyle migration, understood as the quest for a better way of life, therefore effected change. However, it became clear that the migrants continued to pursue a better way of life after migration. In this respect, the act of migration emerges as just one element of the quest for a better way of life, a life project that characterized the migrants' lives before and after migration (Benson and O'Reilly 2009; O'Reilly and Benson 2009) and that was intrinsically linked to the reflexive project of the self (Giddens 1991). Against this background I argue that lifestyle migration can be understood as part of the broader pursuit of happiness that Bauman (2007, 2008) stresses is part of the liquid modern condition.

As Bauman argues, in individualized society, we are all 'artists of life' (2008) who believe that we can make a difference to our lives. By pursuing happiness we hope to escape from the ambivalence of life. For the consumer, happiness is equated not with the fulfilment of needs but with 'possessing and consuming certain objects and practising certain lifestyles' (Bauman 2007: 130). Understood in this manner, the pursuit of happiness is perpetual, as people try to meet their new and increasing desires spurred on by the belief that there is always something more to be had. Individual hunters, in Bauman's terms, thus venture into uncharted territory, hoping that they will find the ultimate in happiness, only to be followed by more hunters pursuing the same dream. In this manner, what individuals seek undergoes continual transformation and is constantly redefined as they respond to and resist external conditions, obstacles to their 'chosen vision of the "good life" ' (Bauman 2008: 53). Indeed, this sense of an individual pursuit was reflected in the migrants' discourses as they stressed their 'pioneering spirit' or the adventure of migration, distinguishing themselves from their compatriots in their self-presentations as lone 'hunters' following the scent of a better way of life.

Despite the parallels between lifestyle migration and the pursuit of happiness, I argue that Bauman's approach cannot provide a comprehensive explanation to account for the nuances of British migration to rural France. First, Bauman stresses the individualization of society. This approach does not allow for the persistence of certain social structures and their influence on individual actions. Bauman (1998; 2000) may hint at some of the distinctions that exist within an increasingly mobile society – for instance, vagabonds who move on irrespective of their own desires because they are no longer welcome as opposed to tourists who move (or stay) as and when they desire – but his recognition of the stratification of society is limited. Atkinson argues that Bauman's replacement of class with a new order of stratification rests on a 'shaky supporting pillar' (2008: 14) and a 'narrow conceptualization of class' (2008: 14). Second, Bauman provides no explanation, beyond the overarching context of liquid modernity, for why people feel compelled to take part in this pursuit.

While it is clear that some of the themes within Bauman's work map onto British migration in rural France, namely the pursuit of happiness, the framework in which this has been developed is not applicable. As the experiences of my respondents in the Lot demonstrate, the act of migration was heavily influenced by, among other things, their class culture. This was evident both in their cultural appropriation of rural France and in their efforts to present their own migration as distinctive and unique. As Atkinson argues, Bauman's 'theorisation may be deeply flawed, but the overall *spirit* of his diagnosis, once viewed through the conceptual lens of whichever class theory one claims allegiance to, might still hold water' (2008: 14). Following this call, when I revisit the persistence of class later in the book (Chapter 7 and the Conclusion), I draw on a conception of class influenced by Bourdieu (1984). Through this conceptual framework, a nuanced understanding of post-migration lives emerges, which recognizes the extent to which class continues to be reproduced even through migration (Benson 2009; Oliver and O'Reilly 2010).

Conclusion

The British living in the Lot are a diverse population who range in age and family circumstances and whose decision to migrate needs to be understood not only as culturally determined but also as the result of particular social, economic and political contexts and more individualized motivations. On the one hand, migration to rural France was a lifestyle choice that reflected their common middle-class culture and had been made possible by their relative affluence (cf Amit 2007). Such insights into the migrants' class background are telling, explaining the choice of destination, but also providing a lens through which further to examine their rationalizations of migration. On the other hand, migration was presented as unique, a way in which as individuals they had changed their lives. This sense that migration resulted in transformation and self-realization was integrated into the justificatory framing of their individual migration stories.

The decision to migrate was presented as a largely individualized action, exclusively undertaken by each migrant. On the surface, it appears to resemble Bauman's pursuit of happiness (2007, 2008). Nevertheless, the residual evidence of class within the migrants' rhetoric and manifest in their claims to distinctiveness, not accounted for by Bauman's individualization thesis, limits the extent to which this theory can explain the nuanced experiences of my respondents in the Lot. However, it is apparent that the spirit of the pursuit of happiness lives on. Bauman claimed that the art of life is never complete; individuals continue to pursue happiness throughout their lives, as they are never truly fulfilled.

While previous research has demonstrated that the social phenomenon of British migration to rural France can be considered as the quest for a better way of life (Buller and Hoggart 1994a; Barou and Prado 1995), how this becomes reality has remained unquestioned. Lifestyle migration is only one aspect of the lifestyle trajectory of an individual; it is neither the beginning nor the end of the story, as it needs to be understood within the context of life before and after migration (Benson and O'Reilly 2009; O'Reilly and Benson 2009). Just as Bauman's (2008) hunters continually refine what will constitute happiness, the migrants revise their desires following migration as they continue in a never-ending pursuit of a better way of life.

Notes

1 I deliberately use the plural to denote the heterogeneity of the middle classes in Britain (see also Reay 2008).
2 This is not to say that there were no families migrating to the Lot after the 1990s. It is just that most of the family migrants interviewed had arrived in the late 1980s and 1990s.
3 At the time of my research, regular flights from the UK to airports in neighbouring departments had commenced, but it was too soon to judge whether these resulted in an increased rate of migration into the surrounding areas.
4 It was rare to find Britons living in the Lot who had not purchased their own home. The exceptions to this rule were those individuals who had chosen to give life in rural France a chance before they committed themselves through the purchase of property. This was

a new phenomenon, which started to become significant in 2005 when I returned to the field.

5 This was estimated at fifty per cent of those who had migrated. However, while I was there I knew of only one couple who decided to return to Britain when it turned out that life was not like it had been on holiday and 'the log fire did not make itself'. There has been little research into the return migration of lifestyle migrants, although Henry Buller (2008) recalls the findings of exploratory research on this topic, suggesting that two-thirds of the people he had researched in the Dordogne in the 1990s had returned to the United Kingdom. I also understand that the Institute for Public Policy Research (IPPR) are currently undertaking research into this form of return migration.

2

Negotiating locality

The imaginings of life in the Lot, understood as the quintessential rural idyll, that prompted the migrants' choice of destination centred around the vision of a discrete rural community characterized by mechanical solidarity and social cohesion (Rapport 1993). My respondents believed that their entry into this idyllic social landscape – an imagined community consisting of the French inhabitants of the villages in which they would reside – would provide them with the antidote to their malaise with life in contemporary Britain (see also Tombs and Tombs 2004; Drake and Collard 2008; Benson 2010a). In this respect, the desire for local belonging emerged as a driving force behind migration, continued as an aspiration for post-migration lives, and was intrinsically linked to the migrants' identity claims.

Focusing on the post-migration lives of my respondents, the ethnography in this chapter reveals the strategies that they used to embed themselves within local social life, demonstrates the role that the local actors took in judging the success of these efforts, and highlights the persistence of a particular (romantic) imagining of locality. Rather than suggest that these claims to local belonging be taken at face-value, I question here why they chose to privilege such claims and how these linked to the greater force behind their migration: the search for a better way of life.

Through migration, the migrants' self-presentations and expectations were challenged as their initial imaginings were confronted by the realities of life within a pre-existing social order. Denying the existence of a migrant community, my respondents in the Lot presented themselves as empathetic incomers who wanted to become part of the local community and, as I discuss later in this book, to highlight the differences between their ambitions and those of others who were happy to surround themselves with their compatriots. As one of my respondents fervently exclaimed, 'We are not migrants! We are not British! We are not expatriates! We are *Sauliaçoise!*' – with the last statement a claim to belonging within the locale. However, whether they achieved local belonging was, in part, beyond their control and they recalled the obstacles to their integration into the local community. As the ethnography in this chapter demonstrates, their experiences forced the migrants to re-evaluate their aspirations for life following migration. Nevertheless, it was rare for the migrants to abandon their initial imaginings of locality; they merely reassessed the measures that they needed to take in order to establish sustainable relationships with local social actors.

It therefore emerges that despite their roles as global social actors, my respondents in the Lot regularly cast themselves as local social actors, their claimed positions characterized by their pretensions to locality. However, while on the surface it seemed that my respondents imagined the Lot as a distinct place where they could uniquely find what they sought, this chapter demonstrates that they often assessed this in terms of their social relations. As a result, the identities that they claimed both reinforced a link between place and identity and demonstrated the extent to which, as Appadurai (1996) argues, locality is a 'property of social life'.

Constituting locality

Previous research has stressed that while the desire for belonging to the community is presented in justification of lifestyle migration (Benson and O'Reilly 2009; O'Reilly and Benson 2009), it is clear that lifestyle migrants often fail to integrate into local societies. Indeed, accounts of such relatively affluent incomers in Spain have focused on the construction of transnational communities that run parallel to the host society (see for example Rozenberg 1995; Rodríguez *et al* 1998; O'Reilly 2000; Oliver 2008), stressing that prolonged engagement with the transnational presents an obstacle to the establishment of meaningful relationships with local social actors. While migrants claim local integration, the reality – often the result of a linguistic barrier – is more likely to be integration into a bounded community of their compatriots. Lifestyle migrants are therefore presented as exclusively leading their lives within a transnational space, with their access to the local limited by their own actions.

In contrast, my own observations revealed that for many of my respondents in the Lot, claims to locality were more than just rhetoric; in fact, they actively worked to effect meaningful relationships with members of the local community (see also Smallwood 2007), highlighting the value that they placed on such social integration. As Buller and Hoggart (1994c: 205) stress, 'value differences' and 'dissimilar objectives in buying a French home' can be read through migrants' choices about whether to integrate into the local community or into an ethnic enclave of their compatriots; indeed, such a value difference was regularly presented by the migrants in justification of their own choices. However, their social relationships were rarely so clear-cut, and for many of the migrants the relationships that they had with their French neighbours often existed alongside those which they maintained with their friends and family back in Britain and with other lifestyle migrants living in the Lot. In this context, following Levitt and Glick Schiller (2004), it became clear that transnational and local relations were not mutually exclusive. In view of this, my respondents' claims to belonging should be read as statements about the individual's position within a wider circuit of relationships (Benson 2010b).

The different values that they placed on their various social relationships were particularly telling of the way in which they wanted their migration to be understood, acting as part of their wider identity claims. While they admitted that it was easy to make friends with other Britons living locally – as one of my respondents explained in specific reference to their experiences of the relationships within the British population of the Lot, 'people get to know each other faster, more, more quickly' – they were always keen to stress that they were still trying, or still had the desire, to make friends with the local French. It is this privileging of relationships with local social actors that is the focus of this chapter: how such relationships intersect with imaginings about local life and their role in how the migrants constituted, experienced and utilized locality.

As Cohen (1982) argues, subscription to a particular locality – an expression of culture – is a claim to insider status and belonging that is intrinsically connected to identity. It is through the interplay between culture and the individual that local distinctiveness may be enacted. In an era of globalization and de-territorialization, such locality can no longer be understood to be spatially grounded (Gupta and Ferguson 1992; Appadurai 1996) but is constituted instead through relationships (Hastrup and Fog Olwig 1997), with locality redefined as a 'meeting place' (Massey 1994). It is unsurprising therefore that my respondents' claims to locality were primarily supported by accounts of their relationships with members of the local community.

As 'a property of social life' locality is always in process (Appadurai 1996). The production of locality resides within the collective imagination, with imagining here understood as a social practice (*ibid*). As a result, there are a seemingly endless number of ways in which locality may be constituted. Building on Benedict Anderson's (1983) 'imagined communities', Appadurai (1996) stresses that imagination works to produce local feeling. He proposes imagined worlds – removing Anderson's (1983) focus on national context – to explain how people mobilize their imaginings of locality. This allows for imagined worlds of individuals who share the same vision for the future. In the local context, such as that which my respondents in the Lot find themselves in, this could include a range of social actors, who are imagined to hold in common a particular understanding of locality imparted from their shared local subjectivity. Furthermore, it is clear that my respondents in the Lot still understood the local as territorially based, claiming local subjectivities that related to their immediate surroundings.

The ethnography presented below demonstrates the value of an imagined world, demonstrating the role that imaginings of and desire for a shared local subjectivity play within the migrants' expectations of life in the Lot. In this respect, imagination can be considered as an important factor both in the framing of migration and in shaping how my respondents understood their post-migration lives. But it is also the case that through their experiences of life in the destination the migrants gradually started to reconsider the imaginings that had brought them to the Lot in the first place. Imagination and experience should not, therefore, be considered as separate from one another in the production of a sense of local belonging; in many ways they are mutually constituting and inextricably intertwined. It becomes clear that, when placed in this framework, the migrants' efforts at the production and realization of locality are ongoing, their experiences of life in the Lot both being informed by their (culturally specific) imaginings of the rural idyll and prompting them to subtly reassess their understandings of locality.

However, this is not necessarily a smooth process. As Gupta and Ferguson have argued, 'important tensions may arise when places that have been imagined at a distance must become lived spaces' (1992: 11). In this respect, it becomes clear that expectations and experiences do not always map directly onto one another; the possible intersections of the two may involve some overlap, and experiences may conform to imagination, while there is a further possibility that imagination may be exceeded. However, what became clear in the case of the British residents of the Lot was that the intersection of long-held expectations and imaginings of local life and community with their experiences in post-migration life brought into sharper focus the various discrepancies and disjunctures that characterize the production of locality.

How can the desire for locality be explained? On a general level, this could be read, as David Harvey (1989) argued, as a reaction to the perceived instability of the globalized world. In this rendering, claims to locality arise as a response to the ontological threats posed by globalization. Locality and the place of individuals within it thus persist as important identity markers in everyday life. However, this generalized interpretation gives little insight into how individuals experience the globalized world, the perceived nature of what they are acting against, and the meanings they ascribe to the localities that they claim. In this respect, Cohen's (1982) focus on how individuals in small British rural communities experience belonging can perhaps help to explain the moral value my respondents placed on locality. With claims to locality acting to reinforce the boundaries between cultures, through their claims to local belonging my respondents articulated the difference between their lives before and after migration, thus distinguishing themselves from their friends and families left behind. Through their everyday practices and rhetoric, they sought to consolidate this sense of belonging.

The ethnography presented below demonstrates the ongoing process through which localities were constituted (Appadurai 1996) in the lives of my respondents. It traces their attempts to realize locality, understood in terms of an underlying cultural logic valorizing community belonging, and it highlights the disjunctures that resulted from the intersections of their initial imaginings and their post-migration experience. As they experienced disparities between their imaginings, experiences and locality, the migrants reconstituted their imagined worlds and subtly changed their expectations for the future.

Une entente cordiale?

For my respondents in the Lot, the rhetoric of migration was founded upon the notion that rural living could uniquely provide a sense of community and a recognizably French way of life. Indeed, these twin concerns were highlighted as the migrants described life within the destination and their efforts to embed themselves within the locality. In many ways, their ambitions rested upon a belief in an 'imagined' (local) community (Anderson 1983; see also Appadurai 1996), with values that the migrants hoped to share.

They approached their lives in the Lot with a preconceived idea of what they would find and how the native community would receive them, with such imaginings framing their depictions of local social life. Such romantic renderings of life in the Lot invariably overlooked the possible obstacles to integration that might result from the different class backgrounds and occupational histories of the migrants and their new neighbours (see also Buller and Hoggart 1994c). Nevertheless, my respondents had a clear vision of their lives in the Lot, which presented acceptance into the rural community as a measure of success. As Robert and Justine Grange explained to me early on in my research, 'it is important to be in the centre of the village and to be part of the village; to know the villagers and to get on with them'. In this respect, it became clear that it was only through lived experiences that locality could be realized (Appadurai 1996). Within the context of the quest for a better way of life, social integration acted as a central component of self-realization (Amit 2007; Olwig 2007; Torresan 2007).

Nevertheless, as the ethnography presented below demonstrates, integration into the local population was complex. David Smallwood (2007) has stressed that for the British living in the Aquitaine region of France there is a relationship between the extent of their desire to integrate, their French-speaking abilities, the degree of 'welcome' accorded to them by the local community, and their success at social integration. As I discuss elsewhere (Benson 2010a), the relationship between linguistic capability and integration can be overstated; speaking French is undoubtedly a useful skill but is no guarantee of integration, and the inability to speak French does not always act as a deterrent to the establishment of relationships.

Through my research, it became apparent that common interest was valued more highly than language skills; these interests became the grounds upon which social interaction could develop, even in the absence of a shared language. The integration of the British living in the Lot into the local community therefore relied on the conjunction of several factors: the degree to which people wanted to integrate; local categories of inclusion and exclusion; scope for interaction; linguistic ability; and shared interests. In this model, while there are some structural determinants to integration, it was also clear that the migrants had to take positive actions in this direction and show their willingness to be involved in the local community. As the ethnographic examples below attest, my respondents in the Lot were not as marginal to mainstream society as their compatriots in Spain were considered to be (see O'Reilly 2000; 2007).

The imagined community of the Lot

The local community that the migrants imagined to be available to them in the Lot was uniquely constituted, reflecting their idealized beliefs about rural living. Their romantic renderings of social relations within the community – reminiscent of Urry's (1990) tourist gaze, and initial perceptions and experiences – reinforced their ideas that the Lot offered 'authentic rurality' and thus contributed to their wider idealizations (and moralizations) of the French countryside. The migrants therefore stressed a localized, bounded 'traditional rural community' based on mechanical solidarity (Rapport 1993: 33), centring on 'immediate family and friendship ties, local community solidarity and supportiveness' (Perry 1986: 22).

Trevor and Susan Sparrow, retired migrants who had spent their lives in London, emphasized the presence of this 'traditional rural community' as they recalled an Occitan dance they had attended the previous week.[1] They drew attention to the extensive local participation – which ranged from children to grandparents (all of whom were dancing) – in the event, arguing that the community was 'just like family'. Furthermore, Trevor and Susan particularly highlighted that they had enjoyed the fact that many of the young people and children from the community had taken part in the event. This reflected a more general belief held by my respondents that these children related to their families and elders with respect and placed value on maintaining good family relations. However, these perceptions of local youngsters were integral to the wider values they attributed to rural French society.

As the migrants discussed the way that local *Lotoise* people related to one another on a daily basis, they highlighted not only their warmth and friendliness (see also Buller and Hoggart 1994c) but also their good interpersonal skills. Robert and Justine Grange, who had owned their house in the Lot for more than fifteen years, explained, 'The French in rural France we find extremely polite, civilised, charming. You know, people talk to you, there's always the greetings – you know, formal greetings.' The willingness of their neighbours to talk to them made them feel that they had made the right choice about where to live and also gave them the sense that they were an albeit small part of the local community. Many of the migrants were also keen to stress the generosity of their neighbours.

> In the country, like here, they give you so much and they think, 'Well, that's normal. If you have a lot, you give'. This week we've had fresh eggs, a bream, mimosa, daffodils … they're just so kind to us. (Susan Sparrow)

To Susan this generosity was evidence of the local community spirit and conviviality. As I argue, evoking lived experiences reinforced the migrants' imaginings that the Lot provided the qualities of the better (and simpler) way of life that they sought. Nevertheless, it is important to remember that the response that they received from the local community could affect the migrants both positively (as above) and negatively. For example, Hannah Blunden, a retiree aged in her early eighties, explained that the local French did not even pass the time of day with her when she entered the village shop, a stark contrast to how she had imagined life within the locality. However, for most of the migrants, at least in their imaginations, the local French were polite and convivial, with 'more value for time, and people and things' (Kay Morris).

Robert and Justine were also keen to highlight the extent to which their neighbours looked out for one another. As Robert recalled, this was one of the reasons why they had chosen to live in the centre of the village, stressing that if he became ill and could not leave the house, or if he fell down the stairs at the front of their house, which was on the main road through the village, one of his neighbours would notice immediately and get help. However, the Granges were somewhat unusual in their expectations, perhaps because they had achieved a level of acceptance that many of my other respondents had not.

While other migrants recognized and valued the respect and care that the local French showed to one another, they did not assume that this would extend to include them. As this demonstrates, the migrants seemed uncertain of their standing in relation to the local community. Through their migration, they had entered into a pre-existing social order, of which they remained uncertain. Their romantic imaginings of the local community and their role within it nevertheless remained a measure against which they were able to gauge their progress *en route* to a better way of life (see Chapter 7).

Making an effort and finding common ground

Even within accounts of the decision to migrate, many of my respondents would highlight their original desire to become part of the local community, to make friends among the French population. Some of the migrants actively sought opportunities to meet with members of the local community, striving to overcome their peripheral position. This required making a conscious effort to get to know local social actors and even initiating opportunities to come together. Samantha Harris stressed, 'you have to work on it ... there are things you can do ... I go to Keep-Fit to mix with the French'. Robert and Justine Grange recalled their initial efforts to get to know their neighbours, 'We were dropping in [to their houses] and introducing ourselves ... you've got to get involved with the community ... and that was quite a deliberate thing, to be part of it [the village community]'.

Unlike the British in Spain, for whom there was 'a British club for every interest and activity' (O'Reilly 2000: 77) and their compatriots in the Dordogne who had set up a range of English-speaking clubs (Barou and Prado 1995), my respondents did not establish or seek out British-run clubs and social groups. They preferred instead to join the existing groups that had been set up to bridge the cultural gap between the French and the British, such as the Association France Grande-Bretagne (AFGB), a cultural association, the object of which was, so the president of the association explained, 'to bring English and French people together'. From its headquarters in the centre of Cahors the Quercy branch of the association offered weekly language workshops (French and English) and organized a range of social activities and (bilingual) cultural and educational visits.

In some cases, my respondents had joined special-interest clubs. Brian and Sally Waites described how they had established friendships with members of the French population by joining the local classic car club, and Trevor Sparrow explained that, as a big fan of rugby, he would attend local games with a group of friends, who were mostly French. Other migrants attended their village keep-fit and rambling clubs, joined sports teams or sang in the local choir. Their participation often extended beyond merely turning up and taking part. These clubs each held regular social events. William Cardew described his experiences as a member of the local rugby club: 'We play once a fortnight for an hour and a half or so, and then we go out for a meal.' Furthermore, several of the migrants acted as committee members or undertook organizational roles. Jane Campbell, for example, was the treasurer for her local keep-fit club, while Brian and Sally had recently organized a rally for the classic car club; and David Lomax held a prominent position within the local choir.

This pursuit of a common interest can be read as a strategy for social integration, regardless of whether the migrants speak French or not (Benson 2010a). Victoria Cardew aptly summarized her logic behind getting involved in the local yoga class, 'it's all part of getting into the community, which is important'. Other migrants explained that it was through the discovery of a shared interest with members of the native community that they had been able to improve their French. Shared interests thus provided common ground around which British incomers and members of the French community could interact. The migrants' participation in these clubs and associations thus created a space where they could develop sustainable friendships with local social actors and allowed for the possibility of further socialization.

While work could have provided such opportunities, the nature of the employment that many of my respondents undertook meant that in the working environment they rarely came into contact with the local French (see also Buller and Hoggart 1994c). First, it was common to find that they were self-employed, running small businesses from their homes. Those involved in tourism, running a *gîte* or offering *chambres d'hôte* (bed and breakfast), were open to the possibility of catering to people from all nationalities. However, with the *gîte* it was common to find that they were occupied mostly by English-speaking visitors, perhaps reflecting the choices that the migrants made about how to advertise their properties, with many of them appearing in British-based publications. The *chambres d'hôte* attracted a wider variety of visitors. Migrants running businesses unrelated to the tourism industry catered to a range of local clients both French and British. However, this contact with local actors did not translate easily into friendship. There were, of course, exceptions: Victoria and William had met an entrepreneurial French woman through their work, with whom they later entered into a business relationship; Jane Campbell, a single woman in her fifties, became close friends with Marie-Claire when she carried out some translation work for Marie-Claire's husband. In general, however, making friends with members of the local population required effort, imagination and perseverance.

There was also the possibility that the migrants might spontaneously develop relationships with members of the local population. This relied on their own efforts, but also on the inclination of their French neighbours. Martin Johnstone stressed that the extensive renovation work that he had carried out himself on his *Quercynoise* farmhouse had sparked the curiosity of many of the local French who periodically came up to the house to examine his progress. On these occasions he would show his neighbours the work he was doing on the house, ask their advice on local architecture, and find out more about the history of the area. His expressed interest in the wider community gave him an *entrée* whereby he was able to establish ongoing social relations.

For those migrants who had brought their children to the Lot, other parents could become friends. Sally Stampton had become good friends with Loïc, another single parent, in the playground as she waited to collect her son Ollie from school. When I returned to the field in 2005, their relationship, a platonic friendship, had developed to the stage where Sally was helping him to organize the birthday party for one of his children. However, the sustainability of such relationships is questionable. My respondents who had relocated to the Lot with their children in the early 1990s had similarly established relationships with the parents of their children's friends, but once the children left home, or at least became more independently mobile, they no longer had an excuse to meet up. Min Jones and Connie Earl, whose children had been educated in France until the age of eighteen, quite clearly linked the cessation of their relationships with the local French to the time of their children's leaving home. It seems that children may facilitate social relations with the wider social community, but, in the absence of the children, these may become difficult to maintain.

Social relations, irrespective of their duration, provided the migrants with many opportunities to learn more about local culture and custom, find out what was going on in the community around them, recognize the complexity of social life in a rural community, and so aid in the gradual embedding of these incomers into the 'imagined community' of the Lot.

Local engagements

While many of the migrants had arrived in the Lot with preconceived ideas about their future lives, their everyday experiences with members of the local population gave them the hope to believe that it would be possible to bring their dreams of local living to fruition, as well as the skills to do so. As they learned more about living in the Lot, they recognized the distance they still had to travel in order to get to their goals. However, I demonstrate here that their relationships with members of the French population enabled the migrants to learn more about local life and think about how to reconcile their experiences with their initial aspirations.

Although they had not always been successful (yet) in their ambitions to speak French, many of my respondents in the Lot were keen to highlight their initial intentions to improve their language skills in order to be able to communicate freely with members of the local population. While some of the migrants had been relatively fluent in French when they arrived in the Lot – a factor in the choice of destination – or made an active attempt to speak the language before they arrived, there were other migrants who spoke little French. For example, Barney Monty told me, in reference to his own linguistic deficiency, that his French did not extended beyond 'asking the *boulanger* (baker) for a baguette'.[2] Very few local inhabitants spoke any English at all, a reflection on the agricultural background of the region and also on the advanced age of many members of the local population. Even within institutions such as the *préfecture* or *mairie*, which the migrants would have to visit in order to obtain official documents (e.g. driving licences, vehicle registration, residence permits), and banks and hospitals, there was no guarantee that there would be an English speaker. My respondents' experiences were a stark contrast, therefore, to those of the British living in Spain, where the strategy for dealing with tourism and international retirement migration has included the establishment of extensive English-speaking services (Rodríguez, Fernández-Mayoralas and Rojo 1998). The ability to understand and communicate in French could, therefore, be an important skill, not only for passing the time of day with neighbours but also for dealing with the practicalities of daily life.

However, at the time of my research, there were very few French lessons on offer in the Lot beyond the oversubscribed language workshops run by the local branch of the AFGB every Wednesday morning and the handful of language schools offering private lessons. Given the scarcity of language provision, the opportunity for interaction with the local French and social relations could play crucial roles in the linguistic development of the British living in the Lot. In this respect, the migrants often found themselves caught in a double bind where they needed French in order to communicate with members of the local population but also required social interaction if they were to improve their language skills.

For those migrants who had been successful in establishing social relations with members of the French population, regular interaction did serve to improve their French. Robert and Justine Grange told me about friends of theirs, a British couple who had also lived in Hong Kong, who had bought a house a few miles further along the valley and, although they had spoken no French when they arrived, the local villagers had encouraged them to take part in community events, with the result that they had quickly started to learn French and socialize. Brian and Sally Waites also recognized the extent to which their French, which they had only properly started to learn once they moved to the Lot, had improved through their social interactions. They recalled how their regular contact with one of their French neighbours had improved their French 'no end'. 'Because he's Parisian, it's easy to understand'. As they continued, 'A couple of French people, when you get to know them … will correct your French', demonstrating that this was a feature of their relationships that they valued.

For others, who had not yet established such firm friendships, participation in local activities also provided opportunities to improve their language skills, particularly aiding in the accumulation of vocabulary. As Victoria Cardew explained, regular attendance at her French yoga class had improved her anatomical vocabulary. In this respect, many of my respondents were similar to Drake and Collard's respondents in Normandy, who were, 'determined to integrate socially, and adopted different strategies to this end' (2008: 226).

The success of certain Britons in establishing social relations with members of the French community was envied and admired by others who had not been so successful; it gave them some hope that it was possible to become friends with members of the local population, even though it might take some time. Alannah

Tapper, who had been living in the Lot for five years and who spoke good conversational French, recalled how she had originally imagined that once living in France she would have a group of French friends whom she could invite round for coffee and a chat, or walk in the woods with. In these romantic visions, she saw herself conversing freely in French and with confidence, but also learning about her new environment with the help of her local friends. Rather than abandon those ambitions, Alannah, as with many of my other respondents, found herself reassessing what was required if she was to achieve them. She concluded that she needed to be patient and continue her efforts in that direction, while recognizing that her success was not only subjectively determined but also relied on the willingness of the local French community.

Social interaction with members of the local population provided the migrants with opportunities beyond the improvement of their French language skills. As they explained, through these relationships they became intimately involved in local life in ways that would not otherwise have been possible and, as one of my respondents aptly summarized, 'learn the French ways'. They therefore developed a more nuanced understanding of local French society. For example, Samantha Harris explained,

> The more I become entrenched in the life, the more I realize the similarities with England … The French people here, I could almost pick them up and I know where they'd fit in the village back in England … They talk about the same things; they worry about the same things.

Beth Macdonald recalled her horror at discovering that her neighbours,

> will just walk in, at any time of day and night, with no advance warning! You could be doing anything – making love on the kitchen table – and they'll just walk right in … But Madame who has money, she's Bourgeois and she telephones ahead.

The distinction between her 'peasant' neighbours and Madame, whom Beth identified as having a higher class standing, demonstrated that she was able to identify the differences between local French actors.

However, as the migrants' knowledge and experience of the local French population increased, so too did their self-awareness. Vivian St. John had made many friends in her village, walking with them daily and joining the 'Wrinklies' club', her nickname for the community association that took older members of the local population on day trips, at the insistence of one of these friends. It was on a trip to Oradour-sur-Glane, a small town whose residents had all been massacred by the Nazis during the Second World War, that Vivian realized that 'the French think differently to us'. Oradour is now a monument to the dead; everything has been left as it was following the massacre. And as Vivian recalled her own reaction to the site, she highlighted how her neighbours had not reacted in the same way.

> I was getting this horrible dread feeling and when we got to the church where they [the Nazis] had locked up all the women and children I felt like I'd come up

against a rubber barrier. They [French friends] thought I was having trouble with
the steps, but it wasn't that. I had to leave … I was really embarrassed by my reaction, I really was. They [French friends] thought I was ungrateful.

In this manner, Vivian became starkly aware of her difference. For her French
neighbours, the visit to Oradour had been a vivid reminder of the horrors of life
in occupied France during the Second World War, which many of them had lived
through. As Vivian readily admitted, her memories and experiences of the war
having grown up in England 'were nothing like what these people experienced'.

Through their relationships with local social actors, my respondents in the
Lot improved their language skills and learned more about the local way of
life, but also became acutely aware of their own difference. It seemed that the
process of embedding themselves within the local community was a longer
process than they had anticipated. When I asked William Cardew whether he
had friends within the local community, he responded, 'starting to, slowly, we're
getting there'.

Making a contribution

Some of my respondents believed that they could establish a place for themselves
within the local community by devoting their time and effort to certain aspects
of local life. As they recalled their efforts to help young French people with their
English, or their role on the local village committee, they presented themselves
as actively involved in the community. Nevertheless, their success depended on
there being ready opportunities for them to contribute. Intention and effort on
the part of the migrants were, at times, not enough to make their contributions
a reality. Hannah Blunden had discovered this in the early days of her life in
France; while she had hoped to help young French people in her village with
their English (and had offered her services in this respect), she found that there
were no willing students. Other migrants, however, had had more success, with
their deliberate contributions helping to emplace them within the local community and, in the process, to make real their imaginings of their lives following
migration.

A common way for my respondents to establish relationships with members of
the community was to help local children with their English (see also Buller and
Hoggart 1994c). In most cases, this was a fairly informal arrangement, whereby
the children would visit the homes of the migrants once a week for an hour or
so, to get help with their homework or to practise conversation. Importantly, the
migrants did not expect financial compensation for their efforts. It was through
such an arrangement that Vic and Anne were able to develop a relationship
with one of the large French families who lived in their village. At the request
of his grandparents, they had agreed to help Jacques, a French teenager, with his
English. To begin with, he had been a reluctant learner, but they soon introduced
him to the English version of Scrabble™, which they then played together every
Saturday morning, building his vocabulary along the way. What had begun as an
exercise to help Jacques with his schoolwork became a social event. Even after he

no longer needed to learn English for school, he continued to come round every Saturday, eventually beating Vic at the game.

It was common to find the migrants explaining that by helping the young people with their English they were making an investment in the future of the individual, who might need English to progress to further study or, as is the case with many French youngsters, to work in London (see Favell 2008). But this was also an investment in their own future within the local community; through their actions they sought to be recognized as valued contributors to local life.

Other ways that the migrants made a contribution to the local community were through their involvement on village committees, participation in local events, inviting local friends to parties, and helping out their neighbours when they were in need. Connie and Harry, for example, had driven one of their neighbours to and from the hospital when she had to have her cataracts removed. Justine Grange was on the village committee responsible for organizing social events such as the annual fête and cinema evenings. She recalled how on one occasion when the committee had been organising a village meal, she had been able to solve what had seemed to be an insurmountable problem. The committee had been faced with the problem of how to cook the six kilogrammes of rice that would be required for the meal. Justine proffered her electric rice cooker as a solution. As she recalled, 'they were all amazed because my rice was rice the way it should be ... and now there is no question. I'm going to be cooking the rice'. In this process Justine succeeded in making herself a valuable member of the local community, carving out a unique role for herself through her own initiative and actions.

By making themselves available to the local population, the migrants often found that they were approached to take on specific roles within the community. Jon and Kay Morris had volunteered to staff the tourist information office one afternoon a week, and this involvement had then led to the invitation for them to join the town-twinning committee. They soon found themselves responsible for seeking out a British town prepared to twin with their local French town. David Lomax, who attended many local events in his area also found himself teaching English to primary-school children at the request of the Mayor, who had approached him at a social event. As with those Britons who helped young French people with their English, these two cases demonstrate that the migrants could make a valued contribution to local society. However, it also became clear that the nature of their contributions was often dictated by the community: the migrants were valued because of their abilities to do things that the locals could not. In this respect, through their activities the migrants were reminded that they were not local, but at the same time were made to feel that they were making a valuable contribution to local life. Importantly, it seemed that at the instigation of members of the local community, the migrants performed an increasing number of roles on a day-to-day basis, demonstrating the extent to which they were becoming part of the complex social life, which, as Frankenberg (1966) argues, characterizes rural community.

In the migrants' opinions, these contributions to local life were valued and encouraged by their neighbours. As Samantha Harris recalled, 'One of the local French said to me, and they weren't joking, "You really ought to offer yourself up for the Municipal Elections. We want some new blood!"' And in one municipality the British incomers had made a significant difference to the population.

> They were saying the other week that the population has gone up quite a bit with all the British coming in [and] retiring here. And it's pushed the population up because it was just in danger of, you know, almost … [dying]. The village would just die out; it seemed to be moving that way. (Martin and Sarah Johnstone)

As Sarah and Martin recalled, the local French villagers also recognized that these incomers had helped to revive a community spirit in the area, in particular due to their commitment to the village association, which organized regular events for the whole community. It was also evident that the migrants felt that they were making an important contribution to the overall image of the department.

> At least, people like us come in and do something … You make the place look better because you do up your house. We're taking things that were comparative wrecks and working on [them] … And so that has made the place look better. In turn, most of us own *gîtes*, which bring in the tourists and money. So actually, we're doing something to help the whole economy of the Lot. (Justine Grange)

Undoubtedly, in this respect, the British population of the Lot had helped to remedy some of the consequences of rural depopulation; derelict properties had been made habitable and local economies benefited from such in-migration (Buller and Hoggart 1994c; Bésingrand 2004). Nevertheless, there were still limits on the extent to which the migrants felt they could contribute towards local life. Hector MacDonald expressed his frustration that the local French were not putting the British living in the area – many of whom had come with useful skills and experiences – to better use:

> I suppose one of the other satisfying things in life is always if you're making some kind of contribution. I have to say that, actually, if you do want to make a contribution to this society, it is actually quite difficult … The French people one knows are quite happy to sit; they are quite happy on occasion to have a drink … But if you go that step further – and you know those conversations, 'Why don't you … ?', to which they reply 'Yes, but … ' – I just get the feeling that the foreigners here, the French are not making the best use of them, because they could probably make a much bigger contribution.

It is clear that through making their contributions to the local community, the migrants hoped that they would be able to embed themselves within local social life and eventually realize locality. As Susan Sparrow described, her work within the local school was her way of 'giving something back to the community'. In this one sentence, Susan implied a system of exchange and reciprocation that lies, as Mauss (1954) argued, at the basis of human sociality; this was a system that she and other migrants actively sought to emplace themselves within. Nevertheless, the security of their position within the locality depended upon recognition and acceptance by the local French.

Local acceptance

For the migrants, the extent to which members of the local community invited them to socialize or were prepared to accept their invitations was a good – although often surprising – sign of the degree to which they were accepted. As my respondents recalled their personal invitations to local events and private dinners, and the response of their French neighbours to the parties they threw, they presented themselves as being recognized and valued by the local community. In this respect, local social actors are seen as having the power to accept the migrants and, in the process, introduce them to a more 'culturally intimate' (Herzfeld 1997) understanding of everyday life in the Lot.

Brian and Sally Waites held a party to celebrate the anniversary of their relocation to the Lot and commented, 'All the French we invited came. You realize that if you try they will appreciate it ... We're a bit surprised by how well it has gone'. Robert and Justine also held a party, this time to celebrate Chinese New Year, and had invited a selection of their French neighbours to experience the occasion and to try Chinese food. As Justine pointed out, all the ingredients they needed to make the dishes she had put together were available locally; it was just that, up until that point, their French neighbours had not been aware of them. Their neighbours enjoyed the event, and one of them was now regularly making the dishes that Justine had served. In this respect, the presence of these incomers could contribute new tastes and experiences to local social actors, who then tried to incorporate them into their own lives. However, and importantly, the migrants had had to earn acceptance by demonstrating through their actions and everyday practices that they really wanted to be part of the local community. Alice Hammond demonstrated quite clearly this process of getting to be accepted as she recalled her experiences with an elderly French man at the local art class.

> I think he thought that I was going to bring in an ex-pat circle and it would become an English art group. And it took, oh, easily six to eight months for him to actually speak to me civilly. And now he kisses me hello, kisses me goodbye.

Jon Morris similarly emphasized that it had taken some time for the local French to put aside their stereotypical images of British incomers as wealthy property investors and get to know them instead for who they were.

> I think we're known now; people know us. When we first came, people thought we had lots of money and all of this. And they were just looking at well, 'What are you going to do to the house?' ... I think that it has taken a while for people to realize that we're not wealthy as in lots of investments and not working ... it has taken quite a while [to], I won't say accept us, because I think we were accepted pretty quickly, [but] to know that we're on a level with them.

Nevertheless, Jon acknowledged that they still had some way to go before they had completely overcome the preconceptions: because they ran their *gîte* complex and greeting cards company from home, it proved difficult to convince their neighbours that they were working.

However, it was also true that localized categories of inclusion and exclusion varied from one *Lotoise* location to the next. In some villages – particularly those whose population was literally dying out as a result of rural depopulation – British incomers were welcomed with open arms. These incomers were encouraged to take part in local community events, having been welcomed into the village and embraced as a necessary part of future of the village. As Martin and Sarah explained, their local village association organized a series of *repas* (meals) throughout the year, which were well attended and where the food was good. Their village was particularly well known for the *chasse* (hunt) dinner it organized twice a year. On these occasions, the village would celebrate the end of the hunt, and the meal would include freshly caught game such as wild boar and venison from the surrounding area. As Martin and Sarah explained, this was a seven-course meal that went on late into the night and served the purpose of bringing the community together, encouraging conviviality among its members (including incomers to the area) and celebrating local farming and hunting traditions. As Waldren found in her study of the relationships between insiders and outsiders in Deià, a village in Mallorca, 'The growth of the village and its path into the future will depend on the continued coexistence of resident locals and foreigners' (1996: 250).

However, in other locations, where the survival of the village was not at stake, my respondents found that the locals did not seem keen to get to know them. The time, patience and effort required, alongside the uncertainty as to whether their efforts at integration would be recognized by the local French, were enough to dissuade some of my respondents from trying any further to become part of the local community. They believed that their integration was completely out of their control, that there was some insurmountable cultural difference that could not be overcome.

Julian and Janet Ford, who had become quite disillusioned with their neighbours, expressed their frustration at the fact that the local French did not seem willing to get to know them, 'The people who live next door but one, they invited all the French people round for *apéritif* so that we could meet them. But they just didn't turn up'. His obvious disappointment was not allayed by his later experiences with his French neighbours. While they were all quite polite when they met in the street and seemed aware that Julian could communicate well in French, invitations to socialize had not been forthcoming. To his evident frustration, this had led to a sense that it was up to him 'to get them here first, but that's wrong. We're the new people, they should be helping us to join the community'. As a result, Julian felt marginalized 'We don't know French people that intimate[ly] … I mean, we know the people around here but we don't socialise with them'. As Strathern (1982) has argued, locals may remain aloof from incomers, unwilling to engage with them.

The failure of his dream for a better way of life had forced Julian to reconsider his choice of destination. He speculated about moving to Spain. In contrast, Beth MacDonald had not given up on the possibility that the Lot could give her what she sought. Not initially realizing the isolation that she would feel in a small hamlet five kilometres from any amenities and unable to drive, after living there for two years she decided that she had to move. When I returned to the field in 2005, she had moved to a small town; her new house overlooked the *pétanque* (bowls) ground, and she was within easy walking distance of all the local amenities. Suddenly, she felt she was at the centre of local life. Others chose patience. Those who saw even a little bit of progress remained determined in their efforts to achieve local acceptance. As Alannah Tapper explained, 'it is not something you can force, you know; and, who knows, it might happen'. While subjective attempts to become emplaced within the locale may have been constrained by the extent to which the local French welcomed and recognized these efforts, Alannah and many of the other migrants hoped that they would one day become part of local social life.

Discrepant imaginings and the realization of locality

As I have argued, the migrants' aspirations for life following migration relied upon embedding themselves within the social relations of the Lot, whereby they were able to realize locality and develop a distinct local subjectivity. By presenting the local community as bounded, stable and homogeneous, my respondents placed the emphasis on their own efforts to pursue connections, assuming, rather naïvely, that local social actors would welcome them with open arms. The 'imagined world' (Appadurai 1996) central to the production of this locality included the migrants as individuals among a wider group of local French actors, excluding their compatriots living locally.

The ethnography presented in this chapter has demonstrated that the migrants initially utilized this particular 'imagined world' to define the locality to which they aspired. They envisaged working alongside sympathetic local French actors towards a shared vision of local life. However, it is evident that the migrants often remained unreflexive about their ambitions, failing even to consider that their new neighbours' ideas about rural living and social relations might be quite different and that community belonging might be dictated by specific categories of inclusion and exclusion. This disjuncture between the migrants' expectations and the local culture rapidly came to the fore following migration, as they started to realize the complexity of social life within their destinations. While the promise of community relations had inspired their migration in the first place, they had not thought through the complex social relationships through which locality was constituted.

As Frankenberg (1966) has argued, complexity of social life and relations is characteristic of close-knit rural communities where everybody knows everybody, but as occupying a number of different roles. For instance, the postman may be your cousin, and he may also run the village shop. Community, in this understanding, includes the production of locality and community sentiment alongside the possibility of co-operation and dispute. While less rural locations share some features in common with the rural community, there are also differences in how these are constituted. Indeed, different communities can have different histories, with the result that they are constituted differently.

Frankenberg's (1966) model, presenting a 'morphological continuum' (to avoid claims to an evolutionist perspective) from rural to less rural societies, is useful in explaining the reactions of my respondents to their lives in the Lot and the different responses of local communities.

First, I argue that my respondents' persistent uncertainty about their position within their new social environment derived from their migration into a pre-existing social order. It is evident that their imaginings do not account for the complexity that Frankenberg (1966) identifies as characteristic of social life within the rural, and, once living in the Lot, they have to come to terms with the ways in which members of the local community relate to one another. Morgan recalls his feeling of 'strangeness' upon his entrance into his rural field site, defining it as not understanding 'the day to day assumptions and practices and the way in which these were rooted in distinct patterns of social relationships' (2005: 647). The hope is that eventually unfamiliarity will be bypassed by a sense of increasing understanding as the stranger becomes more familiar with their surroundings and known to their neighbours. Indeed, such a sense of unfamiliarity permeated my respondents' accounts of their entrance into the local community, but this was often accompanied by the hope that, with time, they would be able to find a place for themselves within the local community. Interestingly, in most cases it was clear that they felt that they were responsible for their success at integrating.

However, in order for successful integration to take place, certain wider conditions need to be in place; in other words, for the migrants to become part of the local community relies, in part, on the response of that community. This brings us to Frankenburg's second point, which highlights the role of local histories – social, economic and political – in the constitution of community. An extension of this argument could highlight that such histories impact on local cosmologies, systems of classification, and the relationship of these communities to the outside world. Recognition of the subtle differences in the constitution of local communities in the Lot further explains the varied ways in which the migrants were (not) welcomed into their new neighbourhoods and communities.

For example, many of the villages in the Lot had experienced extensive out-migration and rural depopulation, and their populations had still not recovered. Many areas were experiencing a lower density of population than one hundred years previously (Bésingrand 2004). In some cases, such locations had an excess of available housing stock and an ageing population, and they expressed the sense that they were losing their history as the population either died out or moved away. Incomers such as my respondents – particularly those who wanted to be involved in local life and learn about the culture and history of the area – were welcomed and actively encouraged to take part in community life.

However, in other parts of the department, local social actors were more ambivalent. For example, an interview with the mayor of Saint Géry, one of the municipalities of the Lot, revealed that while he welcomed and encouraged property purchase, he was uncertain about the future of the village if a distinct English community were to emerge as a result (Bésingrand 2004). In this same municipality, at the time of my fieldwork, it was rumoured that local opposition was building in response to continued British immigration, taking as a paradigmatic case a municipality where the British residents comprised ten per cent of the population. It was clear that this opposition did not take into account the fact that the resident population of that paradigmatic community was a grand total of ninety-two people, or that generally at that time, the British population there were very much invested in the perpetuation of local life.

What is clear is that the different contexts of reception that my respondents experienced require careful attention, but, furthermore, that local responses to in-migration may change over time and in response to changing local contexts (see also Waldren 1996). In this respect, not only did my respondents have to confront the realities of how particular localities were constituted and how native residents responded to incomers, they also had to face the possibility that things might change. These changes could be for the better or for the worse. Nevertheless, the migrants found themselves in a somewhat ambivalent position.

Such ambivalence, in part, originates from the migrants' uncertain position within local categories of inclusion and exclusion. This is made all the more complicated by the fact that systems of classifying insiders and outsiders, as with other forms of identity-making processes, are situational and, as Cohen (1985) argues, are inherent to the symbolic construction of distinctive communities. In her ethnography of Deià, a village in Mallorca that, for over a century, has attracted a large number of outsiders who could be referred to as Bohemian lifestyle migrants (see Benson and O'Reilly 2009), Jacqueline Waldren discusses how categories of inclusion and exclusion shift and change: '[t]he changing composition of those who are considered insiders and others who are seen as outsiders reveals the complexities of Deià society and the ambiguity of these terms' (1996: 205). While the migrants often presented their host communities as unchanging, and their integration into these as, largely, the result of their own efforts, Waldren's presentation of life in Deià highlights that local categories of inclusion and exclusion are dynamic, changing in response to the different needs of the community at particular points in time. In this rendering, it is possible that the boundaries of local belonging may, at times, shift to accommodate incomers such as my respondents. However, the timing of this is unpredictable, as it is dependent on the unique history of each location.

Despite their different responses to the situation on the ground, it is apparent that my respondents' imaginings were not compromised; their idealized visions of local social life and perceptions of locality persisted despite the evident disjunctures. The persistence of these idealizations, which resonate with a representation of rurality that Raymond Williams (1973) claims is specific to the British middle classes (the rural idyll), belied the migrants' position within the British class structure. The ethnography presented in this chapter demonstrates that, rather than abandon their long-held imaginings, the migrants attempted to resolve the disjuncture in other ways.

For some, the solution was to relocate their imagined locality elsewhere – in the green pastures of other migration destinations, or even in other villages and towns in the Lot. These destinations were safe, existing for the time being within the migrants' imaginations, with the result that their ideas about locality could not be compromised by experience. For the migrants who had succeeded in becoming part of the local community and its social relations, locality still bore the scars of their initial imaginings, with warm and friendly locals eventually extending the hand of welcome to incomers who want to blend in. By putting creativity and imagination to work, it seems that my respondents in the Lot redrew the boundaries of their imagined worlds, or approached these discrepancies from two different angles: withdrawal or energetic participation.

Conclusion

My respondents in the Lot commonly explained migration in terms of their dissatisfaction with life in Britain, presenting a narrative of decline that highlights a loss of community spirit and a lack of feeling of local belonging. In contrast, their imaginings of life in the Lot were very much influenced by a particular middle-class representation of rurality as the rural idyll, prized precisely for its 'traditional rural community' and 'mechanical solidarity' (Rapport 1993). When the migrants recognized that to realize locality would require time, patience, and effort, they often looked for solutions, for ways to insert themselves into local life. Their active involvement in local community events, clubs, and associations and their 'contributions' were all part of this strategy. They held onto the belief that, over time and through their continued participation in everyday life, they might overcome the barriers to their integration.

Although the migrants shared in common their hopes to embed themselves within the local community, they rarely acknowledged this within their accounts of life in the Lot; it seemed as though the migrants wanted to present their efforts towards locality as unique. In this manner, they attempted to personalize locality and to make it meaningful in their own terms. As I argue in Chapter 7, the migrants' claims to local belonging can therefore be read as evidence of their continued engagement in processes of distinction. Their efforts were directed at proving to the local actors that they were different from their compatriots and therefore worthy of integration into local life. This particular response demonstrated a level of reflexivity, where the migrants recognized that their subjective measures must be met by the willingness of the local population to accept them. In this respect, the local community determines the criteria for local belonging.

For my respondents, the establishment of meaningful relationships with the local French helped them to measure their success at gaining a better way of life. As the ethnography in this chapter has shown, the migrants were preoccupied with acceptance and social integration, which relied heavily on the judgement of members of the local community. Nevertheless, the significance of the opinions of local social actors, as presented by the migrants, is misleading. While the migrants clearly valued the approval of their new neighbours, they mobilized their successes as a way of distinguishing their lives following migration from those of their compatriots also living in the Lot (Chapter 7; see also Benson

2010b). Ironically, it seems that it was their (British) middle-class consciousness that directed their practices and activities in life following migration, with the local French remaining outside this class framework. In result, the migrants' engagements with the local community served as a way of gaining distinction; my respondents gauged their ultimate success by the extent to which they, as individuals, had exceeded the accomplishments of their compatriots who were similarly working towards the realization of locality. It is thus through these processes of distinction that the migrants accumulated social capital and, consequently, reaffirmed their position as members of the British middle class.

Notes

1 The Lot is situated in the southern half of France, an area where the local inhabitants spoke Langue d'oc before the introduction of a national, standardized language.
2 In recent years, when I have presented some of my work at conferences and seminars, I have often been asked about the level of French spoken by my respondents. I have also been faced with audiences who not only assume that these people as a group do not speak French but also consider that these relatively affluent migrants should know better than to move to France if they do not speak French. As I imply here, they arrive in the Lot with varying levels of French, depending on their age, educational background and life experiences, as well as their desire to speak it. And while they may have the volition to speak French, they often underestimate the amount of time and effort this will take and the resources that they will require in order to be successful.

3

A (persistent) state of uncertainty

This chapter presents a way of understanding and conceptualizing the persistence of uncertainty in my respondents' post-migration lives. While Chapter 2 revealed the continual negotiations involved in the realization of locality and the resulting ambivalence that the migrants felt, this chapter demonstrates that life in the Lot is replete with contradictions: from the mismatch between the migrants' expectations for their new lives and lived reality to the differences between their rhetoric about the lives they lead and their everyday practices. Such contradictions characterized their lives long after migration and cannot be ascribed purely to anxieties over settlement. Irrespective of the length of their residency, my respondents in the Lot experienced uncertainty in a range of situations from their social relationships, their experiences of French bureaucracy and their shift from one lifestyle to another. In this respect, it becomes clear, building on the argument presented in the previous chapter, that many aspects of life following migration are subject to continual negotiation.

How can these contradictions be explained? Other studies of lifestyle migration have explained this feeling of uncertainty in terms of a settlement anxiety, using liminality as a way to characterize post-migration lifestyles (see for example O'Reilly 2000; Hoey 2005; Bousiou 2008; Oliver 2008). Indeed, many of these authors stress that it is precisely the liminality of such lives that makes them appealing to lifestyle migrants, with migration signalling entry into the liminal phase. The ethnography presented below demonstrates that, for my respondents in the Lot, life following migration was experienced in similar terms. However, their overwhelming efforts to escape this sense of uncertainty call for a reconsideration of liminality in relation to this case. Returning to the work of Victor Turner, the principal proponent of the liminal, I argue for a closer reading of the everyday lives of my respondents to explore the extent to which their lives resemble what Turner initially intended. As I demonstrate, there are several points at which these do not match, principally the persistence of ambivalence in the migrants' lives and the co-existence of work and leisure in their new lives.

Against this critical discussion of whether Turner's seminal work applies to this particular case, I introduce the concept of ambivalence as an analytical framework for explaining post-migration subjectivities. I propose that migration signalled not the onset of ambivalence but a significant shift in its terms: ambivalence was a feature of their lives prior to migration – as evident in their recollections of life in Britain and their decision to migrate – that persisted following migration, albeit in a different form. The ambivalence of their post-migration lives was caused not by their disappointments with life – as was the case before migration – but by their struggles to come to terms with the lived experiences of their new lives within the context of their efforts to bring their expectations and imaginings into fruition.

In the course of this chapter it becomes clear that uncertainty and indeterminacy were permanent characteristics of the migrants' lives before and after migration. Migration, once presented as the remedy to the difficulties of life in Britain, did not result in instant gratification, and the process of getting to a better way of life continued long after migration.

Explaining the uncertainty of everyday life following migration

Scholars of lifestyle migration often implicitly attribute the contradictions and ambivalence of daily life following migration to the problems of settlement and adaptation to the new environment. Within this context they variously present liminality as an explanatory concept. They refer to the destination as a liminal and marginal space (O'Reilly 2000; Bousiou 2008); draw parallels between the leisurely lives that the migrants lead and a Turner-esque liminal phase (Oliver 2008); argue that the migrants' experiences connote an interstructural state (Hoey 2005); highlight the presence of a migrant *communitas* (Bousiou 2008; Oliver 2008); discuss the performance of liminality in migrants' daily lives (Bousiou 2008); and introduce the possibility of a permanent liminal condition, or 'liminal subjectivity', as Bousiou (2008: xiii) refers to it. It emerges that the lives imagined, experienced and constructed by the migrants within the chosen destination are anti-structural, contra-normal social conventions when measured against the lives that they would otherwise be leading.

The conclusions of these scholars contribute greatly to wider discussions of lifestyle migration, and the daily experiences of their respondents resonate, in many ways, with those of the British residents of the Lot presented in this book. The image depicted by O'Reilly (2000) of the British in Spain as caught between Britain and Spain, one way of life and another, encapsulates the process of adaptation to their new lives and environments that lifestyle migrants, including my respondents in the Lot, undergo. Similarly, the ambiguity of the *Mykoniots d'élection* towards mainstream Mykonian rituals that Bousiou (2008) classes as evidence of liminality, demonstrates the pervasiveness of the migrants' ambivalence towards the new surroundings and social setting of the destination. Finally, Oliver's (2008) account of retirement migrants living in southern Spain portrays liminality as emerging from the intersection of migration and retirement, with the liminal space offering the possibility of positive ageing. Lifestyle migration, in this respect, allows individuals to take control of their lives. As the stories of my respondents demonstrate, migration was similarly presented as an action out of keeping with normal expectations and thus provided the opportunity for individuals to augment their agency.

The understanding of liminality that underwrites these previous accounts of lifestyle migration is heavily influenced by Turner's (1969) conceptualization and is therefore located between two fixed and immutable points, both of which are defined and agreed by wider societal consensus. Within the liminal phase, liminal beings are gradually socialized into their new status in society. This movement from one social position to another occurs in a strict, linear fashion, where individuals move up the social hierarchy from one well-established position to another. In contrast, my respondents in the Lot had no well-established and commonly attributed end-point, other than the vague notion that they were heading toward a better way of life. Rather than the societal consensus that Turner emphasized (1969, 1982) as fundamental to liminality, my respondents seemed to be on an individual quest, where they themselves constantly redefined the goals. In the absence of a clearly defined end-point and the ongoing nature of the quest for a better way of life, it is therefore questionable whether liminality, understood as the linear progression from one social status to another, can fully account for their pervading sense of ambivalence.

My respondents' experiences, as more individualistically oriented, fit more closely to Turner's (1982) discussion of the liminoid state. This is understood as a transitional phase that individuals enter voluntarily, and through which they experience release from the constraints of industrial society. As Turner explains, people feel compelled to enter this state as a way of overcoming the inauthentic 'communitas of necessity' (1982: 58) of which they feel they are unwilling participants. In the liminoid state, they experience a more authentic communitas based on 'direct, unmediated communion' (*ibid*: 58) and are able to renegotiate the meaning of the social world. Indeed, the fatalistic images of life in Britain that my respondents presented, their elective relocation, and their desire for the rural idyll – which, as the previous chapter demonstrated, centred around the perceived moral value of local community – all contribute to the argument that the experiences of British migrants in rural France demonstrate that they occupy a liminoid state. In this rendering, through the act of migration they became able to define the world in their own terms.

However, it is necessary to remain wary of the extent to which even the liminoid can explain the migrants' lives following migration. Turner (1982) specifically associates the liminoid with the ludic, a leisure space defined in opposition to the working space, that is almost passively experienced by the individual. This model does not allow for the combination of work and leisure – coupled with the migrants' active rejection of the idea that life in the Lot is one long holiday – that characterized my respondents' lives in the Lot. The concept of the liminoid state cannot, therefore, fully explain the migrants' experiences of life following migration.

It seems that while the migrants' presentations of life in the Lot appear to depict liminality, stressing their active decision to reject 'mainstream living to move to marginal geographical spaces' (Oliver 2008: 30), the concepts of the liminal and liminoid, at least as intended by Turner (1969, 1982), cannot fully account for the reality of their lived experiences. Liminality cannot be sustained over a long period of time and is therefore at odds with the unresolved nature of my respondents' uncertainty. Their narratives, where they depicted themselves as standing on the threshold of the better way of life, should instead be read as part of the myth they strive to maintain about their lives in rural France.

In other words, to understand my respondents' post-migration lives as liminal is misleading. By projecting an end to their feelings of ambivalence the migrants created the impression that they had full control over the trajectory of their post-migration lives, when in fact, as this book attests, my respondents never appeared to be any closer to their self-defined better way of life, irrespective of the length of their residence in the Lot. Furthermore, there were many unexpected obstacles in the way of their achievement of the post-migration goals, with the result that perpetual uncertainty and ambivalence characterized their post-migration lives.

It seems that the end-point, the better way of life that my respondents sought, remained beyond their reach. As their accounts reveal, through their small successes *en route* to this better way of life, they gradually redefined their goals. Unlike liminality, which is by definition a temporary phase, the condition of uncertainty in which my respondents found themselves following migration seemed permanent. While Bousiou's (2008) *Mykoniots d'élection* actively sought, 'a space of (structural) liminality where performing subjects can project … their liminal subjectivities … shifting between different subject positions and 'political' self-transformations, a lived-out identity-repertoire which emerges out of their need to transcend every category' (2008: xiii), my respondents in the Lot expressed readily their discomfort and frustration with their ambivalent position and demonstrated their efforts to overcome it.

However, another feature of the migrants' narratives should also be taken into account when discussing ambivalence: their presentations of the lives led before migration. As I revealed in Chapter 1, many of the migrants characterized their pre-migration lives as uncertain and expressed their doubts about what their lives may have held if they had stayed in Britain. A biographical approach to migration (see Halfacree and Boyle 1993), which recognizes the intersections of pre- and post-migration lives, reveals that ambivalence was a constant characteristic of their lives before and after migration. Ambivalence both drove the decision to migrate and was a product of migration. Therefore, the struggle to overcome ambivalence was a persistent characteristic of the migrants' lives before and after migration. This was a highly personalized quest, which had characteristics unique to individual migrants. In this rendering, uncertainty and indeterminacy were reminiscent of the individualized ambivalence which Bauman claims is a feature of liquid modern life (see for example 1991, 2007). Through their accounts of their creative efforts to overcome the uncertainties of their lives, the migrants demonstrated the possibilities of self-transformation inherent to lifestyle migration and highlighted their own efforts to augment their agency.

As the ethnography presented below demonstrates, the migrants seemed to have better control of their lives following migration, despite the uncertainty that they experienced. It therefore becomes clear that the ambivalence that characterized their post-migration lives was demonstrably different from that expressed in their presentations of life before migration. Furthermore, it is clear that there were many aspects of their post-migration lives that caused them ambivalence. In order to reveal the complex constitution of this ambivalence, this chapter presents three areas of my respondents' post-migration lives that can be considered as sources of ambivalence: their position between one lifestyle and another; their status as intra-European migrants; and their relationships with their compatriots. These are not intended as exclusive, and there were many other examples throughout the book that are equally representative.

As I demonstrate through the ethnography presented below, the difficulties and frustrations of learning to live in a different country, of adopting a new way of life, and of rejecting familiarity for difference all operated as sources of ambivalence for my respondents in the Lot. Not only do we find them caught between one way of life and another, it also becomes clear that their ambivalence has emerged from the struggle to reconcile their expectations (as global social actors) and middle-class imaginings with the realities of life in the local.

Between one lifestyle and another

Following migration, the excitement of the migrants' initial expectations was tempered by the realities of life within the destination. While the difficulties of the lives they had led in Britain had prompted their relocation, once living in the Lot, my respondents developed nostalgia for particular aspects of their pre-migration lifestyles. The simultaneous repulsion of and attachment to 'native soil' that McHugh (2000) identifies as a common source of ambivalence among migrants was therefore apparent in the lives of my respondents, although it was more nuanced than McHugh's generalized argument allows for. In the case of my respondents, their nostalgia was directed towards certain features of their cultural lives and various consumer conveniences that they had taken for granted in their everyday lives back in Britain. While the absence of these had not been felt by the migrants immediately after migration, their continued absence reminded them of what they had left behind, of the small sacrifices they had made for their new lives, and of the aspects of their pre-migration lives that they had valued.

For example, it was common to find the migrants drawing attention to the lack of (high) cultural activities in the Lot. Susan and Trevor Sparrow, who had been born and bred in London, working there until retirement, explained that they missed the ballet and the art exhibitions that they had regularly enjoyed in London. They had resolved this, to a degree, by travelling to Toulouse and Bordeaux, the nearest big cities, several times a year when there was an interesting exhibition at one of the many art galleries or if the ballet was scheduled.

Other migrants bemoaned the distance they would have to travel in order to visit the theatre. Victoria Cardew described the change in this aspect of her lifestyle when she told me, 'To actually go out and do things like the theatre, you have to go a long way … I used to go to the theatre a lot and I miss that culture'. As she implied, the distance presented a barrier to her attending the theatre. I suspect that a further obstacle to her theatre-going was her linguistic ability; Victoria had been learning French since moving to the Lot, but it was by no means at the level of fluency that would be required for her to follow and enjoy a French play. Even some of the more proficient French speakers still found it hard to follow. Samantha Harris was particularly proud that her French had reached the level whereby she could visit the theatre with her French friends, but even so she confessed, 'I might not get all the nuances'.

It seemed that, for most of the migrants, the complaint was directed towards that fact that high cultural activities and interests were rarely supported at the local level, although there were a few exceptions to this. For example, one village association organized for small theatre groups to come and perform in the local *salle des fêtes* (village hall). But it was not only the theatre, ballet and art galleries that the migrants missed; there were few opportunities for them to watch films which had not been dubbed into French, no libraries lending books written in English, and very little cultural activity in village life aimed at keeping the mind active. Vivian St. John's description of life in her village accurately captured the sense of resignation I witnessed in many of the migrants' accounts, 'I like Cahors; I love this village. I think that it is beautiful here, but stimulating is not the word'. It was not so much that the migrants were complaining about their lives in the Lot, as demonstrating the sacrifices they had made to live within their ideal destination.

Living in the Lot also led the migrants to reassess the consumer conveniences that they had willingly left behind – the vast high streets full of products, the supermarkets bursting with produce from around the world – but also the smaller conveniences – for example banking services and mobile communications. In many cases, the migrants explained that they had not been well prepared for these small, and at times frustrating, differences. For example, Jon Morris had previously spent six months living in the Savoie, a department located in the Rhône-Alpes region of France, but his efforts to commit to a life led permanently in the Lot revealed what was, in his perception, the idiosyncratic nature of the French marketplace. Jon and his wife Kay described in detail their experiences and the necessary changes to their consumption practices, reflecting a shift in their expectations. From setting up a bank account to purchasing building materials, they presented the ethos of business in France as something that they had had to get used to. In the bank they found that they had to pay for the privilege of having a *carte bleue* (debit card), unlike in Britain where these had been issued as standard. At the builders' merchants the lack of stock regularly meant that jobs around the house could not progress until items they had ordered had been received by the vendor. They argued that there was an informal embargo on competition between businesses, meaning that each shop or vendor had their own niche market.

In their early enquiries about setting up a small lingerie shop in their local town, Jon and Kay came face to face with such restrictions. Their local French adviser told them that one of the women's clothes shops held a small range of bras, explaining that, as long as the shop continued to stock this range, Jon and Kay would not be able to establish their business, as it would be seen as direct competition. As they became aware of the seemingly peculiar dynamics of the local market, Jon and Kay chose to re-evaluate their business plan, later establishing a small business selling handmade greetings cards, an enterprise that had not previously been attempted in the area.

While my respondents presented the rules that governed the local marketplace as peculiar and idiosyncratic, there was a sense that this was how things were in France. To begin with, these services and (in)conveniences were unfamiliar to the migrants, but over time, they became more aware of the economic system that controlled their workings. Unlike Britain, where neoliberal economic policies had resulted in a ruthless and competition-controlled capitalist market, in France the economic system reflected a more socialist and protectionist model and had thus developed in a different direction. As Jon and Kay's experiences demonstrated, drawing on a particular economic and social history, the French economic model sought to protect and preserve the interests of established small businesses by limiting the competition. Unsurprisingly, coming from the highly competitive, consumer-oriented economic environment of Britain, the migrants found the self-serving nature of French businesses difficult to comprehend. Furthermore, their responses to the French economic system demonstrated a longing for certain conveniences – for example, instant access to products, choice within the market, foods from around the world, free banking services – that they had taken for granted in Britain. Paradoxically, their overt rejection of life in Britain similarly focused on perceived products of the neoliberal economy: the rat race, a poor quality of life, ruthless competition and materialism.

European expectations, local realities

Another aspect of the migrants' ambivalence corresponded to their position as European social actors. It is clear that they had held certain expectations about their post-migration lives based on a miscomprehension of what Europe, as a political entity, entailed. One of the advantages, as the migrants presented it, of choosing France as a migration destination was because of its status as a European Union (EU) country. My respondents' European identity – their vague sense that they, as individuals, belonged to Europe – operated as a justification for their migration and continued residence in the Lot, while also forming the basis of their belief that European integration resulted in the universalization of rights. In this respect, the European identity that the migrants claimed to possess was defined by their political affiliation (and thus conforms to the civic dimensions of European identity that Bruter (2005) has identified), while also being situationally applied (see for example Grundy and Jamieson 2007; Savage et al. 2005). As the ethnography presented in this section demonstrates, the migrants mistakenly or unwittingly adopted their experiences of the British welfare state as the European norm, only to face the realities of bureaucratic culture in another

European country with its own political system.

The migrants' political status as Europeans allowed them to take advantage of the laws relating to freedom of movement within Europe, whereby they were permitted to live and work in another European country. Castles and Miller (2003) argue that these intra-European migrants thus occupy an 'intermediate status' between full European citizens and migrants from outside Europe, while O'Reilly (2007) argues that European citizens moving within Europe find themselves caught up in a movement-enclosure dialectic (see also Ackers and Dwyer 2004). On the one hand, intra-European migration is premised upon freedom of movement. On the other hand, however, it becomes clear that certain rights remain contingent upon nation and place. In these respects, being a European who chooses to relocate to another European state results in a particular sense of ambivalence.

Nevertheless, the migrants valued the sense that they were European; they regularly invoked their Europeanness to justify their continued presence within the French countryside. 'We're all Europeans', as one of my respondents explained. Other migrants explained that even their French neighbours understood that other Europeans had a right to live in the French countryside, realizing that this was an aspect of identity that the French and the British incomers shared. Europeanness, in the minds of my respondents and their local interlocutors, distinguished British migrants from other, non-European, migrants in France who have historically experienced a high level of xenophobia from the local population (see for example Silverman 1992; Hargreaves 1995; Noiriel 1996). In this rendering, Europeanness acted as a positive expression of identity, used by Europeans to mark themselves as different from other individuals who do not have the privilege of being European.

The migrants' initial imaginings of life following migration had rested upon a certain myth about Europe: the notion of a fully integrated and homogenized Europe. This misconception of Europe facilitated their migration; as Jon Morris explained, 'You assume, or we certainly did – and that's with quite a bit of knowledge and French friends here – that it's Europe and things will pretty much be the same'. This initial expectation of similarity acted as the source of ambivalence on two levels: in its contradiction to the migrants' claims that they were seeking a different way of life and in contrast to their lived experiences of life in the Lot.

Following migration, there was a sense that the migrants' European identity offered little beyond certain political and legal rights; while it had facilitated migration and their prolonged residence in France, it was little help in their everyday lives. As they struggled to get to grips with the practicalities of life in France, they became all too aware of the differences between life in France and life in Britain and of their own ambiguous position as non-French Europeans living in France. My respondents narrated a seemingly endless saga of the trials involved in fulfilling even the smallest bureaucratic requirement. These included their efforts to get their *carte de séjour* (residence permit), to register to pay tax in France and to organize their medical cover. And as they recalled, they regularly encountered French bureaucrats who seemed unable to advise on the processes involved in the formalization of the migrants' residence in France. However, unlike their compatriots in Spain who used their frustrations as 'excuses for not integrating' (O'Reilly 2000: 153), my respondents continued in their efforts to integrate, disappointed by the obstacles in their way but not deterred from their chosen path.

When Connie decided to renew her *carte de séjour* at the local *mairie* (mayor's office) I witnessed how frustrating these processes could be. Having been through the process before, she had allowed for the possibility of this taking a significant amount of time. She left for the *mairie* around ten o'clock in the morning; it was only a ten-minute walk from the house. She knew that this would not be the only visit she would have to make that day, but this was a reconnaissance mission: to pick up the application form and to ascertain exactly which documents she needed to supply. To be doubly sure, she requested that the clerk in the *mairie* write down a list of all the documents that she needed to return with. She was back home by 10.45 and felt certain that she could collect the necessary documents, fill in the form, and return to the *mairie* before it closed for lunch at noon. And so, within half an hour, she left the house again, believing that she had all the necessary documents (she had been careful to check them against her list) to complete the application.

When she arrived at the *mairie*, it transpired that there was a document missing; the clerk had neglected to add it to the list. No apology was given, and the clerk steadfastly refused to process the application. Connie rushed home, hoping that she would be able to return with the missing document before the office closed and to finish the job on that morning. By this stage she was quite flustered and it took her some time to locate the final document. Nevertheless, she left the house at 11.40 and almost ran to the *mairie*. Once she arrived, however, she discovered that they had inexplicably chosen to close early for lunch.

Other migrants had problems even persuading the bureaucrats that they needed a *carte de séjour*; apparently the obligation for Europeans to register their residence had been removed. However, it emerged that the organization of other aspects of permanent residency, such as health care and taxes, relied on migrants producing their residence permits. For example, Alannah found herself regularly visiting both the *mairie* and the Caisse Primaire Assurance Maladie (CPAM) offices in Cahors when she found that she needed to register herself and her husband Daniel for the French health-care system.[1] As in the case of all British migrants below the age of sixty, she found that they had to be means-tested to calculate the contribution that they would need to make towards their own health-care costs. However, before she could even get to this stage, she had to apply for their first residence permit. This process was made more stressful by the fact that Daniel had recently been diagnosed with cancer and required urgent treatment; without the support of CPAM, they faced paying the full cost out of their own pockets.

Although the process took two years to complete, they did finally succeed in registering themselves within the health-care system and were in the process of claiming back some of the costs of Daniel's treatment. As Alannah explained,

'I'm still having a battle with the French health people; and they're very helpful when you go in there, but they never get it quite right'.

Other migrants had found themselves in a more tricky position with the French health-care system, fearing that they could not afford to pay the compulsory contributions and therefore not registering for health care at all. As the E-111, recently replaced by the European Health Insurance Card (EHIC), only covered emergency treatment for British citizens visiting Europe, they often had no health cover at all. As Betty Monty explained, if anything happened to her husband Barney, she would have to drive him back to England for treatment, no mean feat considering that she did not drive in France and the trip to Dover alone would take thirteen hours. There was also an inherent assumption that the British health-care system would treat them when they got there; they had faith in the welfare state to continue to provide free health care even though they were no longer domiciled in Britain.

My discussions with my respondents also revealed that, despite their efforts to register to pay taxes in France, they struggled to find the information about how to do this. Ron Stampton recalled how he had visited the foreign accounts clerk at his French bank, to be advised that it would be a good idea not to declare some of his British shares, which would mean that he did not have to pay tax on them. This was not a route that he wished to explore; as he explained, he had every intention of paying his taxes. Vic Wilson explained that he had been encouraged by the civil servants at the administrative offices of the *préfecture* in Cahors to visit the *mairie* and collect a form to arrange to pay French income tax on his British pension. The clerks in his local *mairie* had no knowledge of the form and told him to return to the *préfecture*. It was clear that both Ron and Vic were aware that they were liable to pay their taxes in France as it was their country of domicile (they were both permanent residents). However, they found that, as David Hampshire warns in his guide to living and working France, '[i]t's difficult to obtain accurate information from the tax authorities' (2003: 354). Eventually and somewhat ironically, they both found the relevant information about paying their income tax in France by consulting the Inland Revenue back in Britain.

The frustrations my respondents experienced when dealing with French bureaucracy were undoubtedly exacerbated by their sense that this would not happen back in Britain. Indeed, in both the realms of taxation and health care, these processes had been made easier because they were British citizens with National Insurance numbers issued when they were sixteen years old and had paid into the PAYE (pay [tax] as you earn) system, and with permanent UK addresses they had been entitled to free health care. To a large degree the bureaucracy that surrounded health-care entitlements and taxation was different in France because the state organized these systems differently. The migrants were often not aware that their (French) neighbours similarly had to jump through many of the same bureaucratic hoops. Instead, the migrants ascribed their experiences of the French system to their weak position as non-French Europeans living in France; thus their lives in France augmented their sense that they occupied an ambivalent position. As Herzfeld (1992) has argued in the case of foreigners similarly attempting to deal with Greek bureaucratic procedures, the migrants felt that they could not insist that French civil servants and bureaucrats help them in these processes precisely because they were not French.

The examples presented here demonstrate that there is ambivalence inherent both in how the migrants understand Europeanness and in their lived experiences of intra-European migration. Just as Grundy and Jamieson (2007) found in their study of the meaning that Europe held for 18–24-year-olds living in Edinburgh, my respondents in the Lot expressed a persistent uncertainty about this aspect of their identity. This became particularly apparent when they discussed the role of European identity in their everyday lives and their experiences of what social cohesion across Europe actually looked like. The latter was only possible through comparison with their experiences of life within another European Union country, and therefore was specific to their position as intra-European migrants.

Freedom of movement within Europe may be a physical possibility, but in practice individuals find themselves excluded from certain arenas of the host society. By moving, the migrants found their political freedoms restricted and occupied an ambivalent position where 'borders are reasserted through rules and regulations, through cultural and language differences, through social and economic isolation, while assimilation remains elusive' (O'Reilly 2007: 290). While the intention towards integration may be present, the current system of intra-European migration with its contradictory basis does not facilitate this. As my respondents attempted to reconcile their European expectations with local realities, they experienced the ambivalence of European identity. This was further compounded by their position as intra-European migrants free to move while their rights and entitlements remained bounded to place (O'Reilly 2007). The mismatch between their imaginings, where their desires for locality were to be fulfilled precisely through freedom of movement, and their lived experiences – their ambiguous status as non-French Europeans living in rural France – demonstrated to them the obstacles that stood in the way of the better way of life that they sought.

Ambiguous associations

The theme of ambivalence that runs throughout this chapter continues in this final ethnographic section as I reveal the contradictory ways in which the migrants related to one another. On the one hand, these relationships acted as a source of comfort and familiarity (cf Scott 2004). On the other hand, however, the migrants often sought to distance themselves from these relationships, underplaying the role that they played in their lives.

As I discuss in Chapter 7, this desire to distance themselves from their compatriots emerged out of their persistent need, as members of the British middle class, to distinguish themselves from others. It also reflected their wider rhetoric about becoming local and integrated members of the French community discussed in Chapter 2, perhaps believing that by underplaying the extent to which they maintained relationships with their compatriots, their claims to local belonging would be taken more seriously. They therefore reproduced a moral discourse about social integration, believing that their transnational attachments would hinder their efforts at becoming part of the local community.

One afternoon, as we returned from lunch with Julian and Janet, Connie and I discussed the relationships between the British residents of the Lot. From an early stage in my research I had been able to trace the relationships between those I encountered; even those who I contacted independently of my existing networks had relationships that linked them back to my other respondents. As I presented this to Connie, she nodded in agreement and explained, 'We're like family. In the absence of our real families, we rely upon one another'. Indeed, I witnessed how many of the migrants helped one another out. When Harry decided to build his pond, it was Julian who he asked to come and help him; Jane Campbell, who spoke French fluently, was often called upon to translate official documents from French into English. In other cases, younger Britons who were struggling to find work were helped, and through the network of their compatriots they would be offered small jobs. This was how Jack Stone came to set up his gardening and odd jobs business when he arrived in the Lot, which, in result, had initially catered to a British clientele. The evidence therefore demonstrates that my respondents felt a need to support one another in the maintenance of their lives in the Lot.

I argue here that the 'family' that Connie referred to was analogous to community; at times such as these, the British of the Lot were a symbolic community, bounded and defined, not by their ethnicity or in opposition to the native French, but by their shared belief that rural France offered a better way of life. In this respect, they were a group defined in opposition to those who had not moved in search of a better way of life. Furthermore, they were a self-defined and identified group, mobilized in opposition to representations of the British abroad, a category laden with stereotype and negative connotation (see Chapter 6). The migrants' fleeting claims to community therefore acted as a mode of distinction, with community materializing precisely through the migrants' actions, behaviours and words (Cohen 1982, 1985). Just as Cohen (1985) notes in the case of the Norwegian Saami, the migrants claimed a particular local identity as a way of distinguishing themselves from other possible representations over which they had little control. And they did so purposefully and with intent.

Other migrants referred to their associations with their compatriots as being the only solution to the problems that they had experienced in building relationships within the local community. For example, Julian Ford, a British retiree who felt that his French neighbours had ignored his efforts in this direction, regularly invited his British friends round for long lunches or dinner, and they would often reciprocate. In the absence of public spaces where the British of the Lot could regularly meet, it was common to find them inviting their compatriots into their own homes. Many of my respondents would hold dinner parties in order to get to know new people or to spend time with their friends, serving a meal with three or four courses and plenty of wine. The 'dinner-party circuit', as I refer to it, was particularly instrumental in building up the networks between people and consolidating friendships.

As I witnessed, there was a lot of etiquette involved in the organization of these social events. The hosts had to be careful to prepare something different from what had been served at the last dinner party; the guests would bring a small gift for the hosts (in my experience this ranged from a bunch of flowers to homemade chutney), apart from bringing a bottle of wine to contribute towards the proceedings; and there was an expectation of reciprocation: that the guests would invite the hosts to their homes in return and within a reasonable length of time. This was an arena where traditional gender roles might be expected to be played out. Indeed, the women often did the cooking while the men chose the wine, but the rule was by no means set in stone.

These social occasions were opportunities for the British of the Lot to get together. Their actions were evidence of the symbolic community to which they claimed to belong; participation was by invitation only and often restricted to other Britons living locally. I argue here that their decision to host dinner parties was another reminder of the migrants' position as members of the British middle class, and their choices of food and wine became a demonstration of their cultural capital, to be judged by the guests. Indeed, the success of the dinner party pivoted around such choices. I remember one of my respondents recollecting that one host had chosen to serve only British food, imported from Britain; this had not been a success; it was considered a 'tasteless' move demonstrating the unwillingness of the host to integrate, even partially, into French culture. The dinner party may thus serve as a venue for subtle processes of distinction to take place.

The organization also allowed for certain exclusionary practices to occur. Even numbers were often favoured at these events, and this often meant that single people were excluded. Vivian St. John and Hannah Blunden both felt that their status as single women was the reason why they were rarely invited to dinner parties. Furthermore, the fact of having attended an event did not guarantee further invitations. As these occasions were opportunities to get to know one another better, there was always a possibility that people might not get along. As Ron Stampton explained, he was very keen to approach people whom he heard speaking English in the streets. The normal process would dictate that he would first invite them to join him for a coffee. As long as this initial stage was successful, he would exchange telephone numbers and fairly soon invite his new acquaintances to a dinner party. This had varying success, and Ron soon realized that 'being British is not enough', implying that there was a need to have more in common in order for a sustainable relationship to develop. Similarly, Brian Waites explained that he had a lot in common with his new French friends, whom he had met mostly through the classic car club. The situation with his compatriots, however, was different: 'all the English people we know are retired and beyond that, you've got to find something in common'.

This ethnographic evidence demonstrates that many of my respondents were at least partially engaged in networks of reciprocation and exchange with their compatriots also living in the Lot. Beyond the formalized setting of the dinner party, they could call on one another for help, and it was often through their compatriots that they gained information about living in the Lot. However, their accounts demonstrated their ambivalence about these relationships as the migrants regularly underplayed the role that they played in their lives and denied their own membership of a transnational British community. For example, Alice and Keith Hammond, a couple in their early forties, explained, 'we've come to France to live in France and be as much French as we can … we actually don't mix with the English circle'. In other cases, the migrants' actions were influenced by their efforts to distance themselves from other Britons. Several of my respondents described how they had chosen not to join the AFGB because it was 'more British than French'. And in one case, a migrant had actively decided that they would no longer do their shopping in the local town because there were too many British people there.

These actions were evidence of the unease that my respondents felt about their relationships with their compatriots. However, to argue that the migrants did not have any contact with their compatriots would be a gross misrepresentation; their friendships with one another remained a consistent and important feature of their daily lives. While they would refer to the 'British community' in a way that implied that they were somehow external to it, it would become clear that at times they took some comfort in the company of these others. It was therefore common to find that they maintained relatively close friendships with a small number of their compatriots living locally, while also trying to establish relationships with members of the local community.

In this respect a complex picture of the migrants' socialization patterns emerges. Authors such as Scott (2004) and Smallwood (2007) have attempted to typologize their British respondents in France as integrating into either the resident British community or the native populace. However, in the case of my respondents in the Lot, it was clear that while local integration was an emblem of their success at getting to a better way of life, their relationships with their compatriots continued to play a role in their lives. Nevertheless, the simultaneity of these relationships was difficult for them to reconcile with their aspirations to become local, with the result that they were likely to underplay the extent to which other Britons were part of their daily lives. Despite the resulting ambivalence that the migrants experience, this simultaneity is interesting, in that it demonstrates, as Levitt and Glick Schiller (2004) have argued, the co-existence of local incorporation and transnational connections. In this rendering,

> it is useful to think of the migrant experience as a kind of gauge which, while anchored, pivots between a new land and a transnational incorporation. Movement and attachment is not linear or sequential but capable of rotating back and forth and changing direction over time. The median point on this gauge is not full incorporation but rather simultaneity of connection. (*ibid*: 1011)

The ethnography presented in this section and throughout the book demonstrates this pivoting action, but what does this tell us about the migrants' sense of belonging and identity?

On the one hand, following Levitt and Glick Schiller (2004), it could be argued that through the examination of the migrants' lives a distinction between ways of being, 'the actual social relations and practices that individuals engage in' (*ibid*: 1010), and ways of belonging, 'the identities associated with their actions' (*ibid*: 1010), emerges. Depending on the context, these may be combined in different ways. As the ethnography demonstrates, the migrants' claims to belonging, where they self-identified as part of the local community, were often contradicted by their practices, which placed them as part of a wider transnational community incorporating their compatriots both back in Britain and living locally in the Lot. In this rendering, their alternating claims to the locality and their relationships with members of the British community were instrumental, reflecting their sense of self at that point in time. As Cohen argues, 'people assert community ... when they recognize in it the most adequate medium for the expression of their whole selves' (1985: 107).

On the other hand, my analysis demonstrates that the British in the Lot had different measures of self-worth and belonging when compared with their compatriots in Spain. For the British on the Costa del Sol, 'sense of status, self-worth and belonging derive from other Britons; if there are not enough of them, or if the networks are not maintained, many people will feel disempowered and disconnected, lost and alone' (O'Reilly 2000: 153), hence the need for a well-established and continuous sense of community. In contrast, for the British in the Lot it seems that sense of self-worth and belonging are measured primarily by the extent to which they had become incorporated into rural French life. Their relationships with their compatriots could also contribute – and in fact became crucial in the absence of relationships with local social actors – but these were presented as substitutes for their relationships with local social actors.

While the migrant experience may, as Levitt and Glick Schiller argue, be accurately characterized as incorporating 'daily activities, routines, and institutions located both in the destination country and transnationally' (2004: 1003), my respondents articulated these as contradictory to one another. This was in part due to the particular context in which they arose, their imaginings of a better way of life and their desire to live within the local. As a result, competing claims to local and transnational belonging further augmented the sense of ambivalence within the migrants' lives.

Conclusion

This chapter has considered the argument that life following migration can be characterized as liminal, and suggested instead that the permanence of feelings of ambivalence – their presence in life before migration, and the role of both work and leisure in the migrants' lives following migration – indicates that for my respondents in the Lot, the migrant experience cannot be adequately conceptualized as liminal. Instead, I suggest an alternative conceptual framework focusing on ambivalence, which explains and captures more closely the particularities of my respondents' lives. Ambivalence is thus recognized as a characteristic of life before migration that through migration was redefined in terms that the migrants felt they had more control over. In this rendering, the ambivalence of my respondents was not a specific outcome of migration but a reflection of the wider sense of ambivalence experienced by modern social actors.

The recognition of such pervasive uncertainty in the lives of my respondents demonstrates the mismatch between expectations and lived experiences. Life in Britain had been presented as fatalistic and oppressive, with the migrants expressing feelings of ambivalence. Against this background migration was presented positively, understood as a way of resolving such feelings, and therefore as having a transformative potential. This discourse of personal transformation has much in common with discussions of tourism, which similarly present tourism as *'rituals of transformation'* (Franklin 2003; original italics) impacting on the identity of the individual (see for example Abram and Waldren 1997). As an active choice to change their lifestyles, the migration of my respondents was transformative. Nevertheless, the persistence of ambivalence in their lives following migration demonstrates that migration did not fully resolve feelings of uncertainty. The discrepancy between promise and reality that Bruner (1991) identifies within the tourism encounter seems equally to be present in the case of lifestyle migration.

I argue that this difference between rhetoric and action is particularly revealing. On the one hand, it demonstrates that migration narratives were significant as justifications for the decision to migrate. They were formulated in terms instantly recognizable to an audience who were equally dissatisfied with their lives in Britain, and they relied on generalizing statements about the status quo. On the other hand, the migrants' actions demonstrated that the transformative potential of migration was overplayed, just as Harrison (2003) found in the case of tourism. Nevertheless, the migrants continued to emphasize transformation in their communications with friends and family back in Britain, and their reservations about the true transformative potential of migration were expressed only to their compatriots living locally who found themselves similarly striving to come to terms with their new lives. What this demonstrates is that migration itself did not bring instant fulfilment and thus alone did not result in a better way of life that the migrants sought. In this rendering, migration does not represent a rupture between the lives led before and after migration but should rather be considered as an active lifestyle choice, within a series of choices that people make in their lifetime and as part of the reflexive project of the self (Benson and O'Reilly 2009; O'Reilly and Benson 2009).

Although the reality of life following migration did not signal the instant fulfilment that my respondents had hoped for, the search for a better way of life remained significant to them. As I demonstrate throughout this book, they continued to strive towards self-fulfilment, emphasizing their small triumphs and setbacks *en route*. Their progress was not unidirectional, and their goal – a better way of life – remained vague. Unlike Bousiou's (2008) respondents in Mykonos, my respondents did not value ambivalence for ambivalence's sake; they reflected upon it as an indicator of their individual progress on the road to a better way of life. And while lifestyle migrants in Spain may have talked the same talk (see

O'Reilly 2000; Oliver 2008), my respondents in the Lot actively worked towards the achievement of this. Despite the ongoing nature of their quest, it was this expressed desire to reach the better way of life and their frustrations with the ambivalence of daily life that made them unique among lifestyle migrants.

Notes

1 CPAM pays the bulk of health-care costs (up to 70%) for those registered and contributing to the social security system. This contribution is obligatory, and is normally taken directly from an individual's salary. To cover the remaining costs, individuals are advised to take out 'top up' insurance. In the case of many of my respondents, the contribution that would normally be taken out of the salary had to be paid by the migrants themselves, although this was means-tested. This demonstrates that a certain level of social contribution is required for intra-European migrants to gain social entitlements in their host country (Ackers and Dwyer 2004).

4

Life in a postcard

The Lot is a department renowned for its beautiful landscape – awesome lime-stone cliffs with picturesque medieval villages perched at their peaks, verdant green valleys, and vineyards. Indeed, my respondents often cited the environment when they discussed the decision to migrate, perceiving the Lot to offer both beautiful scenery and the promise of traditional rural living (Buller and Hoggart 1994a; Thorbold 2008). This desire to live in a beautiful area reflected the yearnings of lifestyle migrants more generally, with the new landscape offering the antithesis of life before migration (Waldren 1996; King, Warnes and Williams 2000; O'Reilly 2000). While previous research focused on how these perceived virtues of the French countryside and imaginings of the life within it inspired migration, emphasizing the social construction of the landscape and, to a certain degree, the influence of beautiful scenery, this chapter examines how my respondents conceptualized the landscape following migration.

Once living in the Lot, the migrants' perceptions of their surroundings shifted and changed. While their actions within the new surroundings were evidently influenced by their preconceptions, it is also the case that their rural idyll was reconfigured in response to their experiences; their representations and practices were therefore thoroughly intertwined (Bender 1998; Cloke and Jones 2001; Massey 2006). Through their increasing engagements with their surroundings my respondents' understandings of the landscape became more nuanced, complex and even contradictory, reflecting an overwhelming ambivalence towards their new environment. As I argue in this chapter, this ambivalence emerged precisely from their modern way of perceiving the rural as the bastion of tradition. Although they desired a return to the traditional, they brought with them the baggage of modernity. Their migration thus heralded a transformation in the way that the rural French landscape was used.

Traditionally the domain of French *paysans* (farmers with small-holdings) who understand the world through the tension between cultivated land and wilderness, the Lot provided British incomers not only with a beautiful backdrop to their daily lives but also with the space to carry out their (limited) professional activities, for leisure, physical and emotional reprieve and restoration, and investment (Barou and Prado 1995). The migrants therefore presented their new surroundings in a variety of ways: as the rural idyll, with its unspoilt countryside and rustic homes; as a space for leisure; but also as a place where they were able to physically engage with the land and get their hands dirty. Influenced by the argument that the landscape is continuously (re)constructed (Bender 1993, 1998; Hirsch 1995), I consider what these mundane engagements with their surroundings revealed about the migrants and their aspirations, and what their various representations of the landscape did for them.

The Lot: picture postcard and rural idyll

You won't find the tortured geology of, say, the Ardèche or Verdon, or the architectural majesty of the Loire or Dordogne, yet the Lot has something else to offer: for simple, natural beauty and a sense of leafy seclusion, it's unsurpassed. (Moss 2003: 26)

The more rugged and isolated landscape of the Lot is attracting British buyers who like its peaceful rural nature; with its medieval, hilltop villages and more arid appearance. (Buller and Hoggart 1994b)

It was clear that the sweeping vistas of the department, imposing limestone cliffs, wide river valley and wooded hillsides had made an immediate and distinct impression on my respondents. As a result, the aesthetic appeal of the landscape featured highly within their discussions of why they had chosen to relocate to the Lot specifically. As previous literature has emphasized (Buller and Hoggart 1994a; Barou and Prado 1995), the migrants presented the Lot as a quintessential rural idyll. Nevertheless, I discovered that these visions of rurality existed alongside other understandings of their new surroundings. As they pointed out the views from their homes, they presented their rhetoric of migration as self-evident, highlighting the extent to which they had been seduced by the breathtaking beauty of their new surroundings.

The lure of the landscape

I saw those cliffs; I saw the view ... the view across the Vers (river) is absolutely stunning. Why are we here? Because it's so beautiful. (David Lomax)

We came through Saint-Cirq [Lapopie]. He [the estate agent] brought us, we had lunch in Saint-Cirq and then he brought us along the fantastic road from Saint-Cirq to this village. At that stage I think we would have bought the shed because it was ... just so colossal, the view along the edge. To think that we were going to be living 3 km away from that was just something else! (Justine Grange)

These quotations demonstrate the initial impressions that my respondents had of the Lot when they first visited, often when they were searching for homes in rural France. They highlight the impact that the scenery had had on them at this early stage, and the way in which this had become an almost self-evident justification for their continued residence in the Lot.

In this respect, how my respondents in the Lot related to their new surroundings reflected the wider desire of lifestyle migrants for destinations that they perceive to be beautiful (see for example Waldren 1996; King, Warnes and

Williams 2000; O'Reilly 2000; Oliver 2007). The value of this beautiful backdrop in part derived from the contrast with the life left behind. But beyond this lay a narrative of escape, symbolized by the new surroundings. Jacqueline Waldren, in her ethnography of Deià, clearly outlines the link between particular landscapes and salvation. For the incomers to Deià, 'this idyllic setting epitomized the contrast to Western materialist society that most come to escape' (1996:146). As I demonstrate below, this was similarly the case in the migrants' renderings of the landscape as rural idyll. The question then becomes, why was the aesthetic appeal of the landscape so prominent in the migrants' imaginings, and what did it do for them?

I argue here that by looking on the landscape in this way, the migrants could step outside of their everyday lives. This is similar to Urry's (1990) tourist gaze whereby through tourism individuals may escape the ordinary. Smith (1993) similarly argues that through gazing at a beautiful view the, albeit temporary, transcendence of everyday life becomes possible. However, the landscape, when viewed in this way, is not presented in its entirety. As Smith (1993) argues, the landscape in this rendering seems to escape history, to be beyond time, timeless as it stretches unchanged from past to present and on towards the future. As Harry Earl explained to me one morning as he looked out of his sitting room window, 'You can just imagine the cave men running along the valley floor'. Harry's account reflected the wider sense of timelessness contained within the migrants' visions of their new surroundings. Necessarily, this image of the landscape neglected the extent to which the landscape (and indeed perceptions of it) had been shaped by the actions of humans and other actors (Smith 1993). Furthermore, this way of looking on the landscape reflected a romantic veneration of the natural world and a particular conception of nature common to the middle classes (Urry 1990). Therefore, while their perceptions and understandings of their new surroundings resulted in part from the migrants' own subjective experiences, these were refracted through a culturally mediated lens.

As I demonstrate below, this was by no means the only way that the migrants perceived the landscape, but it did continue to play a role in their lives following migration. They often recalled how they could enjoy the scenery at any time as they looked out of the window, stepped out of the front door or moved around the region. As Pat and Jean Porter described, approaching their property and the land around it, which included a vineyard, they were often struck by the visual impact it made. William and Victoria Cardew explained that they could 'just walk out from the house, and there [were] lovely views'. Driving also gave brief glimpses of the beautiful surroundings, as David Lomax recalled: 'The view across the Vers [river] is absolutely stunning. It's actually best if you're moving fast because the trees are quite thick, but if you're moving fast, you can see through the trees'. It seemed that the migrants savoured the permanent availability of these views,

> It's a beautiful area. There's no doubt about it. We still pinch ourselves when we're driving round doing work, even saying, 'Well look! People wait all year to come down for their two-week holiday and we've got it all year round.' (Jon and Kay Morris)

This quotation encapsulates the sentiments of many of my respondents. Jon and Kay aligned their lives in the Lot to living in a dream, where they needed to 'pinch' themselves to check that they were still awake. They also distinguished themselves from tourists, who could only experience this life for a few weeks a year, in the process further highlighting the exclusivity to their migration.

The migrants' representations of the landscape revealed their hopes that through migration they would find a better way of life, characterized in opposition to the life left behind. In this respect migration emerged as a route out of difficult personal circumstances but also as an active choice to escape dissatisfaction with life. The *Lotoise* landscape therefore provided refuge from their lives in Britain (Buller and Hoggart 1994a; Barou and Prado 1995). However, this representation gave little insight into the life available with the Lot beyond this opposition to life in Britain. As I demonstrate below, the French rural idyll offers a slightly more tangible way of life, which, nevertheless, remains meaningful to the migrants in its contrast to life in Britain.

The French rural idyll

Buller and Hoggart (1994a) have argued that British migration to rural France is inspired by the desire for the rural idyll, a desire evident in the movements of many urban dwellers into the British countryside and elevated to an international level as a result of the increasing cost and lack of availability of property in Britain (see also Barou and Prado 1995). This explanation of migration gives an insight into the wider rationalities that may prompt lifestyle migration, providing an explanation of the decision to migrate that particularly focuses on the opposition between the place of origin and the destination. Buller and Hoggart (1994a) stress that the veneration of the rural that characterizes the accounts of British migrants living in rural France is the product of their middle-class imaginings (cf Williams 1973) and is thus a viewpoint that is very difficult to overcome.

For my respondents, the Lot was significant in these terms. This perception of the landscape had framed their initial decision to migrate. In this respect, while the migrants' narratives at times presented a rather individualistic impression of their migration, the recourse to such common imaginings demonstrated the classed nature of their decision to migrate, particularly in the choice of destination. Furthermore, and as I have argued elsewhere in this book, placed within the context of the migrants' lives before migration, this valuation of the rural helped to rationalize and justify their migration.

On the one hand they prized the proximity to nature, recalling their awe and amazement at the sight of a lone deer spotted as the mist rose off the valley floor, the swallows diving on their swimming pools, or the herd of wild boar caught in their headlights as they returned home late at night. These images of nature projected tranquillity and peace, but also a harmony with nature. On the other hand, the migrants demonstrated a more nuanced understanding of their new surroundings, drawing attention to the lives of members of the local community. They prized the close and intimate relationships that their French neighbours had with one another and with their surroundings, their sense of community spirit and conviviality.

> Everyone knows everyone. Everyday dealings are based more on community, sharing things. (Pat and Jean Porter)

> The local community, it's just like family. (Trevor and Susan Sparrow)

> The French in rural France we find extremely polite, civilized, charming. You know, people talk to you. (Justine Grange)

> They are very generous, the French. In the country, like here, they give you so much. (Susan Sparrow)

> They have more value for time and people. (Kay Morris)

In the Lot, the migrants uncovered an idealized village life characterized by authentic conviviality (cf Barou and Prado 1995), a community that valued 'immediate family and friendship ties, local community solidarity and supportiveness' (Perry 1986: 22). As Strathern (1982) argues, the 'natural' community of the rural is a common perception of incomers. For my respondents in the Lot, their readings of the local community confirmed their belief that holistic and harmonious ways of life were available in the countryside. It was thus through their repeated evocation of the virtues of rural communities that my respondents stressed their own search for social harmony, continuity, stability and order (cf Selwyn 1996).

It is apparent that the Lot was attractive to the migrants in terms of its aesthetic appeal as well as its potential to offer a truly rural life. However, it remains important to remember that these representations of the landscape – and, indeed, imaginings of the lives available there – emerged not from experience but out of a particular cultural context: their position as members of the British middle class.

However, it became clear that while these common imaginings had shaped my respondents' initial expectations, and continued in part to frame their post-migration lives, through their experiences of life in the Lot they started to develop different understandings of and engagements with their new surroundings. Post-migration lives, while shaped in part by imagination – here understood as a social practice and therefore derived from structure – and individual biographies, should also be understood as mediated by experience.

In this respect, I argue that Bourdieu's (1977, 1990) concept of practice is useful in explaining how my respondents understood their lives in the Lot, to warn against an interpretation of these lives as being determined purely by the migrants' class status. Indeed, the emic perspective adopted in this research to gain an understanding of the migrants' lives enabled the persistent tension between structure and agency to be revealed. As I demonstrate below, in respect of the migrants' understandings of the landscape, this was evident in the contradiction between their imaginings of rurality and their efforts to realize these, between representation and process. The concept of practice allows for an understanding of the migrant experience, which not only demonstrates the structural forces underwriting these but also incorporates the migrants' own distinct viewpoints.

Process, practice and representation

While the migrants' accounts of their initial migration were dominated by the imaginings of what life would be like, their reflections on their lives following migration revealed the extent to which they were modifying their initial imaginings as they increasingly experienced life in the Lot. In particular, they appeared to have more nuanced understandings of and relationships to their new surroundings.

On the one hand, it could be argued that their increased levels of engagement with the landscape and other actors within it indicated that they were beginning to 'dwell' within the landscape. Following Ingold's (1993, 1995) dwelling perspective, the migrants rooted or localized themselves through their engagements with their surroundings. On the other hand, their narratives demonstrated that the manner in which they related to the landscape was not just a function of their increased engagement with it (indeed, there were times when they were deliberately detached from the landscape). Their accounts of daily life in the Lot revealed the continued influence of the beautiful surroundings on their imaginings of what life would offer them in the future, their memories and nostalgia for the past, and the persistence of the rural idyll imagery. In turn, these impacted on their actions and practices within the landscape. As I argue below, while the dwelling perspective, at first sight, seems to offer a useful framework for explaining the changes in the migrants' relationship to the landscape, its limitations mean that it is not wholly applicable to this case.

Ingold (1993, 1995) uses the term dwelling to explain the way that individuals may become an integral part of their surroundings, ultimately attuned to the unique rhythms of the landscape, and taking their place within the taskscape as they build up relationships with other users, animate and inanimate. The dwelling perspective therefore emphasizes how, through embodied engagements, nature and culture become inextricably bound together, as the individual acquires an unprecedented and intimate knowledge of their local environment. In this manner, engagement results in a sense of rootedness, linking the individual to a particular locale. As I demonstrate, the migrants' narratives clearly reflected this idea that a profound understanding of the landscape could be gained through engagement with it.

Nevertheless, Ingold's perspective has been criticized for presenting a coherent and harmonious image of the landscape, which overlooks the inequalities of power central to its construction and the historical particularity of the social relations taking place within it (Bender 1998; Massey 2006). Indeed, Ingold does not acknowledge, as Carrier (2003) highlights, that engagement emerges out of a particular cultural context; thus, for example, my respondents' idea of what constituted embodied engagement with the landscape may not have been the same as that of their French neighbours. Furthermore, as Cloke and Jones (2001) argue, the inherent localness entrenched within the idea of dwelling, neglects the dynamism and interpenetrativeness of the contemporary landscape. In sum, the dwelling perspective lacks context beyond the present and local, thus privileging practice and activity over representation. As previous discussions of the British in rural France have demonstrated, representation is key to how they envisaged their lives following migration. Simultaneously, my respondents stressed their embodied engagements with the landscape. The question then becomes how to account for both representation and practice, detachment and engagement, when talking about the landscape.

It seems that, unlike the actors in Ingold's accounts (1993, 1995), the British living in the Lot related to the landscape in multiple and contradictory ways. As in the case of Johnson and Clisby's expatriates living in Costa Rica, their migration was explained as the desire for '"traditional" ways of relating to place and surroundings' (2008: 65), no longer attainable in Britain. However, despite their embodied experiences of the landscape, they still referred to it in ways that revealed their modern roots.

On the one hand, their romantic gaze on the rural idyll, a product of modern rather than traditional sensibilities, ironically reveals the extent to which the migrants were in fact detached from their surroundings. On the other hand, their desires for a traditional way of life that in their minds resembled the lives led by their French neighbours were reflected in their efforts in engaging with the landscape and their hopes that they would, through their proximity, absorb the (perceived) authentic local knowledge of these traditional social actors. As Carrier argues, 'some people in the modern west hold a view of their environs that is *more than* the view that is supposed to characterize Modern societies' (Carrier 2003: 10–11; emphasis added). Therefore Ingold's dwelling perspective, resting on the diametric opposition between engagement and detachment, the traditional and the modern, cannot fully account for the migrants' experiences of life in rural France, even though its foundational dualism underscored the migrants' ambivalence.

Contrary to the dwelling perspective (Ingold 1993, 1995) and the social construction of the landscape (see for example Williams 1973), which privilege one way of perceiving the landscape to the exclusion of all other possibilities, Bender (1993, 1998) argues that different perceptions of the landscape may have a combined influence on the way that individuals relate to the landscape. She therefore stresses the intersection of three different ways that individuals might know the landscape: 'the landscape as *palimpsest*; landscape as *structure of feeling*; and landscape as *embodied*' (Bender 1998: 6; original italics). In turn, these have an influence on how individuals understand, interpret, act in relation to, and use the landscape. Bender's conceptualization thus allows for a landscape that is continuously being (re)constructed (Bender 1993, 1998; Hirsch 1995; Massey 2006), while maintaining the residues of its past use; a culturally mediated construction of the landscape, through which the meaning of the landscape becomes embedded in the individual's habitus; and finally, the possibility that landscape may be learned through the individuals' embodied engagement, as they, metaphorically, get their hands dirty. Bender also emphasizes the equal significance of representation and practice, and the recognition that these influence one another to the extent that they are inextricably intertwined (Bender 1998; see also Cloke and Jones 2001; Massey 2006).

In this rendering representations influence practices, and practices feed back into representations. By recognizing the complex and multiple perceptions of the landscape held by individuals, it is possible to reveal the continuing co-dependence of practice and representation that is foundational to the landscape-making process. As I argue, the distinction between representation and practice that lies at the core of Bender's argument mirrors that between imagination and experience that I focus on in this chapter, with a culturally constructed imagination in tension with individual experiences of life in the Lot.

As the ethnography presented in this chapter demonstrates, it is this more dynamic understanding of the landscape that captures the nuances of my respondents' relationships with their new surroundings. In their everyday lives, they attempted to emplace themselves, learning about their new environment through their embodied practices, their tracks increasingly crossing those of other (human and non-human) actors. It becomes clear that their understandings of and relationship to the landscape were complex, shifting and changing in response to their new experiences and encounters with others. Balancing their experiences against their representations, they renegotiated their perceptions of their new surroundings. The combined impact of different perceptions on the landscape and the idea that Bender proposes of the landscape being continually reconstructed is therefore a useful theoretical lens through which to examine how my respondents relate to the *Lotoise* landscape in their lives following migration.

Dwelling in the postcard

The migrants' representations of their new surroundings evocatively recalled the rural idyll with its promise of reprieve and holistic way of living. However, to dwell within the landscape required that they develop a more nuanced understanding of that landscape. As the ethnography in this section demonstrates, this was a gradual process that was made possible by their physical engagements with the land and their careful attention to their surroundings. In part, their perceptions of local actors and their engagements with the landscape acted as a blueprint for how they should relate to the environment. But they also believed that through communion with the landscape and in moving through it, they could learn how to live within it.

Learning the landscape

In addition to admiring the relationships that the local French had with one another, the migrants valued how the indigenous population connected with their surroundings. As Samantha Harris explained, 'The locals are not at all middle class; they're all people of the soil'. Indeed, many local actors engaged in agriculture, from viticulture to arable farming and animal husbandry, and in the migrants' perceptions, they were in tune with nature and knowledgeable of its distinct rhythms, embedded in what Ingold would refer to as a 'taskscape' (1993, 1995). For the migrants, this enviable position of being part of the landscape was exactly what they aspired to; they wanted to dwell in it and thus to directly experience and embody it (see Ingold 1993).

However, while Ingold (1993, 1995) overlooks the cultural dimensions of the way that such landscapes are understood (Carrier 2003), it was clear that for my respondents the desire to be part of the landscape rested upon a particular construction that was not, as Samantha's statement highlighted, shared by their new French neighbours. Despite such differences in the way they perceived and understood the landscape, the migrants' actions demonstrated the extent to which they believed that they were emulating the actions of their neighbours. They therefore acted on the basis of their imaginings of the lives led within the rural idyll and the relationships that residents of this idyll had with the environment.

The migrants' accounts thus expressed a sense that in order to understand the landscape, you had to feel it (see also Tilley 1994, 2006a & b, in relation to gardens; Theodossopoulos 2003a). For example, Pat and Jean moved to the Lot specifically to produce wine. They had carefully orchestrated a plan that included taking courses in viticulture before they left Britain. Their daily lives in the Lot revolved around wine production, which was their livelihood rather than a hobby. They did most of the work involved in the production themselves, from planting the vines and harvesting the grapes to bottling and selling the wine. As they told me, their work in the vineyard required an intimate knowledge of the vines and grapes; for example, they had to inspect the plants for disease, know when the grapes were ripe enough to harvest, and know when and where to plant new vines. They also explained that they needed to keep one step ahead of the weather because of the effect that it could have on their crops. In a part of the world where the weather could be very localized, this required more than checking the five-day forecast; they told me that they had to read the signs from the landscape around them to anticipate the weather. It was clear that their economic dependence on the land influenced the relationship that they had with it (see also Abramson 2000; Theodossopoulos 2003a).

Many other migrants shared the idea that in order to understand the landscape it was necessary to work the land. Their imaginings thus promoted subtle changes in their relationship to the landscape, moving from detached viewers who admired the landscape to (more) engaged actors. Their actions, which were often restricted to their work on their gardens, tending to their fruit trees and large vegetable patches, led to experiences which aided in the cultivation of an embodied relationship with their surroundings. As Chevalier (1998) has argued of the British more generally, 'their relationship to the land is thus created in their garden: they appropriate the land through their practice and skill' (1998: 67).

As I witnessed, the migrants were keen to demonstrate their knowledge and ability of their new surroundings through such gardening practices. Vic Wilson often told me that he had learned to adapt his planting schedule to French rhythms, following the plan of his neighbour Claude. He let me in on the secret: everything could be planted a month earlier than in England, and presumably harvested a month earlier. In this respect, it became clear that he was trying to account for 'nature' within his gardening practices and thus claim it for his own purposes (Chevalier 1998). Vic also made certain that he only planted things that would grow in the Lot, buying his supply of seeds from the local garden centre. He assured me that this was unusual, as many of his compatriots living locally brought seed varieties from Britain and had only rare success in cultivating them. Harry Earl, in contrast, explained how he had learned through his own experiments what would and would not grow in the Lot. This was why he decided to no longer grow potatoes: the amount of work required to produce a reasonable crop was disproportionate to the results.

Over time, many of the migrants had learned more about their surroundings through their own investigations. For example, one afternoon Harold and Min Jones explained to me how they had come to recognize when the seasons were changing, the landscape seemed to change colour as some plants died and others grew in their place. And as I walked with Anne Wilson around her village one afternoon, exclaiming my curiosity at the big craters in a freshly ploughed field, she explained that these were the consequence of the wild boar and their search for roots to eat. This knowledge demonstrated a desire to see beyond the surface and to become more engaged with the local environment.

Both of these examples demonstrate the extent to which the migrants were keen to reconcile their own embodied experiences of landscape with culturally inspired and class-specific imaginings. Through practice, which, as Bourdieu (1977, 1990) argues, accounts both for an implicit practical logic or common sense and bodily dispositions, the migrants mediated imagination and experience.[1] Over time, their knowledge of how to live in the Lot was gradually and subtly transformed. While they did not fully abandon their understandings of the Lot as rural idyll, through their experiences they laid claim to a position within this. In this respect, their engagements with the landscape acted as a further way in which they tried to overcome their position as outsiders and emplace themselves within the local social and physical landscape.

Leisure in the landscape

In addition, the migrants learned about their surroundings through their leisure activities. They regularly took walks into the landscape, at times accompanied by local actors, while others travelled along the river in canoes or through the forests on bikes. In all cases, though, the focus was placed on their newly gained experience of their surroundings, not just on their appreciation of the good view. Nevertheless, as Macnaghten and Urry (1998) argue, their experiences of the countryside, particularly those gained through walking, were premised on the romantic gaze; their leisure activities did not threaten the landscape aesthetic, provided that they did not spoil it through litter or destructive behaviour, or disrupt its peace and tranquillity. Of course, what is considered destructive to the natural environment is culturally designated. As I discovered, the migrants had a clear belief about what the countryside was for and how to behave within it. Nevertheless, this was a moralized discourse, and, as I show in the next section, they often struggled to toe the line. In their self-presentations, however, they were conscious to present their leisure activities as complementary to the countryside.

Their participation in local rambling clubs demonstrated this most clearly. As they explained, walking alongside their neighbours, they could see the landscape through the lens of the locals, explore the environment, learn local history and make new friends.

> We belong to a walking club and stuff and we don't get out there much but it's nice when you do go because you get to see all the places that you wouldn't know with locals and it's a good way to see things. (Jon and Kay Morris)

> Surprising sometimes, you go out for walks and you think you know all the houses in the area, and all of a sudden, you come across a little house in the middle of nowhere ... Jacques, the man who leads us, has got all sorts of plans of the old part of the commune, and he is working out various different routes to find things that are interesting, so we can learn a bit more about the history of the area. (Martin and Sarah Johnstone)

As I walked with my respondents, sometimes tracing the routes through the landscape that they had taken with their neighbours, they demonstrated the extent to which they had incorporated local knowledge into their narratives about life in the Lot. They drew attention to the flora and fauna, stopped at overgrown fields to point out the barely visible ruins within them, and relayed local myths about how the landscape had become what it was today. Moving through the landscape in this way helped the migrants to establish an intimate relationship with it and to gain a distinctive understanding of their new environment.

These leisure activities that brought them into contact with local social actors served a dual purpose; they provided a space for the enactment of a common interest in the area, while also allowing the migrants to gain a deeper understanding of the landscape that reflected the perceptions of their French interlocutors. In the case of the latter, this was a complex process, which entailed the local French, who were an intrinsic part of the rural idyll and who they deemed to have a unique relationship with their surroundings, stepping out of their imaginations and into their experiences. Perhaps it is not surprising, given the way that they had imagined these others, that the migrants wanted them to serve as their guides to their new surroundings; they were thus keen to defer to the knowledge of their neighbours who had an intimate relationship with the landscape derived from years of living within it. However, I argue that this also had the potential to be a risky strategy; the local actors had the power to disrupt, as well as deepen, their imaginings of the rural idyll.

The migrants' presentations of local actors revealed that they too related to the landscape in what appeared to be contradictory ways. While they engaged with it in their daily work and practices, working the land and thus developing intimate relationships with it, they also valued the beauty of their surroundings. The stories of local history that they told to the migrant incomers seemed to convey a sense of nostalgia – 'this is how life used to be' – but also a reverence for their surroundings. The migrants made it clear that these reflections on the aesthetics of the landscape were distinct from the detachment that was suggested to lie at the core of such perceptions of the landscape (see for example Urry 1990). My respondents stressed that for the local French, veneration of the beauty of their surroundings did not derive from a detached gaze on those surroundings; they valued the landscape in these terms precisely because they lived within it. This realization gave my respondents the hope that over time they too would be able to overcome their detachment from the landscape to live within it while still appreciating its scenic qualities. In this respect, they expressed their belief that they would, somehow, be able to overcome the cultural determinants that had, ironically, prompted their migration.

The contradictions of dwelling

Nevertheless, it is clear that their progress in this direction was wrought with contradictions. Their engagements with the landscape revealed further the extent to which their understandings of their new surroundings were contradictory. At times, their paths intersected only fleetingly with those of other users, or they had an appreciation of the environment that was shared by certain users but not all. These evident ambiguities within the migrants' accounts need interrogating, following Cosgrove (2006), to reveal the complex significance that these new surroundings had for them.

On the one hand, there were certain aspects of the migrants' original ideals that were less appealing once they had to live with them. As Beth MacDonald stressed, she had originally been attracted to her house on the edge of a small hamlet at the top of the *causse* (limestone plateau) because of its location and beautiful view. But, as she recalled, she had not thought through the practicalities of living there: 'I didn't realize that when Hector wasn't here, I was going to be completely isolated. The nearest ... village is 5 km from here, so there is no way I can push my trolley 5 km there and 5 km back to do the shopping'. This was also the reason why Trish Greenham had decided to move into a small town; over time, living in a remote location lost some of its shine, particularly if, as in Trish and Beth's cases, migrants could not drive. On the other hand, however, there were other contradictions within the migrants' perceptions of the landscape, which had resulted from their conflicting ideas about how to relate to their surroundings.

The perfect garden

Harry and Connie's garden was a good exemplar of these contradictions. Imagine looking down from their veranda onto a wide patio, the patio table and chairs shaded by a large umbrella in the heat of the day. As you look further down the garden, which stretches down to the bank of an old railway line, you see a large vegetable patch, while to the right you see a large ornamental pond. Beyond these features, the land lies flat and has been covered in grass, an expanse interrupted only by a few small fruit trees and the occasional bush. In the summer of 2005, standing on the terrace, I noticed that the grass was suffering in the heat of the season; closer observation revealed that it had been scorched. Harry had taken the opportunity to kill off all the weeds within it, which left a rather dull brown stretch of dead and dying grass. As he explained to me, he wanted a perfect lawn, which is why he had spent the first few years in France flattening out his land and had invested a lot of his time and energy into sowing the grass seed and tending to the lawn in its early stages. As he was keen to explain, this was not the first time that his plans had been thwarted.

A quick look around the village revealed that no one else had the close-cut, luscious, flat and green lawn that Harry wanted. And when I spoke to other migrants, they explained that the pursuit of such a lawn was misplaced in the Lot. I argue that the lawn was misplaced in terms of their wider imaginings of rural life. Growing vegetables, mirroring on a smaller scale the activities of their French farming neighbours and reflective of their attempts to live more natural and holistic lives, was an acceptable activity. But the lawn, which did not have a place within their romantic representations of the rural idyll, was perceived as a comical undertaking. As I argue, Harry's lawn was emblematic of the conflict between the desire for the rural idyll that lay at the root of migration and his ambitions for his home and garden, which similarly reflected wider, culturally specific imaginings. In many ways, it was clear that Harry was attempting to reconstruct an English country garden; as Tilley (2008) argues, this is evidence of banal (English) nationalism.

For other migrants the contradiction lay instead in their appropriation of French farming practices into the garden-making process. As they tended to their vegetable patches, which were often just big enough to produce a crop that they could reasonably use in their own homemade cuisine, they demonstrated their efforts to understand the landscape as the locals did, by getting their hands dirty. In this manner, they underplayed the different histories that had brought about these practices in order to align themselves with these local social actors. While the migrants living in the landscape continued to reflect their desire for a particularly constructed and embedded rural idyll, the local producers un-doubtedly related to the landscape through a long and hard personal history of trying to tame it and being economically dependent upon it (Abramson 2000; Theodossopoulos 2003a). For the migrants, working on their gardens was a luxury that arguably equated to a leisure pursuit, whereas the French farmers worked the land out of necessity.

The pursuit of the perfect garden was the first example of the migrants' wider ambivalence about how they related to the landscape. While MacNaghten and Urry (1998) argue for a persisting ambivalence in people's relationships with the countryside, referring to the contradictory ways that different individuals believe the environment should be used, I build on this argument to demonstrate that the multi-faceted ways in which individual migrants related to the landscape expose their ambivalence about their new surroundings.

A boar and a horse

Harry's pond was a further symbol of this ambivalence, highlighting the incon-sistency between the rhetoric of migration and subsequent actions. I was there in 2005 when he filled his ornamental pond with water for the first time and sat back to admire his handiwork. But the next morning, when he went out on to the veranda to enjoy his newly constructed pond, he was dismayed to find that one of the edging slabs had been dislodged and had partially fallen into the pond. His immediate fear was that it had ripped the pond's lining, and even though there was no damage on this occasion, he wanted to prevent this accident from happening again. His suspicion was that the wild boar had come down to the valley floor during the night to seek food and water. While drinking from the pond, the boar had knocked the slab with its hooves. That afternoon he erected an electric fence around the pond, its white plastic sheathing and posts posing a stark contrast to the natural surroundings. The following morning, it was clear that the fence had served its purpose; there was no evidence of any further damage from the boar and Harry had achieved a symbolic victory over the wild French fauna.

David Lomax told a similar tale. One morning he had woken up to find a horse in his swimming pool. Luckily, the horse was able to get out of the pool, but the pool's lining, which, as in the case of the pond, kept the water in, had been seriously damaged. It emerged that the horse had escaped from the field where it was kept, probably as a result of badly maintained fences. A closer inspection of the lining revealed that it would have to be replaced. A long and drawn-out debate between David and the local farmer who owned the horse ensued about who should pay for the damages.

These two vignettes demonstrate the nuances of the migrants' relationships with their new surroundings. While Harry put up an electric fence to keep out the wilderness, David was shocked to find rurality in his pool. At the same time, as with many of their compatriots, Harry and David were very knowledgeable about local nature, for example, recognizing the distinctive characteristics of the local birds. The boar and the horse are emblematic of wilderness and rurality respectively, but when they appeared in the pond and the pool they became 'matter out of place' (Douglas 1966). The migrants' resulting actions in response to these incursions into their space demonstrated the contradictions that arise from overlaying different systems of classification. For European farmers, the wilderness is set in opposition to domesticated nature, an opposition maintained by a long and well-established cosmology (Theodossopoulos 2003a). However, for the non-farming migrants, the domains of the wilderness (the boar) and rurality (the horse) existed alongside that of leisure (pond and swimming pool). In the absence of a well-established cultural tradition of relating to the tensions between these three domains, the migrants found themselves in confusion and ambivalence.

A swimming pool with(in) a view

It was somewhat unsurprising that swimming pools, those emblems of leisure, recurred as points of contradiction within the migrants' accounts. My first experience of this occurred before my fieldwork, on a visit to the Lot in 2003. As I looked down from the viewpoint of a medieval village perched on top of a cliff overlooking the valley, I noticed several striking features, but my eye was drawn to the swimming pool on the valley floor. It stood out because of its unusual figure of eight shape and the bright green pool liner (Figure 5). There had been no attempt to shield it from view, and it was the only swimming pool in sight.

5 The figure-of-eight swimming pool

I later discovered that there were other swimming pools on the valley floor, but they had been more carefully hidden so as not to disturb the view. When I returned to carry out my fieldwork in 2004, the swimming pool was still eliciting interest from the local British population. They seemed to unanimously agree that the swimming pool was an eyesore, and they criticized the shape of the pool and the colour of its lining, which were at odds with the natural surroundings. I discovered that the owners of the pool were a British couple who split their residence between the Lot and Britain. As some of my respondents commented sarcastically, there were no flushing toilets in the house, but at least they had a swimming pool.

Despite their derision, many of my respondents also had swimming pools, a stark contrast to the traditional French farmhouses and barns that many of them lived in. Looking around the village where I lived, I found that the only two homes with swimming pools were a *gîte* owned by an English couple and the old coach house, which was owned by a Parisian family who visited the Lot during the summer holidays. If this were a pattern throughout the department, it would strongly support the idea that the British and other incomers to the Lot had different expectations about what these surroundings could offer them their local neighbours had. Although some of the migrants argued that the swimming pools were a necessary addition that helped them to attract visitors to their *gîte*, this did not stop their owners from using them. Others, predominantly retirees, stressed the importance of the swimming pools in their everyday lives. Ron Stampton explained that he eagerly awaited the opening of his pool every spring as he enjoyed not only swimming but also the view from the pool. Julian Ford went one step further, arguing that for him, the pool was part of the view from his house, 'We put the pool there because when the cover is off and the water is sparkling, it's a

6 A swimming pool in the garden of one of my respondents

beautiful sight' (Figure 6). In this rendering, it is clear that the swimming pools were an emblem of the leisure opportunities that these new surroundings offered.

Despite the undeniable association of the swimming pools with leisure, some of the migrants were keen to stress how, unlike the couple who lived on the valley floor, they had made their swimming pools blend as much as possible into the natural surroundings. Martin and Sarah Johnstone had built a state-of-the-art pool hidden within the structure of a ruined barn; you would not know that a pool was there until you were almost on top of it. Another couple stressed that they had had to conform to the planning regulations when they bought their pool liner and to choose a less conspicuous colour. They had also planted several trees to hide the pool from view. But even taking the advice of the planning office was no guarantee that the pool would meet the approval of the inspectors. It was at this stage that the owners of the green-lined, figure-of-eight pool had been ordered to plant three hundred and fifty trees to hide the pool from the view overhead.

The examples presented here highlight the conflicting representations of the Lot, simultaneously emblematic of the rural idyll, raw nature and leisure. Influenced by these contradictory representations, the migrants' engagements with the landscape were subsequently at odds with one another. And yet, they also reflected on the progress of time in the development of a deeper understanding of their surroundings.

> It's funny really because you look around and think it must all be relatively un-
> changed ... but I've come to realize that it's not ... everything has changed.
> Before there was even more agriculture; it's more wooded now than it was ... this

wouldn't have been a garden, would it? And the houses sit so well in the landscape. Over there, there are two scars where the woods have been chopped down;
one for a vineyard, and the other one, they're building something on it. It looks
awful; you can see it from miles away. (Alannah Tapper)

As this quotation highlights, the tension between imaginings of how the landscape should be and how it is experienced, remain pertinent to the migrants'
understandings. In other words, imagination is not completely displaced by experience, the two remain inseparably entangled. The migrants' daily practices in
relation to the landscape reflect this tension, which is manifest in their ambivalence about their new surroundings.

Conclusion

The ethnography presented here demonstrates that the migrants held a series
of contradictory understandings of their new surroundings. As their understandings of the landscape shifted from initial imaginings of the Lot as the rural idyll
to their desires to live within it, a persistent tension between imagination and experience was revealed. As I argue, such tensions can be understood as emerging
from culturally specific understandings of the landscape and the environment;
expectations for lives following migration, framed by wider collective imaginings, but also integrating individual biographies; and embodied experiences of
life within the destination. Therefore, for my respondents in the Lot the landscape became the site for the interface of cultural logic with individual histories
and experiences.

Within the context of the wider literature, this sociological reflection is significant. The unique focus on the intersections between structural conditions
and individual experiences augment earlier understandings of British migration
to rural France as prompted by a middle-class culture valorizing the rural idyll
(see for example Buller and Hoggart 1994a; Barou and Prado 1995). Through the
ethnography presented in this chapter, it has become increasingly evident that
following migration the attempt to realize previous expectations for life in the
Lot was made possible by the tension between the migrants' embodied experiences and their culturally specific imaginings. I therefore argue that in order
to explain post-migration lives, analyses need to be particularly sensitive both
to the structural forces that shape migration and to expectations for life within
the destination, while also paying attention to the role of individual experiences.

Furthermore, this understanding of how my respondents relate to the landscape highlights that through practice, these relationships undergo continual
reconstruction. As the migrants' hopes for their futures in the Lot demonstrate,
they believe that they might eventually overcome the cultural determinants that
dictated the terms of their relationship with the landscape and to adopt a logic
of engagement that is proximate to that of their neighbours. Simply put, they
desire a relationship with the landscape that results from living within it, rather
than viewing it from the outside, their desires reinforcing the dualism between
engagement and detachment.

As the chapters in Part 2 demonstrate, this tension between their imaginings of how to live in the Lot and their embodied experiences frame the migrants' identity claims. They use engagement with the social and physical landscape to distinguish themselves from their compatriots living in the Lot and in other migration destinations. In this respect, the desire to become emplaced, resting on the distinction between engagement and detachment, acts as a measure of the success of these others in getting the better way of life that lies at the core of British migration to the Lot. Ironically, it is precisely this opposition between engagement and detachment that they need to surmount if they are to achieve their goals.

Notes

1 By common sense I do not intend to imply a sense of rational action, but rather to draw attention to the cultural bases on which people often operate, which they hold *in common* with other members of their cultural group.

2

Distinction, identity and the ongoing search for a better way of life

5

At home in the Lot

This chapter explores how my respondents made their houses in the Lot into homes. Through the examination of specific case studies I reveal the process of home-making, from planning, building and modification of the material form of houses to choices over how to furnish and decorate interiors. As these examples demonstrate, there was no standard format, and homes were constructed in a variety of ways. By drawing on the established literature that focuses on the material culture of the home (see for example Miller 1998, 2001; Cieraad 1999), I demonstrate that the migrants' home consumption choices were an expression of their social identities, which revealed their individual journeys to life in rural France, gave insights into the lives they led in the Lot and also reflected their original aspirations for life following migration. Through this examination the intricate relationship between people, objects and consumption is revealed (Douglas and Isherwood 1978; Bourdieu 1984; Miller 1987).

The insights that I present in this chapter are also revealing of the central role that the home played in the everyday lives of my respondents. From the start of my research I was invited to join the migrants in their homes, even when we had not previously met. Much of my fieldwork therefore took place within private homes, as I found myself being invited time and again to join my respondents in these spaces. Significantly, I was not alone in receiving such invitations; it was common to find that the migrants regularly socialized within the home, inviting their compatriots to their homes for long lunches, dinner parties or just for coffee; on other occasions they would have guests to stay, normally friends and family from Britain. While certain rooms might be set aside for such events, there were of course other areas of the home that were considered not to be on public view to visitors or guests. I often had the privilege of being shown these other rooms, particularly if the migrants had recently been doing work on those parts of their homes, and in this respect I ventured into the backstage of their home lives. The use of the home as described here demonstrates that the migrants' homes occupied ambivalent positions as part public and part private spaces.

To illustrate the relationship between home-making practices, identity and belonging; to show the influence of class on the construction of home; and to reveal the home as the locus of social life, I present three case studies. In this manner, I demonstrate the diversity in my respondents' approaches to how they constructed their homes and their subsequent relationships with these. At one end of the scale were the Fords, who had filled their new French house with their British furniture and ornaments, while at the other end, the Johnstones demonstrated a steadfast commitment to a particular rustic aesthetic that they strived to authentically recreate in their French farmhouse. But there was also the possibility of compromise, as the home of the Tappers demonstrated: while remaining faithful to French architectural styles, they had combined these with their unique personal tastes within the home.

Despite this diversity, the home-making practices of my respondents were revealed as foundational to their claims for local belonging, a key component of the better way of life that they sought. Alongside their efforts to emplace themselves within the landscape, through their home-making practices they were able to ground themselves in rural France. This is why the house, a physical representation of their presence in the Lot, was so important to the decision to migrate and to their lives following migration. Nevertheless, their particular choices in home consumption reflected the complexity of their claims to belonging, and the lengths to which they were prepared to go to achieve the better way of life that they sought.

Making homes and selves

As the ethnography in this chapter demonstrates, my respondents in the Lot embarked on the task of home-making in various ways. For some, this involved constructing from the ground up, a house to be made into a home, while for others, the process was different and they co-opted a shell that they then strived to make their own. Tim Ingold has argued that these are two different processes:

> In co-optive making an already existing object is fitted to a conceptual image of an intended future use, in the mind of the user. In constructive making this process is reversed, in that the object is physically remodelled to conform more closely to the pre-existing image. (Ingold 1995: 62)

As Ingold (1995) stresses, drawing heavily on Heidegger, both of these attitudes to home-making emphasize a dwelling perspective (as opposed to a building perspective), with the home emerging as the intersection of people with material forms. Dant (1999) stresses that by applying Heidegger's notion of dwelling in this manner, the material form of home reveals the way of life led by the people who live there, reflecting cultural norms and values, relationships to the land, migratory practices, and size of household. At the same time, these material forms may influence our social actions.

The ethnography presented below demonstrates that my respondents considered both options – co-optive and constructive home-making – when they chose and remodelled their properties. The old French houses that many of the migrants chose were already associated in their minds with quintessential (French) rurality. Any renovation was often done in keeping with this pre-existing image, just as those migrants who had bought new houses off-plan had to invest effort into making their houses conform to their imaginings of rural life.[1] While these practices of home-making demonstrate how both types of property choice can be considered to be a response to the same desires for rural living, this chapter is equally concerned with the material culture of the home: how the migrants chose to decorate, furnish and ornament their new homes and what these choices revealed about them.

The overwhelming suggestion in the related literature is that a sense of home or belonging is constructed through the consumption choices that individuals make.[2] As Miller (1998, 2001) argues, this process of home-making is both ongoing and dynamic and rests upon the relationship between home, consumption and identity (see also Cieraad 1999). In the process of this relationship both the home and its inhabitants may be transformed (Miller 2001). The home is not then a mere backdrop to the life but an intrinsic part of the social relations that take place within it (Miller 2001). The materiality of the home is thus understood as a social process (Clarke 2002; Miller 2002). Therefore, it is through the interactions between individuals, their homes and the materiality of these that meaning is produced (Dittmar 1992; Hurdley 2006).

Against this background, home consumption practices can be understood on several different levels including the expression and creation of particular self-identities: as a reflection of class status, divisions and taste (Bourdieu 1984; see also Veblen 1953[1899]) or as revealing of social aspirations (Clarke 2001); as influenced by social relations (Carrier 1995), moulding relationships between members of the household (Reimer and Leslie 2004) or mediating the relationship between the household and family (Miller 2001); as providing a sense of (imagined) belonging (Clarke 2001; Walsh 2006) or emplacement (Putnam 1993); and lastly, as offering 'an idealized notion of "quality of life" and an idealized form of sociality' (Clarke 2001: 28). In this respect, the objects displayed and used in the domestic setting and the choices over décor are revealing of the lives led within the home on a variety of levels, from the practical to the idealized, and demonstrate a concern over a space that is simultaneously experienced as both public and private.

The context of migration and the displacement experienced are also significant features in the process of home-making, as recent studies of migrants' experiences reveal (see for example Ahmed *et al.* 2003; Walsh 2006). Katie Walsh (2006), in her ethnographic account of the material culture of British expatriates living in Dubai, emphasizes that moving abroad forces even these privileged migrants to reconceptualize and recreate a sense of home or belonging. The continuity of the new home with the past may in part be preserved through material possessions, but each of these comes with its own cultural and individual biography and may stir memories both painful and cathartic (cf Parkin 1999; Hecht 2001; Attan 2006). For Walsh's (2006) expatriates, this continuity with the past was also present in the material objects used and displayed in the domestic space, from the pictures of landscapes hanging on the walls to the DVD box sets of television series. Through their use of these objects, the migrants tried to counteract their feelings of uncertainty and displacement. In this respect, the continuity with their lives before migration acted as an emblem of belonging. This allows for an understanding of expatriate belonging premised on the possibility of being at home in movement (*ibid.*; see also Rapport and Dawson 1998). Walsh's (2006) expatriates in Dubai were thus grounded precisely through their transnational British belonging.

However, the various possibilities for achieving belonging – and a range of 'locations' for belonging that exist simultaneously (Levitt and Glick Schiller 2004) – through material objects and practices should also be considered. In particular, while it is likely that some continuity to life before migration may persist, changes of material objects and practices, whether these are elective or forced, also deserve examination. Indeed, attempts to come to terms with unfamiliar material surroundings may indicate the aspiration for a more localized sense of belonging, a discontinuity with the material realities of life before migration.

It is also possible that people will have no choice but to learn how to negotiate these unfamiliar material worlds. For example, Burrell (2008) demonstrates that Polish women living in Leicestershire (pre-1989) came face to face with the cultural specificity of material goods in their migration from socialist Poland to capitalist Britain. People may also take the opportunity of migration to enforce a change on their material practices and belongings. Such was the case for the Santos family, a Chilean family living in London that Alison Clarke (2001) discusses. They chose to furnish and decorate their house in a modern European style. In so doing, they chose to distance themselves from the Chilean ethnic community in London and from the dominant British culture. Their home-making practices thus reflected the construction of a syncretic identity deemed necessary in their negotiations with the new social environment.

Although there has been a focus on the materiality of home-making within other migrant communities, the literature on the British in France has focused predominantly on property selection (see for example Buller and Hoggart 1994a & b; Barou and Prado 1995; Gervais-Aguer 2004, 2006, 2008). This literature has provided valuable insights into the centrality of the choice of property to the decision to migrate; the investment in property, understood in the context of the quest for a better way of life, was not just a financial investment but also a commitment to the transformation in lifestyle that migration brings about. These earlier accounts also stressed the characteristics of the properties chosen, particularly highlighting the traditional architecture favoured by British incomers and their penchant for restoration and renovation.

In this rendering house purchase is understood as a consumption choice influenced by a fashion or taste for old French houses among the British middle classes (Buller and Hoggart 1994a; Barou and Prado 1995). Although I agree with this observation, unpacking its role within social distinction later in this chapter, I argue that home-making practices had a wider significance in the lives of my respondents. These were intimately entwined with their ideas about life following migration and their efforts to realize this. My interviews and participant observation within the migrants' private homes inadvertently allowed direct observation of the material culture of the home and the role that such objects played in the daily lives of my respondents. It is from this position that I am able to present more nuanced insights into the process of home-making that my respondents engage in on a day-to-day basis, and to reflect on how this was related to their ongoing search for a better way of life.

Making homes in rural France

For most of my respondents, relocation to rural France coincided with the purchase of a property. As the ethnography in this section demonstrates, the migrants appropriated their houses to a greater or lesser extent as they attempted to make real their imaginings of life in rural France. And in this respect, the homes that I visited were revealing not only of the general trends which underwrite this form of migration but of more individualized approaches to life in the Lot.

When Buller and Hoggart (1994a & b) carried out their research among the British living in rural France, they revealed a predominant trend towards the purchase of old properties. Indeed, many of my respondents had chosen this route to ownership. However, as this type of property became sparser and as more retirees moved to the area who were concerned about their future health and mobility, an increasing number of migrants chose to purchase their properties off-plan. This involved selecting the plot of land as well as choosing the building – a lengthy process of a home built from the ground upwards.

Several of my retired respondents explained this route to French property ownership as a response to the lack of old properties on the market and a desire for a modern, easy-to-maintain house. Another added bonus, as one of my retired respondents who lived in such a house pointed out, were that many of these homes were bungalows, an ideal choice for people as they grew older and had greater difficulty negotiating stairs. Indeed, it was mainly retirees who chose these homes. In this respect, property choices can be seen as intersecting with life-course considerations.

There were, however, many other migrants who lived in older houses, having opted for the 'character' of the old as against the relative 'characterlessness' of the new. James Harvey-Browne explained: 'We were looking for an old house with beams, stone walls and stone floors. That was a priority; we were looking for character ... we had had a reasonably modern house in England and it was soulless.' In contrast to the new houses, the old French houses often required extensive renovation and maintenance.

However, home-making was an ongoing process (Miller 1998, 2001) that continued even after migration had taken place. The ethnographic case studies presented below reveal the particular investment that three couples made in making their houses into homes. These have been chosen to reflect not only the different decisions that my respondents made when choosing what kind of property to purchase but also to demonstrate the different ways in which these homes were representative of their identities and rhetoric about their lives in rural France, reflected in their choices of décor and furnishings. In the context of their lives following migration, it is important to recognize that the home was not just a private domain. Against this background, the display of objects within the domestic space takes on a further significance.

Julian and Janet Ford

Julian and Janet Ford, a couple who had taken early retirement in their late fifties owned and lived in a house that was set back from the road. It was only after the turning into their driveway, a narrow strip of gravel bordered by a stone wall on one side, that the house became visible. Once past the sharp ninety-degree bend, the strip opened up to encircle an ornamental flowerbed. Beyond the flowerbed was a low-set bungalow, rendered in off-white *crépi*, as my respondents referred to the roughcast rendering on the outside of their houses (Figure 7). To the right of the house stood Julian and Janet's caravan. In 2001, when the house was being built, Julian and Janet had lived on-site in the caravan, building the swimming pool as the builders worked on the house. They had completed the pool before the house was finished, and recalled swimming in it as the building work continued around them.

When they had first thought about living in France, they had imagined living in an old house, but as they developed their ideas they realized the amount of work that this would entail. As Julian recalled,

> We were going to buy an old house; that was the plan. I'm really handy with bricks and mortar and stuff. I could have done it; I was young enough. I could have gone and bought, in those days, £30,000 worth of wreck and spent £50,000 on it ... but you suddenly think, well hang on, once it's all done you've got to live in it, and you've got to live in it for the next 20 years. And at least here we're warm, we're comfortable, it's a single storey building so I can repair the gutters and roof. This to me was the better deal.

But the choice of a new house was also related to their experiences of life back in England.

> We used to live in this huge farmhouse that had all oak beams, nooks and crannies, and minstrel galleries. It was fairly modernized and more modernized than some of these virtual wrecks, but we moved from there into an estate house so that it would be quick to sell. And that had plastic windows, double glazing, all the things I hated, and I learned to love them. And after a while, I saw how sensible they were. You know, I used to have to repair the old windows with little bits of wood and then the draft still comes through.

Their newly built house in France had come with a five-year builder's guarantee. This was standard for new-build properties. So, any problems with the house, and they could just call the builder, a far simpler option, Julian believed, than having to sort out these problems themselves. He explained that every time his friends with old houses told them about problems they were having, he felt relieved that he had chosen to live in a modern house.

As I recalled in my fieldnotes, the first time I went into the house, I was taken

7 The approach to the Fords' house

aback. I walked in through the front door, straight into a living room, which 'was quite cluttered with ornaments, quite British in appearance. As I sat in the room I realized that there might be a theme to the room of the 1920s or 1930s'. There were Tiffany table lamps and Wedgewood figurines on every available surface. The room seemed stuffed full of ornate furniture that Janet and Julian had brought with them from England. This seemed somehow at odds with the modern architecture of their bungalow. English books occupied every available space in the bookshelves. It was the first time that I felt as though I had walked into a British house, a feeling that continued on my tour around the house. Julian and Janet were very pleased that they were still able to pick up British television; even in their caravan they had been able to receive the Freeview® signal through their satellite dish.[3] While other people had fireplaces in their sitting rooms – even others with new houses had elected for this focal feature – the focal point of this room was the television set.

We sat down to lunch, the first of many that I would have with Julian and Janet. The food was served on British porcelain plates with silver cutlery and included a very rich coronation chicken. This experience demonstrated that Julian and Janet's practices continued the theme of transplantation that seemed to characterize their home. The material culture of their dining table was overwhelmingly British, as was the rest of their house. The only exception to this was the undoubtedly French wine, purchased from the market.

In many ways, how Julian and Janet chose to furnish their house, filling the modern French shell with familiar furniture and knick-knacks collected during their lives in Britain (alongside the material accoutrements of socialization), was reminiscent of how in previous times the British had furnished their houses in colonial India and Africa, 'a type of domesticity that was meant to help reflect and instil the values and dispositions that separated rulers from their subjects' (Glover 2004: 62). Perhaps their particular choices were not surprising given that both of them had lived abroad as expatriates – Julian when he was a child, and Janet with her first husband – and were thus remnants of past experiences that they had not shaken off. Rather than forcing the similarity between lifestyle migrants in the Lot and English colonials in India and Africa, I intend here to draw attention to the similar ways in which the home can become a veritable 'island of Englishness' (Metcalf 1994: 178, cited in Glover 2004).

While walking around Julian and Janet's home, I was left with the feeling that they had bolstered their new lives in France with mementoes of their old lives; the scenery had changed, but they still had the comfort of having all their familiar belongings around them. As Walsh (2006) explains, through the mobility of certain domestic belongings a sense of immobility can be achieved, thus grounding the individual. Just as in the case of Walsh's expatriate respondents living in Dubai, I felt that Julian and Janet, not only in their choices about how to decorate and furnish their home but also in their daily actions, expressed their (almost exclusive) sense of transnational attachment and belonging; this was where they felt most comfortable, most at home. Just as Julian could not make his (French) salad dressing without (British) Colman's mustard powder that he brought from England on each return visit, they could not live without their English furniture.

Martin and Sarah Johnstone

At the other end of the scale was the home of Martin and Sarah Johnstone, who had given up their jobs in Britain to start a new life in rural France. They owned and lived in a nineteenth-century stone farmhouse that they had renovated in keeping with the original character of the building and in which they now ran a *chambre d'hôte* (bed and breakfast) business. The house was located up on the *causse* (limestone plateau). The first time I visited, I was sure that I had taken the wrong route. The drive took me through the open countryside, where the road was little more than a rutted dirt track. There were few houses in sight, and I could not travel at more than 15 km an hour. Sarah had warned me that to get to the house you had to keep going past the point where you thought that you were lost, which turned out to be an accurate description of my sentiments by the time I arrived.

The house was in a very small hamlet of three houses – although there were two more houses about a five-minute drive back along the route I had taken – which gave a feeling of space to the location. The Johnstones also owned a considerable piece of land around the house, where there were a couple of outbuildings. One of these was being used as a tool shed and workshop, but the other was in a state of disrepair. There was a vegetable and herb garden and an above-ground swimming pool, and their chickens and cats were able to roam freely. They explained how the location of their home in the open countryside gave them the feeling that they could breathe again. This was particularly pertinent in view of their experience of life in Britain, where they stressed that they had not had the space to do what they wanted and where they had felt trapped by the walls around their home and garden.

The house and its surroundings were definitely a work in progress. The approach to the house revealed a large stone building partially clad in scaffolding. Martin had spent a considerable amount of time up on the scaffolding with a small hammer drill, removing all the old *crépi* in preparation to re-render the house. Although at the time there was a fashion for bare stonework, Martin and Sarah stressed that the render was traditional to the buildings in the area and would protect the stonework from the elements. As I spent more time with the Johnstones, I learned more of their plans for the future of the property, which included building a swimming pool in the ruins of the old barn (this was completed in 2005), and making the land around the property a little tidier.

My first visit took place on a bright, sunny day in February. As I walked through the front door, the cold air struck me. I had entered a large room, which served as both a sitting room and a dining room. The floor was the original flagstone that Martin and Sarah had uncovered when they were doing the renovation work on the house. In the back corner of the room, they had turned the vaulted *souillarde* (scullery, originally the kitchen) into a storage area and had cleaned out the stone *évier* (sink). But the most impressive sight in the room was the open fireplace, which was large enough to stand up in. When I had dinner with them in that room a few weeks later, the fire was lit, but it still remained cool in the room. Following dinner, along with the other guests, I huddled close to the fire, glad of my warm jumper and scarf. On this first occasion, however, the fire was not lit, and as I moved through the house, I realized that there was little else to heat the large, high-ceilinged room that I had first walked into. Martin and Sarah had decided not to install central heating in the house – they believed that the presence of radiators in their otherwise authentic French farmhouse would ruin the aesthetic that they were aiming for – relying instead on wood-burning stoves and fireplaces in the rooms that they used the most, their bedroom and the kitchen (the *chambre d'hôte* did not operate in the winter months).

We crossed the hallway and entered the kitchen. By comparison with the first room we had entered, the kitchen was warm and cosy. It was a much smaller room, with a low ceiling, and the wood burner in the corner was pumping out enough heat to keep the room at a consistent temperature. On the far wall was the entrance to the original bread oven for the farmhouse. As Sarah made the tea and coffee, Martin explained that he had converted the *cave* (cellar), which had stood at this end of the house, into the kitchen that we were now sitting in. The original floor, simply hewn out of the bedrock, had been at a considerably higher level, and Martin had had the backbreaking task of breaking up and clearing away solid rock so that a proper floor could be laid sufficiently far down for people to be able to stand up in the room. Along the walls, you could still see evidence of the level of the bedrock floor before Martin started work to create the kitchen.

The renovation was a massive undertaking. Martin and Sarah carried out all the necessary work themselves (bar the septic tank, which they had to have installed by professionals). Martin moved the beams in the roof himself so that he could fit further bedrooms into the loft space, and he even made his own windows. The reason they gave for doing the work themselves was to avoid what they called the 'French builder' phenomenon. As Martin described it, French workers would finish off work in the way they wanted, without regard for the desires of their clients. Martin had seen this happen many times. For example, they would put layer upon layer of plaster on a wall in an attempt to make it flat, but this gave the wall a rough finish rather than a smooth one. Martin and Sarah explained that by carrying out all of the work themselves they had managed to get their house to look the way that they wanted it to look, rather than be forced to accept someone else's interpretation of how it should look.

While the house was being renovated, it had become something of a talking point, and many of the local people would stop by to see the work in progress. As Martin and Sarah recalled, their French friends felt that they had restored the house in a way that was sympathetic to local architectural styles. In this respect, it was not just that the house had embodied their vision of rural living; it was a statement about the lifestyle that they wanted to lead.

Martin and Sarah had deliberately chosen to buy an old house. As Martin explained, he found new houses lacking in character by design and felt also that they were not built to last. Their house, in contrast, oozed character that had built up over its long history. As Miller (2001) argues, old houses are often haunted by such ghosts, but the people who live in them have the choice over whether to connect with them or not. Indeed, Martin and Sarah had risen to this challenge and tried to make the house as authentically French as possible. All the furniture in the house had been bought from local *brocante* (junk shops) and auctions. On each visit, they would proudly show me the new work that they had done on their home, from the new rustic shelves in the kitchen, 'made from old wood complete with woodworm', to their work on the land around the house. As Martin explained, they worked hard to maintain the aesthetic of an old French house. For example, he was rather apologetic about the modern doors on the kitchen units, 'We've got modern units, but they're temporary doors … I'm planning to replace them with oak doors'. It was almost as though by living in this house, which they had made true to their understandings of local rurality, they could emplace themselves within the local community.

Unlike Janet and Julian's home, I felt that the Johnstones' home reflected their desires to start anew and to make a new life for themselves in France. There were few reminders of their life back in Britain beyond the extensive library of English books. The house acted as a statement of their intentions and reflected the philosophy of their life in France. They had gone out into the local community with the express intention of making new friends and were regular participants in community events. However, it was also clear that they had a taste for rustic French living, despite the fact that this was in many ways a stark contrast to their lives in Britain.

Importantly, Martin and Sarah had chosen to live this way; there was no necessity involved (they could have installed central heating if they had wanted to, or renovated their property in a very different way). While Julian and Janet remained attached to their lives before migration, surrounded by all their familiar belongings, Martin and Sarah seemed to have completely left these behind in their efforts to start a new life. Their home belongings demonstrated their desire for an attachment to the local rather than the transnational. I noticed that they even carried in their pockets folding Laguiole knives (a brand of table knife originally from the neighbouring department of Aveyron). They used these at every meal. They consumed exclusively local products, many of which they had produced themselves. In many ways, their choices about the domestic space and their everyday practices within it reflected their desire to escape the superficiality that had, in their opinions, characterized their lives in Britain. While their home-making practices were clearly aspirational, they differed from those of Clarke's (2001) Chilean respondents in that they seemed to reject wholesale their past system of values and mores in exchange for an idealized new system. Furthermore, the house played a central role in how they imagined their lives in rural France, an idealized and romanticized emulation of the lives they imagined as having been led in the past in the same space. As the nexus of all their daily activities, a living and working space, their home appeared to both accentuate and inspire their ideology for living.

Daniel and Alannah Tapper

The first time I pulled into the driveway of *Le Tournesol* (The Sunflower), the home of Daniel and Alannah Tapper, I was worried that I had come to the wrong place. On either side of the narrow driveway were piles of sand and stone. The building in front of me looked derelict and run down, and there were no sounds or indications of any life on the property. I continued down the driveway and, to my relief, found two further buildings. While one was still in a state of disrepair, the large French farmhouse fronted by a stone staircase leading to a covered balcony appeared to have been renovated. I crossed the yard and climbed the stairs, and by the time I reached the top Alannah had come to the door, having heard my footsteps.

We went down to the kitchen and Alannah switched on the electric kettle, the first I had seen during my fieldwork as many of my other respondents boiled their water in kettles on the stove. I was surprised to see that, unlike the other kitchens I had seen in old buildings, Alannah's kitchen was modern-looking with contemporary glass-fronted cabinets. The glass doors leading out to the courtyard between the three buildings had small curved feature windows above them, which Daniel had decorated with small stained-glass birds.

Once the coffee was made, we carried it upstairs with a plate of biscuits and settled ourselves in the alcove seating area on the first floor. On one wall, a large selection of small watercolours and pastel pictures were displayed; behind Alannah was a large bookcase stretching from floor to ceiling, and apart from the top shelf, where there was a collection of very colourful pottery, it was full of books piled on top of each other where there was no longer room for them to stand upright. I sat by the window, which looked out onto the trees that surrounded the front of their property. On the wall next to the window was a huge copper-framed mirror. In front of this was a small stool on which stood two Harry Potter books, one in French and the other in English. And to my left was a large decorated dresser. For the first hour or so I could not stop looking around me. I kept seeing new things; there was just so much to see. The old sat alongside the brand new, Daniel and Alannah had mixed styles seemingly effortlessly and without care. I felt that Barbara and Ron Stampton's description of Daniel and Alannah as bohemian was quite fitting. The clutter and exoticism that characterized the interior were a stark contrast to the austere living conditions that their house could stand testament to.

My initial impressions demonstrate that Daniel and Alannah's home was in many ways different from those of my other respondents. While it was an old house, the Tappers had chosen to instil it with their own character rather than sticking rigidly to the aesthetic style that such a house might encourage. Daniel, who had been an architect back in Britain, had an artistic mind; he had drawn and painted a large proportion of the artwork in the house. I later discovered that he had painted a huge and colourful mural on the wall of the master bedroom, which Alannah proudly showed me. There were also mementoes of the lives that they had led before moving to France. Daniel had spent some time living in Fiji, and his artwork at times reflected this. The books were a reflection of Alannah's interests. I also realized that the furniture they had put in the house was a mixture of beautiful antique pieces and comfortable old items that they could not part with. So for example, under the stairs on the lower level of the house, in a dark corner assigned to the television, stood a threadbare sofa.

When Daniel and Alannah bought the house, they had to do some work in order to make it more comfortable. Alannah explained that for a while they had slept in the loft space (now converted into rooms) on an old bed which had been left behind by the previous owners because it was too heavy and large to move. At that time, the loft was accessible only by a makeshift ladder that had also been left behind in the house. Over time, they had acquired more furniture and made many improvements to their home. As Alannah explained, Daniel had a particular enthusiasm for renovating old properties and was, as I observed, in the process of converting the barn – the building that I had originally thought was derelict – into a guest house and workshop. He had ambitious plans to construct a *pigeonnier* (pigeon loft), an architectural feature that was characteristic in the Lot and Quercy region, for the front of this building, and over the course of the year I witnessed his progress with this project. I was there a few days after the massive solid oak frame of the *pigeonnier*, which Daniel had designed himself and commissioned from a local company specialising in traditional-style buildings, was put in place at the front the building; and I returned to see him meticulously filling the spaces between the oak beams with small bricks, following the traditional method of constructing the walls of the *pigeonnier*.

As I repeatedly visited Daniel and Alannah in their home, I learned to appreciate that their home-making practices were an investment in their lives together. It was first and foremost a statement about their relationship, although there were elements that suggested their intentions about their lives in France. The decision to move to France had coincided with their (early) retirement, but also with their decision to live under one roof – they had been together for only five years when I first met them. In fact, they married after their permanent move to France, starting their married life in a new place. On the front of the *pigeonnier* a small stained-glass window read *carpe diem* (seize the day), and had both their names scribbled on it, a poignant reminder of the mark that Daniel and Alannah had made on their house and reflecting their feelings about their lives in France. By their own admission, they had not been overwhelmed by this house when they had first viewed it, but with time and effort, they made it into their dream home.

The material culture of Daniel and Alannah's house was telling both of their home-making practices and of their relationship. Although Alannah expressed her feeling that she had lost her a way a little since living in France, and regretted her lack of artistic talent, she was keen to let Daniel express himself in this way. The process of home-making thus became a locus through which they were able to express their love for one another – Daniel through his home-making practices, and Alannah through her encouragement of his efforts.

Deconstructing homes and home-making practices

The differences in the types of property that my respondents chose and their decisions over furnishings and decorations reflected the complex and nuanced nature of the better way of life that they sought. For some, their homes were clearly symbolic of their desires to become part of the local community, while for others, they demonstrated the comforts of the familiar. Homes also spoke of the identity of individual migrants and revealed the quality of the relationships within the homes. In many ways, it was clear that the migrants' homes provided further justification for migration and were foundational to their narratives about their new lives. Although these narratives were largely idealistic, reflecting their early aspirations for life after migration, it was evident that their relationship to their home acted as a blueprint for these lives.

However, it should not be assumed that the migrants related to their homes on the same terms. For both the Johnstones and the Tappers, work on their respective homes was an attempt to engage with and appropriate the history of their new houses. In this respect, they recognized the agency of the home, particularly its role in a set of historical processes (cf Miller 2001). This was most clearly demonstrated by Martin and Sarah Johnstone's interest in the history of their property. In the *gîte* that they had restored, they displayed a photo of the villagers taken at the turn of the twentieth century, where the house had served as a backdrop. They also renamed the house to reflect its previous incarnation as the home of the village *charron* (cartwright). Indeed, both couples demonstrate an attitude of care towards their homes, a commitment towards the creation of home. Home and garden in this respect were the vessels for the better way of life that they sought, expressed in the way that they moulded the house to their needs as well as in their manner of responding to the building itself.

Of all my respondents, Martin and Sarah's desire for local belonging was the most closely integrated with their sense of home and was writ large on their property. But as they presented it, the house itself had, from first sight, appeared to offer them the better way of life that they sought. They took up the challenge and mastered the techniques required to restore the house to its former glory. It was difficult to differentiate Martin and Sarah's aspirations from the lifestyle and identity that the house offered them. The home itself could therefore be active in its own construction, exerting agency and causing the owners to adapt their lifestyles accordingly (Miller 1998). In this case, it is difficult to read the identity of the migrants as distinct from the identity of the house. But furthermore, by taking great care to restore and preserve the character of the house, the migrants presented themselves as connoisseurs of French rural living, understood here in Bourdieu's terms to imply,

> an unconscious mastery of the instruments of appropriation which derives from slow familiarization and is the basis of familiarity with works … a practical mastery which, like an art of thinking or an art of living, cannot be transmitted solely by precept or prescription. (1984: 66)

In this respect, the migrants' relationship with their home depicted the depth of their understanding of their property. As Martin and Sarah demonstrated, rather than a case of passive consumption, the choice of each piece of furniture had been carefully made to reflect the authentic French rusticity of their property. And in their discussions of new properties, they not only demonstrated the extent of their knowledge about local architectural styles, they distinguished themselves from others with different approaches to property consumption (cf Bourdieu 1984).

In contrast, Julian and Janet Ford's home clearly demonstrated the superimposition of a particular identity onto a property. They had fully appropriated their house and it made a very evident statement about the transnational nature of their homing practices. While there were brief insights into the lives led before migration through the objects displayed in many of my respondents' homes – the Tappers with their books, carefully selected from the *Times Literary Supplement* and purchased during return trips to the UK; and the Johnstones with their penchant for English television series, which they watched through the DVD player on their computer hidden in a corner of their bedroom – the Fords' belongings were almost exclusively remnants from their lives before migration.

Walsh (2006) argues that material belongings from before migration are used as a form of grounding, to counter any feelings of uncertainty that mobility might entail. Even when they spent time in the caravan, Julian and Janet would take with them several of their belongings from the house. This demonstrates that they considered home to be mobile, founded upon the familiarity of their belongings, which happened to reflect, more than anything, their transnational belonging. In a way, however, their home consumption choices could equally be read as distinctive. They had maintained consumption practices that had been meaningful in their lives before migration and that would be recognizable to some of their acquaintances living locally; they remained engaged in a process of distinction, but on different terms from those of my other respondents.

Finally, the relationship of the Tappers to their home demonstrates the possibility of a compromise between the agency of the house and that of its owners.

They had maintained the external image of a French farmhouse but had furnished and decorated it to reflect the identity that they wanted to project. Similarly to the Johnstones, Daniel and Alannah demonstrated a certain connoisseurship about *Lotoise* architecture, but they were also keen to marry this with their own unique style. This compromise, however, was an ongoing negotiation. On one level, they demonstrated their aspiration to be seen as sympathetic to the local architectural styles. On another level, they wanted their home to reflect their individuality, in the process displaying the distinctiveness of their lives. But furthermore, as a private space, their home became the embodiment of their relationship, from the colourful and romantic mural that Daniel had painted on their wall of their bedroom, to the small stained-glass window in the *pigeonnier* through which they left their mark (and their name) on the house. In this respect, it was not only that their relationship with the house reflected their desires to be part of the local community; the better way of life that they sought centred around the idea of their starting a new life together. As Alannah explained on more than one occasion, living in France was about living with Daniel. If anything happened to him, her dreams would be shattered and she would probably return to Britain.

The home-making practices of my respondents in the Lot were revealing in the way that they gave insights into the individualized rhetoric of post-migration lives, identities and relationships within the home. As the migrants remained engaged in these ongoing home-making practices (Miller 1998), from structural work to small aesthetic changes, they refined and consolidated their migration narratives.

Conclusion

The ethnography presented in this chapter has demonstrated that, while the materiality of the home is reflective of British middle-class trends for French property ownership (Buller and Hoggart 1994a & b; Barou and Prado 1995), it is also revealing of the migrants' identities and aspirations. The three case studies presented in this chapter represent the variety of home-making practices that were undertaken by my respondents, the material form and culture of their homes acting as a further demonstration of the diversity of the British population currently residing in the Lot. From the examination of their home-making practices, it became evident that choices over how to turn a house into a home were influenced by individual life histories, philosophies about a better way of life, the social relations within the home and individual identities. The home, in this rendering, became a vessel that mediated the migrants' identities, aspirations, histories and relationships.

In part, the centrality of property selection to the decision to migrate helps to explain why the migrants invested so much of themselves in their homes. The investment in a particular house signalled the start of a relationship between the migrants and a particular place and was therefore about emplacement. But additionally, the purchase of a property structured the decision to migrate and was the first stage in the realization of a better way of life. Through the presentation of their efforts to make themselves a home in the Lot, the migrants variously laid claim to a particular lifestyle. In this respect, the migrants' relationships to their homes may also be read as an attempt to achieve cultural capital (Bourdieu 1984), operating as the basis for their further pursuits of distinction.

Although it is undeniable that the process of social distinction remains an important dimension of the migrants' post-migration lives, a topic that I will explore further in Chapters 6 and 7, it has also become clear that the homes of the migrants are the primary loci of their social life with their compatriots. Socialization within private homes not only provides space for distinction to take place, but also allows for the constitution of the migrants as a group of individuals all seeking a better way of life. Such entertainment within private homes provides the contexts for the migrants to present to an audience, and therefore authenticate, their own ideas about the constitution of a better way of life. Their choices over décor and furnishings and the food and drinks that they serve are all under scrutiny. In this respect, their homes are more than merely the setting of socialization; the materiality of their homes stands as an exemplar of the lifestyle that is sought. It is thus through socialization with their compatriots that they put to the test their own individualized rhetoric of migration.

It is evident that the purchase of property in the Lot provided the initial impetus for migration and the foundations upon which the migrants organized their lives subsequently. Yet in time these homes became the centre of their social lives and an articulation of their post-migration lifestyle choices. By inviting their compatriots into their homes, they opened up their private spaces to inspection. Within this space, they found opportunities to discuss their lives in the Lot. In conclusion, the homes of my respondents epitomized and defined a space in which to realize migration, but they also became a public, visible context for articulating a discourse about their new lives at home in the Lot.

Notes

1 An off-plan purchase refers to the purchase of a property from a property developer before or during its construction.
2 There has been a spate of literature concerned with the meaning of home which I have chosen not to address here, focusing my analysis instead on how the migrants construct a sense of home and what this reveals about their aspirations for life in France, their identities and their social relationships. However, Mallett (2004) provides a good review of the related literature on the meaning of home.
3 Many of my respondents had also worked out how to pick up digital television from the UK, claiming that French television had nothing to offer them.

6

The unexceptional lives of others

This chapter presents my respondents' stereotyped representations of 'others', a term used to designate tourists and lifestyle migrants living in other destinations. It questions the ends to which these representations were employed and what they reveal about their authors. In particular, it became clear that the discussions of others were heavily influenced by the migrants' moralized framing of a better way of life, focusing on such issues as social integration, linguistic ability and the value of local knowledge. By drawing on the established anthropological literature on stereotypes and 'othering' (see for example McDonald 1993; Herzfeld 1997; Theodossopoulos 2003b), I argue that such observations of others provided a platform for my respondents to emphasize the peculiarity of their own post-migration lifestyles, in the process rationalizing and justifying their migration choices, and gave them a basis on which to enact processes of social distinction.

As the ethnography below demonstrates, the British living in the Lot frequently presented their compatriots in other destinations in two ways: as indistinct and as destructive. Presented as indistinct, these 'others' were considered to be indistinguishable from one another and lacking the desire or knowledge that would facilitate their entry into the local community. In this manner, it became apparent that my respondents did not value the lifestyle choices of these others; the choices that the latter had made did not map onto the migrants' own ideas of what constituted a better way of life. In this respect, it became clear that my respondents felt that the choices of others were lacking in good taste, although they did not articulate such feelings in precisely those terms.

Presenting these others as destructive, my respondents drew attention to the possibility that under certain conditions – a critical mass of lifestyle migrants who did not share the desires for either social integration or a deep knowledge of local life – such incomers could alter fundamentally the way of life available in particular destinations. The migrants presented examples of locations where this had already occurred, Spain and the Dordogne, to demonstrate that, in some cases, lifestyle migration had resulted in making destinations indistinctive; just as MacCannell (1976) has argued in the case of tourism, as a result of lifestyle migration what is sought may be destroyed. Through the contrast between their own aspirations for post-migration life and their perceptions of the lives of other lifestyle migrants, the migrants further confirmed the Lot as a distinctive destination that still offered a better way of life.

Their perceptions of tourists were articulated along similar lines, as they sought to distance themselves from the negative connotations of tourism. While careful not to reject their own provenance as tourists, whose visits to rural France had inspired the decision to migrate, they stressed the knowledge that they had gained through migration, solely as a result of their position as *permanent residents of rural France*. Their relationship with tourists was ambivalent because of their own discovery of France through tourism and because in many cases their livelihoods following migration relied on tourism. In this respect, their reflections on tourism were largely restricted to the differences between their experiences of everyday life and those of tourists who were only temporary visitors, and to mild complaints about how life in the Lot changed at the peak of the tourism season (July–August).

It became clear, as with the use of stereotypes more broadly (see McDonald 1993; Herzfeld 1997; Theodossopoulos 2003b), that my respondents' 'othering' practices revealed more about the lives and identities to which they aspired than about the lives of such others. As I argue in this chapter, my respondents used stereotypical representations of tourists and other lifestyle migrants to project and confirm the distinctiveness of their own lives in the Lot. In this respect, it becomes clear that these representations of others should be understood within the context of the wider processes of distinction in which the migrants engaged. Furthermore, it was apparent that they were aware that other people pigeonholed them similarly; my respondents therefore distanced themselves from the often negative associations ascribed to tourism and expatriate living precisely through their discussions of how tourists and lifestyle migrants in other destinations were different. Therefore, their representations of others were one way in which the migrants strived to displace and resolve their persistent feelings of ambivalence, claiming the knowledge of how to 'really' live in the Lot.

Stereotyping people and places

The ethnography presented in this section demonstrates the migrants' persistent use of stereotypes, taking primarily as their subjects their compatriots in Spain, lifestyle migrants in the Dordogne and tourists. To a lesser degree, my respondents also stereotyped particular places, highlighting the extent to which these locations could not offer the distinctive way of living that lay at the core of their quest for a better lifestyle. Through their discussions of other people and places, the migrants thus engaged in a process of othering.

Indeed, stereotypes are often used in this manner. However, there is a danger in assuming that they reflect an objective reality. It is rather the case, as Brown and Theodossopoulos argue, that '[s]tereotypes ... reside not in the world, but in the eye of the beholder' (2004: 4). They are thus partial representations that aim towards evaluating and categorizing social life (Theodossopoulos 2003b).

Against this background it becomes pertinent to question why people use stereo-types, and what it does for them. As McDonald (1993) argues, examining how particular stereotypes are constituted may reveal more about the people using them than about the subjects of the stereotype. In this respect, I argue that my respondents' use of stereotypes has a self-evaluating and self-defining potential: it reveals important information about the migrants' identities in life following migration.

The ethnography below highlights certain common features in the way that my respondents stereotyped others. In the case of their compatriots living in other destinations, their representations focused on the persistent social engage-ment and interaction with other Britons, the creation of a 'little England', and the inability and perhaps unwillingness to speak the local language. In part, the migrants ascribed these aspects of their compatriots' lives to the destinations that they had chosen, drawing attention to the accommodations that such places had made to facilitate the inflow of these migrants. But my respondents also high-lighted the different mentality of these people, stressing that these other migrants did not strive for a different way of life in the same way, comfortable with the relative familiarity of their lives abroad. In relation to tourists, they were keen to highlight how although they occupied the same space (the Lot was a popular holiday destination), they could not in their limited engagement gain the deep knowledge of how to live in the Lot; the engagement that my respondents had cultivated through their prolonged residence there. In these respects, it became clear that stereotyping others reflected how the migrants understood their own lives. Through their narratives, they projected the lives of these others into the public arena as a way of laying claim to belonging, identity and a better way of life.

However, it was also the case that through these discussions the migrants engaged in a rare demonstration of their (albeit fickle) solidarity with other Britons living locally. In many ways, their use of stereotypes was significant in defining the criteria for belonging to an imagined community, the British of the Lot. The stereotypes that they used thus plotted and reinforced the boundaries of inclu-sion and exclusion of this group identity, acting, as Brown and Theodossopoulos have argued, 'as a means of affirming social solidarity and membership' (2004: 7). The conviction that held them together was their belief that the Lot – as opposed to other destinations – was unique in offering the better way of life that they sought. In this respect, the use of stereotypes was central to the migrants' con-tinued engagements in processes of social distinction, whereby they attempted to present their own lives as distinctive and unique, by highlighting their relative successes at getting to a better way of life. Therefore, how my respondents spoke of other people and places was revealing of their own ambitions for life after migration, reinforcing their claims to place, ways of life and a sense of belonging.

The success of stereotypes lies in their significance for a particular cul-tural context. Presented in performance to an audience, stereotypes require validation in order to be put to use in the way described above. As Brown and Theodossopoulos argue, stereotypes 'make sense to specific audiences because they relate to existing sets of knowledge ... and it is this connectedness to tak-en-for-granted truths about the world that grants stereotypes authority' (2004: 12). In this respect, it is not surprising that my respondents drew on archetypal models of tourists and expatriates that had a value easily understood by the transnational audience of their friends and family. This was undoubtedly a risky strategy, because they were simultaneously trying to distance themselves from the same images.

The examples presented below demonstrate the various ways in which the recourse to stereotypes was used to affirm the distinctiveness of the migrants' migration and lifestyle choices. As I argue, these played an important role within the processes of status discrimination common to the British middle classes that my respondents regularly engaged in. In this respect, the migrants' use of stereo-types was one indicator that their original class status was still embedded in their post-migration practices.

Brits in Spain

The British residents of the Lot commonly drew on stereotypes when discuss-ing their compatriots living in Spain. They particularly focused on an alleged colonial style of living, the idea of a 'little England in the sun', and the over-whelming lack of integration of the British living there. These are images that are regularly transmitted through the British media (King, Warnes, and Williams 2000; O'Reilly 2000; Oliver 2007) and which seem to have become pervasive in the national imagination despite the attempts of academics to dispel them (see for example Betty and Cahill 1999; King, Warnes, and Williams 2000; O'Reilly 2000; Oliver 2007). In this respect, the British in the Lot continued to be influ-enced by the British media.

As Sian Harvey-Browne explained, Britons who move to Spain enter

> a community where they do not need the language. A prime example is my parents. They moved out to Spain; they've been there eighteen years. They can probably order a couple of things in the supermarket, and that's about all ... They've even got their own English butcher... And you think, why bother going out there? It's only because they've got sunshine and cheap booze.

In this quotation, Sian highlighted her belief that her parents had not integrated into Spanish life. Furthermore, there was no impetus for them to integrate; the implication was that there were English service providers to respond to all their needs. It seemed that the British in Spain, of whom Sian's parents were presented as exemplary, did not need to have any contact with the local population or culture in order to live there. Sian later stated adamantly that her life in the Lot was in no way similar to the life that her parents led in Spain.

Ironically, in an earlier interview Sian and her husband James explained that they had decided to leave Britain whilst on a holiday visit to Sian's parents in Spain. Sian described how the idea had come to her one morning when her father, who was still working despite having retired to Spain, laid down tools and said, 'let's go and have coffee'. In contrast to their busy lives in Britain, this more laid-back (working) lifestyle had appealed to James and Sian. Since living in rural France though, Sian had become more critical of the British in Spain, distancing herself from these negative representations through her assertions that her life in the Lot was in no way comparable. She was particularly keen to highlight the sparseness of the British population and their efforts not to create an insular community but instead to integrate into the local community.

Sian's observations of the British in Spain were representative of many of my respondents' references to these other lifestyle migrants. Their representations of the lives led by the British in Spain were presented explicitly as the antithesis of their own lives in the Lot, a perception based in part on their knowledge of how the Spanish had responded to the British population. As my respondents presented it, in contrast to the French, the Spanish weren't as protective of their culture; they had been quite happy to have huge building developments taking place and embraced foreign money. As Simon Glass explained, 'in the banks, even the cashiers speak English as the Spanish understand that it is the international language of finance'. Many of the migrants also emphasized how easy it was to migrate to Spain and how little effort incomers had to invest in order to establish their lives there. They also clearly demonstrated a belief that the Spanish did not expect the British moving to Spain to want to be involved in the local culture; as Rodríguez et al. (1998) highlight, the Spanish had laid on services to specifically cater for the British population (see also O'Reilly 2003).

This theme was also evident in the account of Sally Stampton, whose sister had been living in Spain for many years, working as the headmistress of an English-speaking school, which prepared British and local Spanish students to take examinations for British educational qualifications (GCSEs and A Levels). These English-speaking schools were common in Spain, so Sally told me, where the Spanish authorities encouraged their children to be bilingual. This meant that it was easy for British children living in Spain to get an education without speaking the local language. In contrast, Sally had registered her son Ollie at the local French school when they first arrived in France. As she recalled, he had at first struggled because his lessons were in French. Recounting this to her sister in Spain had elicited the suggestion that she move him to an English-speaking school. Sally asserted that there were none in the area, which her sister found very hard to believe given her own experiences in Spain.[1] Two years after migrating, Sally was very proud when Ollie gained the highest mark in his class for French spelling and grammar.

This argument that lifestyle migrants in Spain are marginal to Spanish society is common within the work of lifestyle migration scholars:

> British migrants live on the margins of Spanish society, not residentially but economically, socially, structurally and ideologically. They take what they want from each culture – their own and their host's – enjoying their marginality to its full advantage. (O'Reilly 2000: 160)

> [A]n expatriate society has been created parallel to the Spanish society, in which

most of the retirees' social relations are with people of their own nationality, whereas their relationships with the local population are limited. (Rodríguez, Fernández-Mayoralas, and Rojo 1998: 195)

However, as I have demonstrated here, my respondents considered that this was the result not only of their compatriots' lack of desire to integrate but also of the Spanish population's lack of encouragement for them to do so. From the English-speaking infrastructure (Rodríguez, Fernández-Mayoralas, and Rojo 1998; O'Reilly 2003) to the critical mass of British people living in and visiting Spain, there were structural constraints to these migrants' integration into the local community. While the ambivalence of my respondents in the Lot could indicate that they too occupied a marginal position in relation to the local French community, as I argued in Chapter 1, their rhetoric and practices demonstrated their efforts to overcome this and to become local (see also Chapter 7).

These representations of the British in Spain were further significant in terms of what they implied about Spain as a migration destination. Janet and Julian Ford, for example, said that their friends who lived in Spain could not leave their house without fully securing it, pulling down the heavy metal shutters over all the doors and windows, and locking them in place, even if they were only heading to the shop down the road to buy a bag of sugar. In this manner, Spain became the antithesis of the Lot. I heard similar tales from many of the respondents, who claimed that the British enclaves along the Spanish coastline were the regular targets of thieves. In contrast, my respondents demonstrated their belief in the relative security of the area and its lack of crime, rarely locking their front doors when they were in the house or garden. Some people even left their front doors unlocked when they were away from the house.

Through the use of these stereotypes about the British in Spain and the life on offer there, my respondents reasserted the cultural logic that underwrote their migration, highlighting that rural France was unique in offering the better way of life that they sought. Furthermore, by presenting the British in Spain as separate and detached from the local Spanish population, my respondents drew attention to the uniqueness of the lives they led in the Lot. Stereotypes, in this example, operated to confirm the distinctiveness of my respondents' post-migration lives while also displacing their anxiety about their own ambivalence. Their discussions of these others thus confirmed their rhetoric for choosing their migration destination: it uniquely offered them the potential for a more fulfilling and better lifestyle.

Dordogneshire

Buller and Hoggart (1994a) argued that the many of the British living in the Lot had chosen it as their destination because of its similarity to the Dordogne – which neighboured the Lot to the northwest – and the lower cost of property. Against this background, it may be surprising that my respondents were keen to distinguish themselves from their compatriots in this neighbouring department, claiming the Lot to be the corner of rural France which uniquely offered a better way of life. As I demonstrate below, their representations of the Dordogne stressed that it was like a British colony, that their compatriots there did not want to integrate (and did not speak French), and that it was comparable to the southern (home) counties. In these respects, the migrants once again adopted common clichés about the British living in the Dordogne. As Barou and Prado found,

> During the meetings we had in Brittany and Normandy, the British residents cited to us the case of their compatriots in the Dordogne as an example not to follow. The condemnation of this type of 'colonial' behaviour was for them the best gauge of their will to integrate. (1995: 135; cf Buller and Hoggart 1994a)[2]

As the ethnography below shows, it seems that the flavour of these representations has changed little in ten years. Through their discussions of these other Britons who were similarly attracted to the rustic French landscape, my respondents in the Lot implied that they had a more appropriate attitude to post-migration life; as I discuss later, they believed they were unique in having the knowledge of how to live in rural France.

While Buller and Hoggart (1994a) found that 13.8 per cent of their respondents in the Lot had considered living in the Dordogne, the majority of my respondents emphasized keenly that they had actively and deliberately not chosen the Dordogne. They stressed that its reputation for having a high number of British residents had been the primary deterrent. It was common therefore, for the migrants to draw attention to the large expatriate groups that they perceived to dominate in the Dordogne, and with which they had not wanted to be associated. The statement of one respondent was representative of the comments of many of the other Britons living in the Lot, 'I certainly wouldn't want to live in the areas I've heard talk about in the Dordogne … it's like a British colony'. In this manner, they drew upon a particular cultural understanding of colonial living, where the colonists distanced themselves from the local population and reproduced their own cultural values and norms. Indeed, as the migrants highlighted, their compatriots in the Dordogne did not attempt to integrate with the local population:

> You know [in the Dordogne] they speak English … you get people who come into the post office and say, 'I want a stamp', and if it's not understood, they say it a bit louder [raises her voice], 'I want a stamp'. And you think, you've just said that … but they [the French] like you to make an effort. I mean, even if you make mistakes, they'll appreciate it. (Sian Harvey-Browne)

These negative discourses about the British residents of the Dordogne were particularly meaningful in the context of the migrants' efforts to promote their own lives in rural France. One afternoon, I joined Martin and Sarah Johnstone for coffee in their home. During my visit, some of their friends, a Scottish couple who lived in the same *commune*, dropped by to return a tool that Martin had lent them earlier on in the week. They stayed for a coffee, and as we sat talking, Martin explained, 'There is one thing we do say here; normal people do not come to the Lot.' Bob, his friend, continued, 'Normal people go to places which are like England except warm. There are apparently villages in the Dordogne where fifty per cent of the population are English'. Sarah and Bob's wife Sylvia joined in the conversation, listing the different English clubs in the Dordogne, and stressing that life in the Lot was so much better than the life on offer in the Dordogne. The Dordogne, at least in the opinion of those present, was for 'normal people', with the implicit suggestion that life for Britons living there could continue as it had in England, but in surroundings that were more scenic. The Lot, however, was only for those who wanted something out of the ordinary from their lives. While those living in the Lot led distinctive lives, their compatriots who had chosen the Dordogne led largely indistinctive lives.

Jon and Kay Morris spoke similarly of the Dordogne: 'It's known as Dordogneshire ... [British people in the Dordogne] have got their own shops; there are village cricket teams.' As in the accounts of many of the migrants, there was an unspoken agreement that cricket was a quintessential emblem of Englishness. Jon and Kay agreed with Martin and Sarah that they and others among their compatriots living locally had deliberately chosen the Lot because it offered a different way of life, while the Dordogne did not. However, their narratives about the Dordogne continued, highlighting that British migration had transformed the area to the extent that it was no longer recognizably French:

> We had some Australian people staying in one of the *gîtes* last summer who were touring a bit, and they'd been to the Dordogne. And they said to us, 'It's bloody awful. Everywhere we moved or went ... we went to the baker's and it was an English person who owned it; we went to get canoes, it was an English person who owned it. You know, no offence, but it felt like we were living in England. And, you know, we wanted to be in France'. (Jon and Kay Morris)

The Dordogne was considered to be no longer French but another British county, 'Dordogneshire'. Even tourists, temporary visitors to rural France, could see the extent to which the local population had changed. By drawing on the accounts of their Australian visitors, Jon and Kay confirmed their perceptions of the Dordogne as unexceptional because it has become anglicized.

It is apparent that such representations of the life available in the Dordogne became a measure against which my respondents judged their own lives in the Lot. In particular, they drew attention to how their lives were different, typically arguing that they had chosen not to migrate to the Dordogne because they had not had any intention of becoming part of a group of English people and that they wanted to be integrated into the local population. In contrast, the Lot was valued precisely because the emblems of Englishness – such as the cricket clubs – that were present in the Dordogne were largely absent. By living in the Lot, my respondents felt that they could lead distinctive lives in contrast to their compatriots in the Dordogne and Spain. The migrants articulated this as having been made possible by their unique efforts to become insiders (see also Herzfeld 1992).

However, the proximity of the Dordogne to the Lot had sparked a further fear among some of the migrants. Their efforts to distinguish their lives from those of their compatriots living in the Dordogne demonstrated their concerns over their own identity. In addition, as was the case for Bruillon's (2007) respondents in the

Lot, they feared that the presence of a high number of Britons (or other lifestyle migrants) in the Lot would bring about social transformation as had happened in the Dordogne. In this respect, they feared that they would be complicit in the destruction of what they had moved for.

> We, unwittingly, by coming here, are helping to destroy this, and we do it – and I have to say 'we', the foreigners – because what we are doing is buying up the houses, which means that young people can't afford to buy the houses. (Hector Macdonald)

> What we have come here for we will gradually destroy, as there will need to be more commerce, more houses, more this, more that. Service ethics will change; you'll get more English people … or more Dutch people running things. So it will change, but it will probably destroy what we came here for in the first place. (Jon and Kay Morris)

These statements reflected the migrants' concern over the future of the local culture, reflecting wider discourses about the destruction of local culture through, for example, tourism (Greenwood 1989); the possibility of social transformation resulting from lifestyle migration (Buller and Hoggart 1994a; Barou and Prado 1995; McWatters 2008); but also their quest for a better way of life, which, in the process, destroyed what they sought. They projected a knock-on effect, concerned that any changes might deter tourists from visiting the Lot. As many of the migrants relied upon tourism for their income, this was a concern that they took seriously.

> If things change like that, the popularity of France could slip in this area, literally, a lot, and people would think, there's so many English people there, or Dutch. Pretty much every campsite along the Lot is Dutch … that's the thing. It's another thing we need to watch out for. We certainly wouldn't go on holiday, personally, to somewhere in Spain where it was all English-speaking and Fish and Chips. (Jon and Kay Morris)

The attitude of my respondents in the Lot to change is as Waldren writes in the case of the foreigners living in Deià, a small village on Mallorca: 'They see progress only as destructive to the idyllic setting they so admire' (1996: 204). However, such negative attitudes to change do not account for the dynamic way in which local communities respond and adapt to such social transformation. For example, Waldren (1996, 1997) demonstrates that the people of Deià benefited from the incoming population while managing to maintain a sense of their local culture. In this respect, it becomes clear that there is another possible way to understand the impact that such incomers have upon local culture. Following the literature which stresses that local cultures are reconstituted and adapt in the face of tourism (see for example Boissevain 1996; Abram and Waldren 1997; Coleman and Crang 2002), I argue that these more dynamic understandings of local culture suggest that destruction of culture is not the only possible result of mass lifestyle migration.

Nevertheless, it was apparent that my respondents believed that Britons living in the Dordogne and Spain had destroyed the distinctive way of life that may once have been available there. This resulted partly from their high numbers and partly from the attitudes of these impartial incomers. In the migrants' opinions, these popular migration destinations had become little more than 'Britain in the sun', as the result of the colonial behaviour and failure to integrate of their compatriots. In contrast they presented the Lot as still offering a distinctive way of life.

In this manner, they presented a moralized discourse about how to live and behave after migration. Their discussions of their compatriots, particularly those living in Spain and the Dordogne, revealed how the migrants wanted to be seen. They took control of their self-representations to present themselves in a more favourable light, in the process confirming both the rationale behind their decision to migrate and the distinctiveness of their lives in the Lot.

The trouble with tourists

Many of my respondents had had their first experiences of rural France when on holiday. Indeed, elsewhere lifestyle migration has been considered as a form of tourist-informed mobility (Williams and Hall 2002), with holiday experiences inspiring potential migrants to buy property and to pack up their lives back in Britain. It seems that holiday memories play an important role in this form of migration (Buller and Hoggart 1994; Barou and Prado 1995; King, Warnes and Williams 2000; O'Reilly 2000, 2007; Oliver 2007; Benson and O'Reilly 2009). These British lifestyle migrants living in rural France were initially attracted to the relaxed pace of life and the good food that they previously experienced on their holidays (Buller and Hoggart 1994a; Barou and Prado 1995; Gervais-Aguer 2004, 2006; Depierre and Guitard 2006). While to a certain extent their lives in the Lot resembled their experiences from holidays, their accounts demonstrate that they actively distinguished their lives from those of tourists in the area.

This desire to distance themselves from tourists is common among lifestyle migrants, as O'Reilly (2000, 2003) and Oliver (2007) reveal in the case of Britons living on the Spanish coast, and Waldren (1997) highlights in the case of long-term foreign residents in Deià. Indeed, O'Reilly argues in the case of her British respondents living on the Costa del Sol:

> they put a lot of effort into identifying as not tourists by sharing jokes about and constructing stereotypes of tourists that symbolize the boundaries between them; by overtly expressing their differences from tourists in terms of dress and behaviour; and by demonstrating the effects long visits to Spain have had on their bodies in the way of acclimatization and deep tans. (2003: 307)

Through this example, O'Reilly (2003) draws attention to how such boundary-construction becomes internalized and embodied (literally) by her respondents. I build on this to argue that for my respondents in the Lot, long-term residence in the Lot had led to a deep understanding of life in the Lot, perhaps captured in O'Reilly's use of the term acclimatization, that had been central to their rhetoric about migration. Using their knowledge as a measure of belonging, they focused on the relative superficiality of the tourist experience, presenting a binary opposition between residence and tourism. The following quotation from Peter Mayle's autobiographical account of life in Provence provides a vivid and humorous illustration of these contrasts between British residents in rural France and tourists. It seems that living in France was *not* like a holiday.

> The greatest problem, as we soon came to realise, was that our guests were on holiday. We weren't. We got up at seven. They were often in bed until ten or eleven, sometimes finishing breakfast just in time for a swim before lunch. We worked while they sunbathed. Refreshed by an afternoon nap, they came to life in the evening, getting into high social gear as we were falling asleep in our salad. (Mayle 1990: 85–86)

For the Britons living in the Lot, interactions between migrants and tourists were frequent. First, there were those friends and family who, taking advantage of the 'cheap' holiday, came and stayed in the homes of the migrants. Many of the Britons living in the Lot worked closely with tourists, relying on them to fill their *gîtes* and *chambres d'hôte* during the summer months. Their stories were often reminiscent of Mayle's accounts, highlighting the difference between living and just visiting. They drew on their encounters with these others to present an overall image of them, the antithesis to how they wanted their own lives to be understood. In this manner, they stressed that they were different from tourists precisely because they knew how to live in the Lot.

> We get friends from the UK coming out. They want to eat all day. They want to drink at lunch, which is fine, but we're working. And you can't do it everyday; you've got to keep up with all the bits and pieces that are going on. (Jon and Kay Morris)

While the migrants may once have been visitors to the Lot themselves, they highlighted how much more they now knew:

> When you go abroad, it's on holiday; it's an association that builds up in people's minds, understandably. Abroad equals leisure, equals fun, equals, you know, relaxing … the reality is never, of course, quite like that. (David Lomax)

> It's real life isn't it? Like when you go on holiday somewhere and say, 'Oh, I'd love to live here.' It's totally different when you actually live here. (Jon and Kay Morris)

The migrants therefore stressed that tourists could not access real life in the Lot; it was always beyond their reach (Urry 1990). However, they also drew attention to their own journey from tourists to residents, implying that they had learned about life in the Lot through this process.

In contrast to the actions of tourists visiting the Lot, the migrants often stressed that their own actions more closely resembled those of their French neighbours. For example, they explained that in the summer months they arranged to visit the weekly market early in order to avoid the traffic and parking problems and buy the best products. As they often explained, the only other people there at that time in the morning were other permanent residents. The tourists also enjoyed the produce from the market, but they did not arrive early enough in the morning, because they did not know how to live in the Lot. Once again, my respondents made a distinction by highlighting that they, unlike tourists, participated in the life of rural France.

On the whole, they presented the tourists as disruptive to the slow pace of life and tranquillity in the Lot. For example, my respondents often complained about how busy the roads became when the tourists were around, how they had to book their favourite restaurants in advance during the summer months rather than just turn up as they would do during the rest of the year, and that they would not visit certain places during peak season because there were so many tourists. And the tourists had other adverse effects. As Harry once explained, his favourite ice cream cost more in the summer; the local supermarkets raised the price to benefit from the increased demand. My respondents in the Lot thus presented the tourists as disruptive to the way of life available there, just as they did in relation to their compatriots in the Dordogne and Spain.

Through their anecdotes, the migrants reproduced the distinction between themselves and the tourists. It is as though they were saying, to quote the title of Jacqueline Waldren's (1997) article about foreigners living in a Mallorcan village, 'We are not tourists – we live here' (see also O'Reilly 2000, 2003; Oliver 2007). In this manner, they laid claim to a sense of local belonging through their knowledge of how to really live in their rural idyll. Furthermore, these representations expressed a range of other relationships, meaningful precisely because of the relationships that they expressed within them. In particular, they highlighted the relationships between themselves and the local French, the local landscape and way of life. And their claims gained further weight from the specific binary opposition that they drew between residence and holiday. It was not unusual, therefore, for the migrants to refer to their compatriots either living in other locations or more locally in the Lot as resembling tourists. As Jon and Kay so aptly commented, 'for a lot of English people living here, it's just one big holiday'. As I discuss in the next chapter, the migrants' desire to be different could even be traced in their discussions of others like them who had chosen to move to the Lot, but with whom they had not reached a consensus over how to live.

However, it must be noted that the discovery that life in the Lot did not resemble their holiday memories was not received positively by some of the migrants. Within the first two weeks of my fieldwork, I met Paul, a man who had been living in the Lot for only eighteen months but who had decided to return to Britain. Despite initially buying into the model of 'life as an eternal holiday' (Bruillon 2007: 133) in rural France, Paul and his wife 'soon discovered that living in the Lot was not like [their] holidays here. The log fire did not make itself'. It was rumoured that they were not alone; while I was doing my fieldwork, many of my respondents told me that fifty per cent of migrants returned to Britain (see also Buller 2008).[3] Many of my respondents told me similar stories of people deciding to return to Britain after only a short stay in the Lot, speculating that they did so because the cultural difference was too much to handle. I argue that these presentations were also instrumental in that they enabled the migrants to emphasize once again that they were different: they had managed to overcome the difficulties of living in the Lot, while others had not.

By the end of the winter, I fully appreciated the feelings expressed by Paul. I had observed how Harry built and tended to the fire in the living room every day, and how he emptied the ash from the grate and carried out the dirty work of cleaning the fireplace on a weekly basis. The fire was not purely decorative either; it provided warmth to a house that otherwise relied on a fifty-year-old central heating system, where the radiators all had plastic containers strategically placed under the pipes to catch the all too frequent leaks. The long and the short of it was that it seemed hard work to maintain the 'idyllic' log fire. It was a long process, which involved going outside on cold winter mornings to collect wood from the woodpile before you could sit back and enjoy it (often before Harry's first cup of tea). Before my fieldwork, I had never fully appreciated the work that went into maintaining a fire, both to keep it burning at a constant rate and to keep the fireplace and chimney clean. Seen in this light, the log fire was an apt analogy for the constant efforts that migrants had to make in order to learn how to live in the Lot and to build and maintain social relationships with members of the local community.

Nevertheless, at times the migrants would again adopt the detached gaze of the tourists (Urry 1990), at least in respect to the landscape. Stepping back from their daily efforts they would recognize that they were lucky to live in such a beautiful place.

> It's a beautiful area. There's no doubt about it. We still pinch ourselves when we're driving around doing work, even saying, 'Well look! People wait all year to come down for their two-week holiday and we've got it all year round.' (Jon and Kay Morris)

Although this quotation presents the idea that these migrants could be seen as permanent tourists, gazing on the landscape (cf Urry 1990), placed in the wider context of the migrants' discussions of tourists and their compatriots living in other destinations, it is evident that the migrants occupy an ambivalent position somewhere between tourist and local, outsider and insider. While their experiences of rural France had begun when they were tourists, as I show in the next chapter, following migration they took an authoritative position on how to really live in the Lot in their continuing pursuit of a better way of life.

Self-awareness and solidarity

As my ethnography demonstrates, the British residents of the Lot took great care to distance themselves from such stereotypes as those often used to describe tourists and other Britons living abroad. Most commonly, the migrants rejected the idea that they were like expatriates or tourists. This was evident when I had dinner with Martin and Sarah Johnstone one evening. We were joined by some of their British friends whom I had not previously met. One couple showed interest in my research but did not like the terms I used to describe migrants such as themselves. As I mentioned in Chapter 1, their response was captured in this following statement: 'We are not migrants! We are not British! We are not expatriates! We are *Sauliaçoise!*'.

This quotation shows a subtle change in the migrants' narratives, for in their descriptions of the initial decision to migrate, many of the migrants had originally stressed that it was because of their peculiarly British sense of adventure that they had been able to up sticks and move to another country in the first place (see also Bruillon 2007). However, I argue here that in their lives following migration many of the Britons of the Lot rejected the category of migrant and instead took on an alternative local, regional identity. In their perception, distinctiveness emanated from their status as insiders of the local community; they identified themselves as different precisely because they felt that they were integral members of the *Lotoise* population, while others were not. This reflects Herzfeld's (1992) argument that claiming insider status is a way of asserting distinctiveness.

The migrants' representations of their compatriots were largely symbolic, revealing the migrants' emic categorizations and self-classifications. Although the stereotypes at first sight appeared self-evident, the particular way they were defined and used bore the signature of the migrants as their authors. Specifically, the system of classification that migrants produced and maintained was organized in concentric circles, with the self as the author at the centre. Closest to the centre were the migrants' compatriots in the Lot (whom I discuss in the next chapter), followed by the British residents of the Dordogne, Britons in Spain, and then tourists. The migrants' discussions about the British still living in Britain suggested that they also place them in the outer circle, at a safe distance. How my respondents chose to classify others was therefore a reflection of their self-presentations as 'different', 'not normal', 'adventurers' and 'pioneers', as fundamentally unlike other Britons. Although this depiction of the migrants' unique system of classification makes it seem as though the stereotypes that the migrants employed were discrete, these circles at times overlapped, representing the actors within them using the same characteristics. For example, the British in Spain and those in the Dordogne were equally characterized as expatriates or associated with tourists.

Despite their reified presentations of others, the migrants still engaged in friendly relationships with those that they stereotyped (see also Waldren 1996; Brown and Theodossopoulos 2004). In evidence of this point, many of the migrants told me about friends who lived in the Dordogne and Spain, or their interactions with tourists. The migrants' claims to distinctiveness were therefore premised on their relationships with, and first-hand knowledge of, others. The migrants who ran *gîtes* drew on examples of how they had had to explain to their visitors how to use the compost heap in the garden, or how to separate rubbish for recycling. This information about 'how to live in the Lot' (albeit temporarily in the case of tourists) was often collated in a file somewhere in the *gîte* for visitors to read through at their leisure. During the summer months, Connie, Harry and Jane continually reminded me that they knew how to live in the Lot better than their *gîte* visitors; why didn't the visitors 'get up early to avoid the heat of the day'? Why didn't they 'shut the shutters during the day to keep the heat out of the *gîte*'? As this example shows, tourists provided my respondents with an affirmation of their way of life; in other words, for the British in the Lot, the presence of tourists was a constant reminder that they knew more about life in the Lot. Their self-understanding was, therefore, contingent on the presence of these others.

The categorization of tourists and other lifestyle migrants by my respondents thus resonates with Boissevain's argument that the presence of tourists promotes both self-awareness and solidarity among the hosts,

> brought about by the regular presence of outsiders, which automatically creates categories of 'we' and 'they', insiders and outsiders, hosts and guests. By being looked at, examined and questioned by strangers, locals become aware of how they differ from the visitors. (1996: 6–7)

Therefore, while the migrants gained a degree of self-awareness and came to know themselves through migration, their encounters with tourists and their perceptions of other lifestyle migrants were in fact reflections on their own identities and categories of belonging. By comparing their lives in the Lot with the experiences of tourists and other Britons living abroad, the migrants presented themselves as a group, the 'British of the Lot'. This is an imagined community (Anderson 1983); while they did not know all of the other British living in the area, they claimed solidarity with them, emphasizing that they had all had the same motivation behind their migration: the search for and eventual achievement of a different way of life.

As I argue in the following chapter, this solidarity was fickle, as my respondents frequently drew attention to how their compatriots living locally did not have the necessary knowledge of how to live in the Lot. Indeed, in discussions about their compatriots in the same department they displayed more antagonism towards them than they did towards tourists and other Britons living abroad. I argue that this difference in the way they related to others mapped onto the distinctions they drew between insiders and outsiders. They perceived their compatriots in the Lot as insiders. Their narratives thus revealed that the migrants believed that they were in direct competition with one another; they all claimed their lives in the Lot as distinctive, but the presence of their compatriots served as a constant reminder that they were not so different after all. The rivalry that the migrants presented in their accounts, in opposition to the laid-back way that they related to outsiders such as tourists and other Britons living overseas who lead indistinct lives, resonates with Herzfeld's (1992) argument that ambiguous insiders are a greater problem than outsiders. Their talk of tourists and Britons living in other overseas destinations therefore demonstrated that in their minds these others posed no threat to the distinctiveness of the lives they led. Instead, drawing on stereotypes of these others, my respondents living in the Lot claimed, 'this is what we are not'.

Conclusion

The ethnographic examples in this chapter show that the migrants referred to specific 'others', such as tourists and Britons living in other overseas destinations, by using stereotypes. Such use of stereotypes reveals that, in the migrants' perception, these others did not have the desire or the knowledge of how to live a distinctive and exceptional way of life. While the migrants perceived that tourists and their compatriots in other destinations were noticeably different from the local population, they highlighted the distinctive contrast of their own lives. They claimed this on the grounds of their efforts to become part of the local community. Social integration was thus a characteristic of the different way of life that Britons living in the Lot sought. This desire for integration in order to achieve distinction resonated with Herzfeld's (1992) argument that, in claiming insider status, distinction is achieved through belonging, a point that is further apparent in the ethnography presented in the next chapter.

By recounting my respondents' classifications of others, I show how the stereotypes they used were significant to them and revealed more about how Britons living in the Lot wanted to present themselves than about the others they referred to. How they presented others can be understood as an effort to displace their ambivalent position as incomers to the local community, caught between their imaginings of life after migration and their experiences of life in the Lot. The migrants' presentations of tourists and other British migrants as 'destructive' and leading unexceptional lives thus reflected their awareness that their own presence in the Lot in part destroyed the uniqueness of the way of life available there. Their discussions of their compatriots, while a product of their heightened consciousness of the moral value of integration (particularly as this has been applied to discourses of the British abroad), also served to resolve some of their feelings of ambivalence.

To conclude, the migrants' classifications confirmed their beliefs that they led distinctive lives. They used stereotypes to say, 'this is what we are not'. Tourists and Britons living in other destinations may have been 'destructive' in their minds, but they did not pose a threat to the migrants and their self-presentations of the unique and distinctive lives that they led. Instead, they confirmed the peculiarity of the migrants' lives because, by using stereotypes, the migrants revealed what they believed they were not. However, as I discuss in the next chapter, their compatriots in the Lot presented a much greater challenge to these self-perceptions.

It is evident that the way of life that my respondents led was a central feature of how they wanted to be recognized. They therefore claimed to lead a different way of life, and their classifications of others confirmed those assertions. It seemed that the focus on the distinctiveness of their lives in the Lot was a key feature of the migrants' narratives, although it manifested itself in a variety of ways. In particular, as the following chapter traces, this engagement in apparent processes of social distinction was indicative of the continued influence of their class background and culture on their everyday practices and behaviour. Status discrimination, entangled with processes of self-identification was, as the examples presented here attest, also intrinsically related to their claims that through migration they had achieved a better way of life. Their culturally specific use of stereotypes was thus very much part of their wider self-realization projects.

While it seemed that the migrants had more control over the terms of their distinctiveness after migration, it remained evident that they had not fully escaped from their British middle-class processes of distinction. David Lomax's statement one afternoon perfectly captured this paradox:

> The interesting thing about the British abroad is that we all do it. We all come out here and like to pretend that we're the only people here. We all like to say 'I hope the British invasion stops soon.'

Notes

1 The nearest international school offering instruction in English was in Toulouse. For British children living in the Lot, attendance at this school would have necessitated a daily round trip of three hours or more.
2 Translated from French: 'Au cours des rencontres que nous avons eues en Bretagne et Normandie, les résidents britanniques nous ont cité le cas de leurs compatriotes de Dordogne comme l'exemple à ne pas suivre. La condamnation de ce type de comportement "colonial" était pour eux le meilleur gage de leur volonté d'intégration.'
3 I never tracked down the official records for this, nor did I come across any further examples during my fieldwork.

7

En route to authentic living

This chapter builds on the argument presented in Chapter 6 to highlight the relationship between post-migration lives, processes of social distinction and the quest for a better way of life. It recognizes that the search for a better way of life does not stop after migration but is an ongoing process, through which my respondents redefined their goals. Nevertheless, the ideology of a more authentic way of living remains at the core. The concept of authenticity thus serves as a lens through which to examine the migrants' everyday lives following migration.

Against this background, the chapter highlights the role that status discrimination plays in the process of getting to a better way of life, while also stressing that this quest could indeed be understood as reflecting the migrants' desires for distinctiveness. In this rendering, it becomes clear that, for my respondents, these processes of distinction were rooted in their ideologies of living rather than purely in their consumption practices. Furthermore, it is apparent that status discrimination was put to work creatively in the designation, constitution and realization of a better way of life.

Such processes were apparent in the way that my respondents in the Lot related to one another. Their reflections on the lives of their compatriots living locally, the gradual changes in their tastes, and their efforts to present themselves as having insider knowledge of life in the Lot, revealed their efforts to articulate their progress *en route* to authentic living. By contextualizing my respondents' post-migration lives within the broader notion of authenticity, I demonstrate in what ways they constituted authentic living and what this revealed about the relationship between lifestyle migration and migrant subjectivities.

Despite the rhetoric of transformation inherent in my respondents' migration narratives, the act of migration alone did not bring about the better way of life that they sought. Their increasingly nuanced understandings of life in the Lot demonstrated that, over time and through residence, they gradually refined their ideas about how authentic living was constituted. In this respect, their particular migration is better understood as one step among many that they undertake in their efforts to get to a better way of life. The end-point of this quest – authentic living – was therefore constantly re-defined, and they remained in the process of transforming their lifestyles. The irony is that, as the length of time that they lived in the Lot increased, the migrants became more aware of the conceptual distance they had yet to travel in order to reach their particular 'holy grail'. In this rendering, just as in tourism, authenticity – and therefore the better way of life that they pursued – remained elusive (MacCannell 1976; Handler and Saxton 1988), gazed upon but not fully realized (Urry 1990).

Chapter 6 demonstrated the way in which my respondents, through their use of recognizable stereotypes, participated in subtle processes of distinction, whereby they valorized their post-migration lifestyle choices and practices. This chapter demonstrates further the value of such distinctions; through their discussions of their compatriots living locally – from those who integrated into the local population to those whose efforts in this direction were perceived to be failing – the migrants affirmed and legitimated their own position *en route* to authentic living. In this respect it becomes clear that authenticity and social distinction provided mutual reinforcement: by presenting the authenticity of their post-migration lives, the migrants laid claim to distinction, but it was only through such claims that authentication could be achieved.

About authenticity

The quest for a better way of life that underwrote my respondents' migration and subsequent experiences of life in the Lot was heavily influenced by their perception that in rural France they would find authentic living and would be able to be themselves. This particular lifestyle migration promised much of what they sought in their quest for authenticity. As Handler and Saxton (1988) argue, this is the desire for 'real' lives and 'real' selves, which, as Lindholm asserts, is reflective of 'a heightened concern with cultural and personal authenticity' (2008: 5). In this respect, my respondents' narratives confirmed Crang's argument that the quest for the authenticity lies 'at the core of modern subjectivities' (1996: 418), where the search for authenticity is viewed as a matter of existential concern, fundamentally linked to self-expression and identity. It is against this background that the persistence of the quest for a better way of life following migration, and the nuances of my respondents' post-migration lives, become more meaningful.

The quest for 'authentic living' evident within my respondents' accounts resonates with the search for 'pure cultures' characteristic of early anthropological enquiries, where anthropologists searched for cultures that were unspoilt by Western influences (Bendix 1997). Subsequent calls for the deconstruction of these presentations of other cultures as authentic have argued that this is necessary because it is a romanticizing, essentialist, and fundamentally racist discourse, which assumes cultural fixity and the possibility of purity (Lindholm 2002; van de Port 2004; van Ginkel 2004; Anonymous 2004).

As a result of such criticisms, there have recently been efforts to renegotiate a position for authenticity within anthropology. This renegotiation draws on a particular conceptualization of authenticity that resonates with Handler's (1986) definition of authenticity as culturally constructed (see also Bruner 2005) and functional to those who claim it. As Handler (1986) argues, the 'search for authentic cultural experience ... says more about us than about others' (1986: 2). Handler's statements focus on the anthropological search for authentic cultures, but I argue that they can be adopted to interrogate the experiences of those who search for 'authenticity' in their everyday lives. Indeed, many recent discussions of authenticity stress that it is a concept that people regularly draw on (see for example, Anonymous 2004; van de Port 2004; van Ginkel 2004). It is therefore time to examine 'what quests for authenticity *mean for* and *do to* its seekers' (2004: 59 original italics), emphasizing the importance of noting how individuals construct and perceive the authentic in everyday life (see also MacDonald 1997; Anonymous 2004; van de Port 2004).

Throughout this chapter I examine the migrants' lives through this framework of authenticity, questioning what constitutes authenticity and what role is played by the quest for this particular sense of authentic living – identified by my respondents' claims of the knowledge of how to *really* live in the Lot. Some of the answers to these questions may be found in a comparison with the tourist's quest for authenticity (see for example MacCannell 1976; Cohen 1988; Graburn 1989; Urry 1990; Selwyn 1996; Franklin 2003). Just as tourists search for the authentic on their travels, so do the migrants in the different way of life that they seek. The link between tourism and authenticity, as Lindholm (2008) summarizes, is premised on the idea that 'real life is elsewhere', allowing for the possibility of self-realization – the discovery of the authentic self – precisely through the journey to 'elsewhere'. Indeed, this was also evident in my respondents' lives, from the decision to migrate to their discourses about how life had, subtly, changed following migration.

The tourist's perception of authenticity is imbued with a particular meaning that contrasts with the superficiality of modernity. For MacCannell (1976), it is a response to the feelings of inauthenticity that permeate the modern world and an effort to (re)construct meaning in an era of instability and fragmentation. Other scholars have similarly stated that tourism, understood as the quest for authenticity, is an attempt to reclaim what modernity has destroyed and lost (see for example Cohen 1988; MacCannell 1992; Lindholm 2002; Franklin 2003). In part, and as became clear in Chapter 6, the way that my respondents explained the rationale behind migration reflected this interpretation of the quest for authenticity. As I have demonstrated elsewhere in this book, rural France became the rural idyll, a curiously British representation. Furthermore, the migrants emphasized a desire for community values and a sense of belonging, claiming that this was no longer available to them in Britain. However, despite this resonance with the tourist's quest for authenticity, there were points at which my respondents' experiences differed. In particular, the quest for authenticity has been described as taking place outside of everyday life, beyond the mundane:

> the journey and stay are to, and in, sites which are outside the normal places of residence and work. Periods of residence elsewhere are of a short-term or temporary nature. There is a clear intention to return 'home' within a relatively short period of time. (Urry 1990: 3; see also MacCannell 1976)

The search for authenticity, in this rendering, is thus only fleeting. In this respect, it was the persistence of my respondents' quest for authentic living and its articulation in everyday life that distinguished them from tourists – and from second-home owners who similarly associate authenticity with their holiday homes (Hall and Müller 2004). How then can we explain my respondents' quest for authentic living, which not only motivated their migration but continued to characterize their lives in the Lot? As the ethnography presented in this chapter demonstrates, it is the process of getting to authentic living which is meaningful to my respondents.

'Genuine' French living

For my respondents living in the Lot, the quest for authentic living was a comparative and relative endeavour. As the ethnography presented in this section demonstrates, they judged the authenticity of their own lives against those of their compatriots living locally. Broadly, as I highlighted in Chapter 2, authentic living was defined as becoming local, reflecting their early aspirations for life in the Lot. Those whom they considered to lead the most authentic lives – in the sense that they were deemed to have genuine and credible knowledge of how to live in the Lot – were those whom they believed to have socially integrated into the local population. Through their discussions of the lives of these others, they revealed a continuum of authentic living – from less authentic to more authentic – and their position within this.

The pinnacle of success – those whom they deemed to have the most authentic lives – was reserved for those who were indistinguishable from the local population. At the other end of the scale, the migrants identified their compatriots who, in their opinions, had less or the wrong knowledge of how to live in the Lot. Their representations of these others drew upon similar tropes to those they had used to describe their compatriots living in Spain and the Dordogne, demonstrating that the solidarity conferred by their descriptions of those living in other destinations was fickle. My respondents' perceptions of the lives led by their local compatriots acted as a further measure by which they could gauge their own progress *en route* to a better way of life and could claim their lives as being more or less authentic; only through these discussions could they gain some idea of their progress and the distance that they still had to travel. However, the position on the scale of authenticity was by no means stable, and as they learned more about what was entailed in leading a truly authentic life, they found that they needed to re-evaluate their position in relation to their goals.

The migrants' discussions of others who (they implied) led more authentic lives than they did revealed the characteristics of 'authentic living' that my respondents valued. Interestingly, while they valorized the lives led by local social actors, they gauged their own success through a comparison of their own lives with those of their compatriots living in the Lot. By noting the extent to which these others had managed to integrate into the local population, the migrants articulated their own understandings of how to master life within the destination.

In many respects, it became clear that my respondents measured their success against an 'ideal type', embodied in the individual Britons who had become so integrated into the local population that they were almost indistinguishable from it. These others had lived in the Lot for upwards of thirty years, often marrying into the local population.

Furthermore, these long-term residents were elusive; on the rare occasion when I had the opportunity to meet one of them, she explained that her migration had nothing in common with these later migrants; her migration had had different motivations. Her initial travel to the Lot had been part of a greater tour through France, as she tried to learn the language and experience another way of life, a 'coming of age' (Korpela 2009b). In this manner she clearly distinguished her migration choices and life in the Lot from those of later migrants. The irony was that in this process she too revealed the extent to which she was still engaged in the processes of distinction common to the British middle classes.

In conversation, many of my respondents discussed one woman, Catherine Duval, a British woman who was aged in her seventies, holding her up as a paradigmatic case of how to live in the Lot. I compile the following romanticized account of her migration and subsequent life in France from the stories that a number of my participants told me. Catherine first came to the Lot as a student during the 1950s when she was in her early twenties. She was studying French at a British university and stayed in France to teach for a year. By the end of the year, she had fallen in love both with Cahors and with a man who lived there. Although she returned briefly to Britain, the pull of the Lot and the man she loved proved too strong and she soon decided to try and make a life for herself in France. She married her sweetheart, set herself up as a professional translator and had lived in the Lot ever since.[1] Her career and her marriage were a great success. Her skills as a translator were always in high demand. She had children and then grandchildren. She had been on the committee for the AFGB for many years, but had recently given up this position.

By the time of my research, Catherine's reputation had reached mythical proportions. She had successfully integrated into the local population – this was an assessment made by other British migrants on the basis of her ability to speak French and the fact that she socialized as easily with the French population as with the British, seeming to bridge the gap between them effortlessly – and many of the migrants upheld her as a role model. Each of them seemed to have a story to tell about her.

Primarily, many of my respondents told me of moments when she had been their saviour. One couple recalled an incident when they had had problems with their car. When they reached the garage, they did not speak French and the mechanic had no English. Fortunately, the mechanic knew Catherine and rang her, requesting that she come down to the garage to act as a translator. The way the couple presented it, she came straight down to the garage to help them out, accepted their thanks, and then went home. They wanted to return the favour with a drink or a meal, but Catherine declined. The couple never saw her again.

The accounts of some migrants revealed that they were protective of

Catherine. One hot summer day I sat with Harry, Connie and Jane on the terrace of their house while a journalist interviewed them. At some point, Catherine's name entered the conversation and Jane expressed admiration for what she had achieved for the British living in the Lot, as well as her success at becoming accepted by the French. The interviewer took great interest; where could she find Catherine? The response was immediate and was the same as the one given to me months earlier: over the years Catherine had been inundated with media attention and now it was time to leave her in peace. This was an interesting reaction as there was no indication that this respect for her privacy was at Catherine's own request; it seemed as though Jane, Harry and Connie had taken it upon themselves to speak in her place.

I argue that both the awe and the protection expressed in the migrants' statements about Catherine reveal more about what she signified to my respondents than her actual character. With their stories, the migrants implicitly presented her, and others who had lived in the Lot for similarly long periods of time, as leading the most authentic lives of all their compatriots. As their accounts demonstrated, they admired her ability to switch between two cultures and languages and the seemingly effortless integration into local life. My respondents presented these pioneers as having transcended their position as outsiders. In this manner, their lives operated primarily as a blueprint for the authentic living that my respondents aspired towards.

It is interesting that the ideal position to which the migrants aspired, the authentic living that they continually pursued, was that of their metaphorical and idealized ancestors, the pioneers. While they undoubtedly admired the lives of their French neighbours, their accounts demonstrate that they followed the example set by these original migrants. It seems that my respondents' goals for their new lives in the Lot were that they would one day be able to escape their migrant status through the demonstration of their cultural fluency.

Learning authentic living

Although the migrants expressed their ambitions to be socially and culturally integrated members of the local community, their accounts revealed that this was not a straightforward process. Mastery of the art of 'really' living in rural France took time and experience as they built up their knowledge of how to live in the Lot, in the process distancing themselves from certain material reminders of their outsider status. How they then incorporated this newly found knowledge into their daily lives was, however, idiosyncratic, contributing towards their individualized awareness of life in the Lot. It seems that not only were quality-of-life considerations culturally specific, as Findlay and Rogerson (1993) outline, but furthermore that these had a more personalized and individualized significance for the migrants. By confidently stressing the value of their understandings of how to live in the Lot over and above those of certain of their compatriots, the migrants continued to differentiate their lives from those of others.

The following ethnographic examples outline some of the ways in which my respondents measured their own progress en route to authentic living. As they reflected on what they had learned about how to live in the Lot, they realized the distance that they – as individuals – had travelled, judged the progress of their compatriots and realized how much they still had to learn in order to achieve their goals.

A taste for rural France

For many of the migrants, return trips to England provided the opportunity to stock up on foodstuffs that they could not buy in France. These included Marmite™, tea bags, mango chutney, baked beans, salt and vinegar crisps, McVitie's™ choco-late biscuits, and Angel Delight™ instant dessert. However, they could not easily transport other goods. Primary among these was meat, and I often heard people complain that they just could not get bacon or sausages that resembled those back in Britain, as the French had a different way of butchering their animals, with the result that different cuts of meat were available. Indeed, returning to England following fieldwork, I remember a friend teasing me as I filled my fridge with sausages and bacon, so much had I missed the taste.

In other areas of France popular with British migrants, British entrepreneurs had responded to the desires and demands of the British population. For example, in the Dordogne, there was at least one van that brought in goods from Britain. However, at the time of my research, there was no such supply of British foodstuffs to my respondents in the Lot. During the summer the supermarket in one of the towns stocked some British produce, but my interlocutors in the area derided the efforts made, stressing that it was clear that this was old stock from the amount of dust that had built up on the many bottles of lime cordial over the years. It seemed that lime cordial was not one of the products regularly sought by the British of the Lot.

Living without the comforts of their familiar British food, many of my re-spondents eventually discovered locally produced alternatives. Vic and Anne Wilson, yearning for their full English breakfast complete with bacon, found *poitrine* (finely sliced meat from the breast of the pig). In their discussions of the locally available substitutes for their favourite British products the migrants stressed that they made these discoveries themselves through trial and error and that their efforts to live with what was locally available located them more firmly as living their daily lives in France rather than indecisively between the two countries.

> When we first moved here, we kept saying, 'Oh, I want that from England'. Now we've found alternatives and substitutes, or as good as, just by looking and finding something … People will say, 'Oh, you must want something from England'. No. You know, we've got a life here now. (Kay Morris)

It seemed that the challenge was to eventually live without the crutches provided by food treats from Britain. Some of the migrants' narratives recounted how they had eventually achieved the ideal situation where they wanted no supplies from Britain, gradually changing the contents of their cupboards, fridges and freezers.

To highlight the virtue of their actions, they would frequently draw attention to how other lifestyle migrants living locally continued to stock up from abroad.

> There's a lorry that comes from Holland that goes around the villages as well ... There's a guy I know who was working at a Dutch person's house one day, and she wanted some soap powder and she said, 'I'm just going across the road to borrow some soap powder. The lorry's coming tomorrow.' (Jon Morris)

Similarly, the local Dutch estate agent stocked his office with Dutch goods:

> When we bought the house, we bought it from a Dutch estate agent ... and everything in there – the tea, the coffee, the sugar, the chocolate bits – everything was from Holland. There was nothing in French. (Jon Morris)

Ron Stampton told me similar stories about a British man who had a second home in the area. Whenever he visited his house in the Lot, he would bring his food from Britain. Ron thought this was ridiculous, given the quality of the local produce.

Recalling these instances and comparing them to their own ways of living in France, Jon and Ron implied that they led very different lives from those of other migrants who lived on imported goods; while they lived on what was available locally, others appeared to be caught in between France and their country of origin. In this manner, they implied that their lives in the Lot were more authentic, in the sense that they strived to live rural French life to the full, buying products that were readily available.

Another way in which the migrants distinguished themselves from their compatriots living locally was through the discussion of wine. Conforming to the stereotype of life in France, wine played a big part in the daily lives of the migrants. As many of them reminded me time and again, a bottle purchased in a French supermarket would cost twice as much on the shelves of a British supermarket. As well as contributing to their reasons for moving to France (Buller and Hoggart 1994a; Gervais-Aguer 2004, 2006; Depierre and Guitard 2006), the ready availability and affordability of good-quality wine contributed further to the migrants' representations of the Lot as paradisiacal and idyllic. However, the migrants were unanimously keen, at least in their narratives, to distance themselves from the image of expatriates as constantly inebriated. Once again, by evoking the (inebriated) other, they were able to present their own practices as an exercise in restraint. However, as I witnessed, this highlighting of the weaknesses of their compatriots was often hypocritical. For example, many of them would reprimand their friends for drinking and driving but would themselves get behind the wheel of the car when significantly under the influence.

The migrants' discussions about drinking habits may broadly be split into three categories: what they say about themselves, what they say about other migrants, and what they say about the French. They most frequently presented other British migrants as an example not to follow, contrasting these, often negative, images with their self-presentations. As Jon and Kay Morris told me, 'If we drink at lunchtime, we just can't do anything in the afternoon'; their comment was part of a more general discussion about the habits of retirement migrants who, according to Jon and Kay, start drinking at lunchtime. This was not a problem, as Jon and Kay continued, but while the lives of retirement migrants consisted of leisure time, they still had to work. Even drinking one glass of wine with lunch interfered with their abilities to continue working, so they did not drink until the evening.

Harry also discussed the drinking habits of his retired acquaintances. He told me how they regularly got 'stoned', by which he meant that they got very drunk. Harry said they were 'sozzled' daily, starting to drink before lunch and continuing throughout the day. He claimed to know people who drank a bottle of wine (each) on a daily basis. In his opinion, he had a more moderate approach to alcohol. He was also dismissive of his compatriots' purchases of wine *en vrac* (in bulk) from local co-operatives. This involved taking five-litre plastic containers to the market to be filled from a barrel by the vendor. In contrast, Harry selected his bottles of wine carefully from the selves at the supermarket, reserving some in his *cave* (cellar) for special occasions. Harry also instructed me on what to drink when I went to the homes of other migrants that he knew. On one memorable occasion he told me not to touch the rosé; I forgot, and had an enjoyable lunch accompanied by what I thought was a nice and refreshing rosé wine, tasting very different from the paint stripper that Harry had described. What he implied by drawing attention to these different drinking habits and tastes was not only that he had a more responsible attitude towards alcohol but also that he had discernment when it came to wine, at least in contrast to certain of his fellow Britons.

While the reputed behaviour of their compatriots served as a reminder of how not to behave, the drinking habits of their French neighbours could serve as a model of appropriate social drinking. As several of my respondents explained, the common British perception that the French drink a lot of wine was unrepresentative; in other words, heavy drinking was not part of everyday French life. It also seemed to be the case that there was a particular (French) etiquette about how to drink that many of the British incomers had not grasped. Time and again I heard about how members of the British population had disgraced themselves when invited to take *apéritif* with their French neighbours, outstaying their welcome and drinking too much; courtesy dictated that they should have one drink and then leave. It seems that there was, in many cases, a fundamental lack of fit in the drinking practices of the British and the local French, drawn partly from misrepresentations but also as a result of the failure to recognize that drinking practices and habits are often socially constructed (Douglas 1987). That many of the migrants highlighted the inappropriate drinking behaviour of their compatriots was a further way in which they implied that they had greater knowledge of the local culture and ways of doing things.

This was also the case when migrants drew parallels between their drinking practices and those of their French neighbours. For example, Connie Earl and Jane Campbell, who drank moderately and only with meals, explained that their habits were in line with those of their French neighbour, Thérèse, a Parisian woman in her seventies who owned a holiday home next door. During her stay

8 The local market

each summer, Thérèse would invite Harry, Connie and Jane to the house for *apéritif*. On these occasions, Thérèse would have only one drink. Connie and Jane explained that they understood that this was the culturally appropriate way of drinking for a French woman of her age and status. Connie and Jane aligned themselves with Thérèse by explaining that they drank moderately following the example set by this sophisticated French woman. It is interesting that, rather than refer to their neighbours who lived in the village all year round, and possibly had different drinking habits, Connie and Jane chose instead to discuss the practices of a Parisian. This example once again demonstrates the complexity of the processes of distinction in which the migrants participate within the new social nexus.

In some cases, alignment with local French actors was further evident in the choices that the migrants made about where to buy their food. Indeed, most of my respondents in the Lot bought certain goods from the market and others from the hypermarket. Most commonly, they would buy fresh, locally produced fruit and vegetables from the market (see Figure 8) and pick up bread from the *boulangerie* (bakery). The products in the market were, as my respondents explained to me, the fruits of local people's labour and were finite, unlike the products in the supermarket. 'Here everything is local,' Alannah told me one day. 'They're proud of it and rightly so. And I think it's a good thing that vegetables are seasonal.' My respondents also explained that, as with the food they grew in their own gardens, these local and seasonal products tasted better.

The village market attracted all residents of the area – the French *paysans*, the Parisians, the Dutch and the English – as well as tourists. It was an event in the weekly calendar of each village and an opportunity for socialization. In order not to miss out on the best produce, as I witnessed, it was important to get to the market early in the morning. By supporting the local producers and traders, the migrants implied that they contributed to, and were involved in, the greater community of the Lot. Through their attendance at the market, they also had the chance to meet up with their compatriots living locally, sometimes taking a coffee together in the local *café*, and with their French friends and neighbours. And while tourists also attended, as I discuss later in this chapter, they did not have the knowledge of how to use the market. They stood out because they did not have a relationship with local vendors and residents.

But the migrants were also knowledgeable about local food production, particularly the *produits de terroir* (regional specialities) – ranging from the full-bodied AOC Cahors red wine and the *magret de canard* (duck breast), to *cabecou* (a small, round goat's cheese) and *foie gras* (goose-liver pâté). They became self-appointed ambassadors to the Lot, introducing their friends, relatives and other visitors to their products. And through their discussions of the processes involved in the production of these delicacies for the market, the migrants demonstrated that they had an appreciation for them that extended beyond consumption.

The migrants' developing cultural understanding of food production in the Lot and their increasing taste for and appreciation of local products demonstrated how they were gradually refining what constituted authentic living. As David Howes emphasizes, 'we relate to and create environments through *all* of our senses' (2005: 7; emphasis added). Howes continues that to become emplaced, to feel at home within the physical and social environment, is the result of the 'sensuous interrelationship of body–mind–environment' (*ibid.*: 7). In this rendering, the migrants' multisensory experiences, and the values that they give to these, contributed towards how they constituted the Lot as a specific place, as their home (see also Feld and Basso 1996).

Learning from the locals

While at times the migrants presented their knowledge of how to live in the Lot as the result of their own experimentation, at other times they stressed that they had had native teachers. They would explain how they deferred to their French neighbours whose years of experience had equipped them with better knowledge of how to do things.

Bob and Mary Potter explained that their neighbours had taught them how to prepare local products; as they presented it, their neighbours had introduced them to, and initiated them into, a different way of life. Bob and Mary proudly recalled that in their first year of living in France they had raised a pig under the watchful gaze of the farmers next door. They saved their kitchen scraps to feed the pig, went to feed it twice a day and regularly cleaned out the stall that it shared with another pig until, at the end of the year, they took it to the abattoir to be slaughtered. Their neighbours then showed them how to make sausages and pâté, and taught them how to cut up the carcass. Bob and Mary used every part of the pig, giving some away to their friends, but storing most of it in the deep freeze; the meat in its various forms lasted for a whole year. In Britain they had worked as an accountant and a lecturer, so had not previously had the opportunity to participate in such activity. As they told me, they loved this new lifestyle, revealing their desire to live a truly rural way of life. The maintenance of a sense of authentic living, it seems, was a central feature of the migrants' daily lives.

The humble attitudes that the migrants adopted towards the knowledge of their French neighbours were often contrasted to those of their compatriots who were less respectful of local knowledge and tradition. 'There are people who come down here and think they're better than them,' Susan explained. She went on to remark that on the contrary, the local French knew 'far more than we do about living here'. It had, however, taken her a while to realize this herself, as she revealed when she later recalled a story about her and Trevor's early days of living in the Lot:

> We bought a lot of fruit trees ... the old lady next door said, 'What are you doing up there?' I told her we were planting fruit trees and she said, 'You'll get no fruit'. I said, 'Oh well, perhaps', and she said again, 'You'll get no fruit'. So I said, 'Well, perhaps the blossom will look pretty?' 'No', she said, 'You'll get no fruit' ... We never had a piece of fruit; she was quite right.

While initially some of my respondents seemed unwilling to concede that their neighbours were right, later they would draw on the knowledge they had derived from local French actors to criticize the actions of their compatriots in the Lot. In this manner, the migrants made it known that they were truly on the path towards more authentic living, while their compatriots still had a lot to learn. Vic, for example, expressed his opinion about Harry's efforts to cultivate a lawn (see Chapter 4), stressing that, as incomers, he and his compatriots should open their eyes to the practices of their neighbours. As grassy lawns were not a common feature of French gardens, the logical conclusion would be that the climate was not right for this type of cultivation. The local French grew vegetables in their gardens, and maybe a few flowers, but a lawn was a hopeless venture. In fact, most of the local land of any size was used for agriculture.

In contrast, Harry stressed that he had learned through trial and error what would grow and what would not, thereby aligning himself with the locals who had gained their knowledge by working the land and by engaging intimately with it (cf Theodossopoulos 2003a). These subtle differences in the migrants' descriptions of the processes by which they learned how to live in the Lot demonstrate that the perception of what constitutes an authentic life differs from one migrant to another. However, it is also evident that the quest for authenticity was a comparative project; by contrasting their own knowledge and beliefs about authentic living with those of their compatriots they made an implicit judgement about who had the greater knowledge about how to live in the Lot and, further to this, which of them led the more or the less authentic lives. Through such claims the migrants revealed the relationship between the quest for a better way of life and their ongoing pursuit of distinction. The examples presented here demonstrate the extent to which, through their judgements about their compatriots living locally, the migrants championed their own lifestyle choices, laying claim to progress *en route* to a authentic living. Indeed, the claim to possessing distinctive knowledge of how to live in the Lot was further supported by their migrants' revelations about local social life.

Although my respondents in the Lot often aligned themselves with the local French, it is important to recognize that they did not see all of their French neighbours in the same way. I encountered one example of this when Connie and Jane talked to me about the local suspicions concerning a farmer who lived just outside their village. Apparently he had collaborated with the Vichy government during the Second World War, while many people in the area had been involved in the resistance movement against the occupiers. Connie and Jane, who could see his farm from their house, also told me of local suspicions, which they also held, that he was smuggling something in the trucks of hay that originated from his farm, travelled down the valley and came back to the farm. As they continued, this farmer was not French but German – a judgement based on his mixed parentage – and could therefore be considered to be an outsider to the local community. As this example demonstrates, the manner in which Connie and Jane talked about this farmer reflected their knowledge of local history, while also demonstrating their ideas about local categories of inclusion.

By drawing parallels between their post-migration lives and those of their French neighbours, the migrants laid claim to local knowledge and accessed an authentic life that was intimately embedded in local practices. Through their appropriation of the authentic lives of others, the migrants, as Handler (1986) argues, renewed their sense that they too led authentic lives. They subsequently drew on this local knowledge to distinguish themselves from other migrants and to place emphasis on their relationships with members of the local population. Further to this, however, their possession of alleged local knowledge helped them to build a discourse of distinction that authenticated their social position in their new surroundings.

Authenticity as distinction

The migrants' discussions about what they believe to be the 'real' or genuine way to live in the Lot show that they were very confident in their views about what constituted authentic living and what did not. However, as the ethnographic examples in this chapter have demonstrated, the migrants did not always hold the same ideas about how to live in the Lot, and thus they challenged one another's understandings of how to live an authentic life. Despite this lack of consensus among my respondents, I argue that, through identifying those who were either more or less authentic than them, the migrants invoked a particular notion of authenticity which, as Fine states, equates it to the 'recognition of difference' (2003: 155). Thus, as Handler (1986) and van Ginkel (2004) assert, in presenting the authentic in their accounts, my respondents demonstrated the distinctiveness of their own lives. Therefore, locating the migrants' accounts within the context of broader discussions of authenticity brings to light the processes of distinction that they use in their everyday lives. This resonates with Bourdieu's (1984) argument linking class distinction, classifying practices and taste.

There has been an overwhelming reluctance to apply Bourdieu's ideas about the role of culture and cultural capital in the perpetuation of class distinctions in contemporary British society. This is largely based on a misconception of the British middle class as lacking culture (Gunn 2005). Researchers in the early 1990s began to argue that culture and consumption had in fact been historically significant to the British middle classes (Brewer 1997; Kidd and Nicholls 1999); cultural capital is thus an undeniable feature of the processes of distinction and systems of hierarchy engaged in by British middle-class actors. As Bennett *et al.* demonstrate in their study of contemporary cultural practices in Britain, Bourdieu's (1984) discussion of distinction 'offers a powerful and incisive account of the relationship between cultural tastes and activities, and contemporary social inequalities' (2008: 11). While they argue that the way social distinction has been conceptualized needs to be more pliable – suggesting for example that it is necessary to account for intersectionality rather than class exclusively – nevertheless, Bourdieu's argument provides a good basis for understanding the role of cultural capital in modern inequalities. This comprehensive study (published as *Culture, Class, Distinction*) provides some interesting insights into processes of distinction, which can help to explain further the quest for authentic living that was common to my respondents.

Firstly, Bennett *et al.* (2008) recognize that it is possible to transplant cultural referents and imaginaries in the pursuit of distinction. In this respect, distinction need not be bounded on a national level, as Bourdieu (1984) presented it, but may have transnational characteristics (Bennett *et al.* 2008). In this framing, my respondents' accounts of their lives following migration and their quests for distinctive or authentic living emerge as part of the (transnational) middle-class struggle over identity and social position. Furthermore, Bennett *et al.* (2008) argue that among the middle class there are those whose tastes exemplify reflexivity and self-awareness rather than reproduce established cultural boundaries. This sense of reflexivity was characteristic of my respondents' lives as they reflected on their own practices and those of their respondents, as well as their progress *en route* to authentic living.

Over time, it seemed that the migrants were developing a taste for life in the Lot, a budding taste for a life they regard as distinctly authentic. As I argue, their assessments of what was considered to be an authentic way of living, and thus that which could be considered distinctive, were dictated by their subscription to particular ideologies of living rather than purely to consumption practices (although these did play a role). In this respect it became clear that status discrimination among my respondents relied on demonstrating the ability and desire to live appropriately in the Lot.

This understanding of how authenticity operates as a marker in processes of distinction reveals that through their individualized claims to authentic living the migrants revealed the extent to which their post-migration lives reflected their renewed ideologies for living. In this respect, it was out of choice that they enacted a uniquely authentic lifestyle which, ironically, was how their French neighbours lived out of necessity. This was possible because of the migrants' possession of a certain level of cultural capital, derived from their position as members of the educated middle class. It was thus the case that despite the migrants' claims to the similarities between their lives and those of their French neighbours, their routes into these ways of living were significantly different. Undoubtedly, the post-migration lives of my respondents superficially resembled their neighbours' lives – e.g. they worked the land to produce some vegetables – but it was their relatively privileged economic position that enabled them to pursue this lifestyle. Their realization that they had not yet reached the pinnacle of authentic living demonstrated that they still had some distance to travel until they reached their goal. Their participation in this process was therefore an intrinsic part of their daily lives.

In engaging in these processes of social distinction – understood as the struggle over the power to define and classify (Bourdieu 1984) – through which they differentiated their lives in the Lot from those of their compatriots living locally, the migrants laid claim to and sought legitimacy for their new lifestyles. In this respect, they placed themselves in a position of authority to define the authentic. Thus, while status discrimination continued to characterize their post-migration lives, they appeared to have more control over the terms by which they and their compatriots were judged. By telling their stories, which distinguished them from certain of their compatriots, my respondents drew parallels between their lives and those of local actors and demonstrated the progress that they had already made *en route* to a better way of life. Over time and through the accumulation of knowledge and experience, they refined their understandings of authentic living. While they aligned themselves with the local French, laying claim to a position within the (imagined) local community, this did not undermine their understandings of themselves as distinctive social actors. In this respect, and as the ethnography presented here demonstrates, what was exceptional about their lives was not their insider status but the process of becoming an insider.

Conclusion

The exploration of post-migration lives presented in this chapter has revealed that the quest for a better way of life that prompted migration, and which was ongoing thereafter, was intrinsically connected to processes of social distinction in which the migrants engaged. As I have argued, the two should be understood to be mutually reinforcing, with status discrimination playing a role in the migrants' assessments of their progress *en route* to a better, more authentic way of life, while the quest itself, underpinned by particular ideologies of living, further reflects the desire for distinctiveness. In this rendering, migration and related lifestyle choices can result in the accumulation of cultural capital. Furthermore, the concept of authenticity serves as an appropriate lens for understanding this relationship between distinction and the quest for a different way of life, not only in what it reveals about the nature and constitution of the quest, but also in explaining the process by which the migrants strive to authenticate their actions.

The ethnography has demonstrated that my respondents' claims to the authenticity of their own lives pivoted around their judgements of the lives of their compatriots also living locally. Importantly, it became clear that, despite my respondents' experiences of life in the Lot, their judgements were based on their initial imaginings of what the rural idyll had to offer. In this respect, claims to more or less authentic living, and therefore distinction, rested upon certain ideologies about how to live in the Lot. As such, their judgements of the degree to which their compatriots had achieved authentic living demonstrated that while the quest for a better way of life had originally appeared to be individualized, in fact, their progress in that direction relied upon its nature as a comparative endeavour.

Undeniably, the processes of distinction that my respondents engaged in were an intrinsic part of the self-realization project that lay at the core of their migration. The migrants' discussions of where they positioned themselves in relation to their compatriots revealed their self-presentations. They admitted readily that their quest for the authentic had begun when they were tourists. Inspired by their holiday experiences, their ambitions for life following migration had been naïve. However, following migration they soon realized that living in the Lot could offer much more than what it had seemed to offer at first sight. Their narratives thus demonstrated that, even after migration, they remained involved in the process of acquiring the authentic – a goal which constantly shifted as they gained more and more knowledge of how to live in the Lot. In this respect, the process of getting to distinctive or authentic living was integral to the production of a particular migrant subjectivity.

As the ethnography presented in this chapter has demonstrated, it did not appear to matter whether they had achieved authentic living (or indeed, whether they would achieve it in the future); it was the process of getting to it and their continued engagement in this process that appeared to be significant to the migrants. I argue that given the importance of this engagement, it was likely to characterize their lives permanently. As a quest for personal authenticity, the migrants' desires were of an existential nature, and thus the significance of their position *en route* to authenticity lay in understanding how this intersected with and affected the migrants' understandings of themselves.

The interrelationship between processes of social distinction and authenticity was significant in terms of what it revealed about the quest for a better way of life. Through their recourse to the political economy of taste, the migrants asserted their new identities and strived to justify their lifestyle choices. As I shall argue in the concluding chapter, their engagement in these processes was indicative of their struggles over the power to authenticate. It seems that although they privileged a rhetoric of migration that highlighted the individualized quality of their choices and actions, their quest for a better way of life was, on closer examination, revealed to be a comparative project.

Notes

1 Catherine Trundle (2009) identifies how cases such as this, where the migration is also tied up with intimate relationships, are related to lifestyle migration. In her examination of English-speaking women who migrated to Italy to marry their Italian partners, she argues that the initial travel to Italy – which led to them meeting their partners – can be understood as a form of lifestyle migration as it shares in common many of the identified characteristics, but the particular circumstances which later bring the women to settle in Italy also incorporate marriage and family. The result of this, so Trundle argues, is that the explanation for the migrations of these women needs to account for their position in the life course and their motivations at that time.

Conclusion:
distinction, ambivalence, authenticity

Through the pages of this book we have travelled with my respondents, British residents of the Lot, as they left their lives in Britain behind; gained insights into their imaginings of life in rural France; and examined the extent to which these were realized (or not) in their post-migration lives. My analysis has moved beyond the explanation of the phenomenon of migration to rural France as motivated by broader middle-class trends (see Buller and Hoggart 1994a; Barou and Prado 1995), to demonstrate how it is underwritten by a more pervasive cultural logic, while also revealing the individualized motivations and imaginings that prompted migration. While migration can broadly be understood as the search for a better way of life, a quest that my respondents held in common with many other lifestyle migrants (Benson and O'Reilly 2009; O'Reilly and Benson 2009), I have questioned the transformative potential of migration and critically examined the presence of a recurring mismatch between the migrants' expectations and lived experiences.

The discourse surrounding migration, and the particular characteristics of the better way of life sought by my respondents, reveal the migrants' tastes, understood here – following Bourdieu (1984) – to denote cultural preferences and aesthetic judgement. The aesthetic dimension of these consumption practices indicates that individuals aspired not only to a particular sense of identity but also to a lifestyle (see Bourdieu 1984; Featherstone 1991). In the case of my respondents in the Lot, on one level they demonstrated by their choice of destination, property selection and resulting lifestyles the extent to which their lifestyle migration was part of wider cultural practices of consumption associated with the British middle classes. On another level, however, the ideologies for living that underwrote such consumption practices and wider everyday practices were the true measure by which they distinguished their lives from those of others and thus laid claim to symbolic capital. This is confirmed by the ethnography presented in this book.

Ong (1999) has argued for the recognition of the cultural logic that drives migration, demonstrating that in this rendering, migration strategies intersect with capital accumulation. As she demonstrates, this is particularly pertinent to understanding transnationalism and gives rise to a more nuanced understanding of international migration, which allows a role for individual agency as well as structural determinants. In the case of my respondents living in the Lot, it became clear that migration was made possible by their relatively high levels of cultural and economic capital, but they also sought to augment these through various means: property ownership; living appropriately; learning French; and distinguishing their lives from those of others. They thus laid claim to the distinctiveness of their post-migration lifestyles, in the process reinforcing, justifying and authenticating the decision to leave Britain and settle in the Lot.

Taste, however, is dynamic and can therefore change over time (Bourdieu 1984; Featherstone 1991; Bennett *et al.* 2009). As the ethnography presented in this book has demonstrated, over time the migrants' conceptualizations of a better way of life were subtly refined in response to their increasing experiential knowledge of what the Lot could offer and their perceptions of the lives of others. Their everyday practices and actions correspondingly changed, resulting in incremental transformations that fed back into their understandings of their lives in the Lot as they worked towards the goal of authentic living.

The story thus far

Through the chapters in this book, I have introduced my respondents, their migration narratives and their everyday experiences of settling into their new lives in the Lot. In their efforts to renovate their houses and work on their gardens, as well as in their relationships with local social actors and compatriots living locally, the migrants encountered the challenges of emplacing themselves in a new physical and social environment. The ethnographic investigation also reveals that the decision to migrate was inspired by – but also subsequently inspired a powerful discourse about – the search for a better of life. This was a discourse that moved beyond the migrants' desires for material improvements in their lives – captured in the research on British migrants and property selection conducted by Buller and Hoggart (1994b) and Gervais-Aguer (2004, 2006, 2008) – and additionally projected their self-belief in their own powers to transform their lives.

Understood within the broader context of the lives led before and after migration, the act of migration emerged in many cases as part of a broader project of personal development and self-improvement. My respondents often saw their migration as a turning point in their lives, a watershed moment (see also Hoey 2005, 2006). And it was common to find that migration coincided with an abrupt change in life circumstances – redundancy, retirement and children leaving home. The migrants presented these as critical moments in their lives, with migration serving as a way to temper the discomfort of such transformations. It emerged that migration was often an affirmative action that alleviated the feeling that they had lost control of their lives and identities. In this respect, insights into the search for a better way of life not only revealed the migrants' ideological motivations but also demonstrated its ontological significance.

Articulating a better way of life

The myth of the better way of life uniquely available in the Lot was common to the accounts of all my respondents. Certain characteristics were prized. Above all, the migrants placed a particular value on rurality, with its tranquillity, slow pace of life and community spirit, reflecting the British middle-class idealization captured in the rural idyll (Williams 1973). Rather than being exotic, the Lot emerged as familiar to my respondents, capturing perfectly their rural longings. Indeed, it seems that they gained comfort precisely from the familiarity of their surroundings; there was a sense that, armed with their ideas about rural living, they were not venturing into the unknown. Furthermore, their post-migration aspirations centred on the desire 'to evoke, even possess, the 'ordinary' and the 'real' through the act of cultural appropriation itself', which Bennett *et al.* (2009: 71) argue is characteristic of the educated British middle classes. In this sentiment, the Lot can provide 'the real thing', while this was perceived as not being attainable elsewhere.

In this respect, the perceived qualities of rural living became representative of the better way of life that the migrants sought, and their entrance into the local community correspondingly gained significance. By presenting rural life as bounded, the migrants reflected certain discomforts that had prompted both their decision to migrate and their choice of destination. In particular, they explicitly identified their dissatisfaction with the increasingly impersonal dimension of the globalized world, manifest in the loss of community and the diminution of personal relationships. Despite the migrants' discomforts with these perceived consequences of globalization, they remained largely uncritical of their own position as global social actors with freedom of movement within Europe, which had initially facilitated their migration.

Despite their shared ambitions for a better way of life, whose loose definition reflected the qualities of rural living, the migrants presented their individual lives as unique, demonstrating how they had approached their lives in the Lot in different ways. In part, this reflected their provenance 'from all walks of life' (although as I have shown, this was restricted to all walks of life within the British middle classes) and their individual interpretations of what the better way of life would do for them. But also, as I have argued, it reflected a desire for difference and their continued engagement within processes of distinction.

In this rendering, the search for a better way of life is a relative and ongoing endeavour, through which individuals attempt to distinguish their lives from those of others, and in the process accumulate cultural capital to consolidate their social status. Lifestyle migration is therefore part of a process by which individuals attempt to achieve their better way of life and should be understood within the context of other consumption or lifestyle choices. Correspondingly, the act of migration emerges as just one action among many that my respondents undertake before and after migration in their efforts to get to a better way of life (Benson and O'Reilly 2009; O'Reilly and Benson 2009).

However, the route to a better way of life was not clearly defined; it was not simply a case of following the yellow-brick road. After migration my respondents continually reflected on their successes and failures, demonstrating that while they might have had ideas about what they needed to do to progress further, realizing those ideas was much more complicated. Accordingly, their accounts demonstrate (echoing the findings of Bennett *et al.*), 'a sense of being uneasily installed between two cultures, sharing elements of both but being completely at home in neither' (2009: 238). Nevertheless, their daily lives were characterized by their efforts to escape this sense of uncertainty. Life following migration saw the migrants continuing to work towards authentic living, gradually redefined in response to their lived experiences, but still operating as the motivating goal in their lives. Everyday life was thus fraught with ambivalence and restlessness as they continued on their quest of self-fulfilment, with the end-point signalled by their social integration into the host society. They thus continued to experiment, altering their everyday practices and reflecting on their relationships with others in their efforts to get closer to their lifestyle goals.

Imagination, migration and lived experience

The persistent influence of imagination on the migrants' lives – evident both in the decision to migrate and in its role in shaping their post-migration lives – calls to attention the need to examine the location of what seem to be individual imaginings within wider cultural and historical frameworks. Indeed, as has been revealed throughout the book, the migrants' understanding of their lives in the Lot emerges out of the tension between imagination and lived experience. In this rendering, imagination is understood as being collective – as an everyday social practice (Appadurai 1996, 2000) or as having a social quality (Bourdieu 1984) – and thus indicative of structure and emerging from particular cultural frameworks. As Castoriadis (1987) argues, such imaginings, which reflect a sense of collective agency, are also central to the reproduction of society. In this understanding imagination is not only the product of society but is also central to its perpetuation. Society and imagination are thus mutually constituting and reinforcing.

Understanding migration through this lens reveals that the imaginings that framed my respondents' migration were indicative of wider structural conditions while also reproducing these. In this respect, although they had presented their migration as individualistic, the migrants' actions reflected and reproduced a wider cultural logic. The myth of the rural idyll, indicative of their continued membership of the British middle classes, prompted migration and shaped expectations, but also legitimated their actions. Furthermore, understanding imagination as social practice, it becomes clear that through migration my respondents also set the conditions for further British middle-class migration to the Lot.

While imagination provided the structural conditions under which their migration was possible, it is clear that more individualized circumstances prompted the act of migration. This explains, simply, why some British middle-class actors who think of migrating do so while others do not. Such circumstances were the culmination of individual biographies. Indeed, such biographies stretched into the migrants' post-migration lives, their embodied encounters within this new social and physical landscape also contributing towards their understandings of life in the Lot. I argue, therefore, that it is necessary to consider the intersections of imagination and subjective experience, accounting for both structure and agency in the ongoing constitution of a better way of life.

As the ethnography presented in this book has demonstrated, my respondents acted neither on the basis of their culture nor on that of their more individualized experiences. Instead it has become clear that imaginings and experiences intersected in the way that they understood their lives. Following Bourdieu (1977, 1990), I argue that it is therefore appropriate to consider the migrants' actions as evidence of a logic of practice, whereby their understandings of their lives result precisely from the interface between structural determinants and their own embodied experiences. Everyday practices mediated between the desire for a story of post-migration life that was specific to the individual, and expectations that were culturally designated. While this accounts for the process by which they developed their understandings of life in the Lot, the particular nature of the migrants' pursuit of a better way of life – a culturally prescribed desire for self-realization and distinction – brought the tension between imaginings and experience to the fore.

Ambivalence, transformation and middle-class dispositions

In part, post-migration ambivalence may be considered to emerge from the mismatch between lived experiences and ambitious expectations, and from the uncertainty as to how these may be reconciled. However, as can be seen in the migration narratives of my respondents, migration was often presented as the resolution of such feelings, leading to the question of what resemblance, if any, there is between post- and pre-migration ambivalence. As I have argued, it is possible to understand the ambivalence that characterized my respondents' lives as a more general ambivalence typical of the lives of contemporary individuals (Giddens 1990; Bauman 1991). This is one possible explanation for why the search for a better way of life was ongoing in the migrants' lives, even after migration, and for the constantly changing constitution of the end-goal. It also draws attention to the need to understand the intersection of this quest with processes of self-realization.

When considered within the context of original migration narratives, this persistence of ambivalence compromises the rhetoric of transformation underwriting the decision to migrate. It emerges that at most the life-changing potential of migration is discursive. Rather than being realized fully, it acts as a justificatory mechanism that consolidates the reasons behind migration. The full extent of the transformations the migrants had initially imagined was therefore unattainable. This is not to deny that migration results in significant changes in the migrants' daily lives. However, I argue that these subtle transformations were not just the result of the change of scenery; instead, these were brought about by the migrants' deliberate efforts to effect a change in their lifestyles.

Nevertheless, my respondents' belief in the transformative potential of migration had both purpose and meaning. In particular, it reinforced their overly idealistic perceptions of life in the Lot and made their migration possible. However, this rhetoric neglected the persistence of certain ways of thinking and behaving that were difficult to shake off and that remained inscribed on the migrants' bodies. Effecting the transformation that they desired was thus a considerably more complicated and time-intensive process than they had imagined initially. The migrants' class status and their familiarity with the workings of the globalized world therefore acted as barriers to the achievement of their alleged goals. This is somewhat ironic given that it was their middle-class predilection for rural living that had prompted their migration in the first place.

Following migration, the ideology of rural living and the desire for local belonging remained constant in the migrants' lives, framing their definitions of a better way of life. In particular, they associated it with the lives of their French neighbours, recalling their efforts to learn from these local actors and adhere to the principles and practices of the latter. On the one hand, the migrants' adoption of local cultural practices can be understood as indicators of their efforts to bridge the social distance between themselves and their French neighbours. In this respect, the migrants presented themselves as having a taste for necessity. This was in fact the product of their desire to distance themselves from the lavish tastes of luxury and once again locates them within the middle classes (see also Brooks 2000). While they presented rural living as a French aesthetic, it is understood better as a British middle-class taste for a perceived French aesthetic. Indeed, for some time, the purchases of a French property and long-term residence in rural France have been a part of the British middle-class cultural canon (Buller and Hoggart 1994a; Barou and Prado 1995; Tombs and Tombs 2007).

Viewed from this perspective, this form of lifestyle migration can be considered to be a culturally specific practice that favoured a particular aesthetic outlook and served to support and even augment the social status of individual migrants. The migration of my respondents was undoubtedly the result of their already relatively high levels of cultural capital. As I have argued elsewhere, lifestyle migration can be understood as the migration of relatively affluent individuals in search of a better way of life (Benson and O'Reilly 2009; O'Reilly and Benson 2009), where their affluence is reflected in levels of both cultural and economic capital. Their existing levels of capital thus allowed them to experiment with new ways of improving their social status. As I argue below, by mobilizing cultural, economic and social capital within a social space – their networks of friends and acquaintances acted as an audience for them to promote their new lives abroad – the migrants sought to acquire more capital. Nevertheless, my respondents' efforts at capital accumulation remained firmly rooted in their British middle-class dispositions.

Lifestyle migration as consumption

As the ethnography presented in this book has shown, while there were certain characteristics of a better way of life that my respondents agreed upon, their quests had an individualized quality about them. In other words, while the migrants appeared to agree on the ideal components of their improved lifestyle, they had very different ideas about how to achieve these and about the extent to which they would have to abandon their prior identities and practices. Their consumption practices in life following migration therefore reflected a variety of tastes; even on the level of the individual, in most cases these can be considered to be eclectic. Furthermore, their tastes concerning their lives in France changed over time (and subsequently their everyday routines and practices), in response to their lived experiences and as they built up their cultural competence.

As Bennett *et al.* have argued, 'the educated middle classes seek to position themselves through demonstrating competence in handling a diversity of cultural products' (2009: 178). In this rendering, distinction may be realized through competence at a range of cultural practices. Ongoing reflections about how to live in the Lot therefore acted as aesthetic judgements through which my respondents distinguished themselves from their British middle-class compatriots living in Britain and in other destinations, but also living locally. It therefore appears that my respondents' claims to distinctiveness lay in their ideologies for living, reflecting their unique beliefs about what constitutes a better way of life.

To a certain degree, through migration and their residence abroad, the migrants found themselves in a position where they had greater control over processes of distinction and status discrimination. It appeared that, to an extent, they were able to dictate the terms of their distinctiveness in ways that they had not felt were possible back in Britain. Through migration they had augmented their levels of symbolic capital, acting on imaginings that were significant to their peers. However, precisely because their migration was somewhat unusual when considered within the life-course trajectory of most middle-class Britons, and because they were operating outside the national boundaries of such class processes, my respondents had the power to reconstitute practices of status discrimination in ways which were of benefit to them. To a degree, these remained framed by their culture – indeed, they served to legitimate these lives led abroad – but they were more dynamic and negotiable than the processes which had characterized the migrants' pre-migration lives.

As I have shown, within their processes of social distinction it was not simply that the migrants identified people who did not have the knowledge and taste to live appropriately in the Lot; they located themselves on a continuum heading towards a better way of life. This was the aesthetic judgement of their own success in relation to that of their compatriots. At the far end of this continuum stood other migrants whom they revered for having achieved a better way of life. It was therefore possible to read their progress *en route* to their self-defined better way of life through their reflections on their position on the continuum from less to more authentic living. While the distance they had travelled could be measured, they were uncertain of how far they still had to go. It is clear that through these various processes of distinction, the migrants narrated their progress *en route* to a better way of life.

Throughout, the better way of life sought by my respondents maintained its idealized quality. Even when faced with the realities of life in the Lot, their goals for the future did not diverge from the established trajectory. However, the examination of the way they negotiated their daily lives revealed a more complex scenario, which often resulted in a curious mixture as they tried to combine their British tastes with French rural living. On the level of social relations, it became clear that the migrants maintained connections with their compatriots, both back in Britain and living locally, while at the same pursuing relationships with members of the local populace. While these were the nuanced realities of the migrant experience, my respondents nevertheless continued to aspire towards a better way of life characterized by full social and cultural integration. As I argue below, this reveals the extent to which an underlying middle-class cultural logic inspires my respondents' beliefs about the migrant experience. Whether full integration in their terms is achievable or not, this is the culture of migration within which they function and operationalize their claims for distinctiveness.

For the British living in the Lot, lifestyle migration was one step in a wider cultural process, broadly understood as the quest for a better way of life, whereby they continued to strive for social distinction among their peers (Benson 2009). The persistence of such classed dispositions demonstrates that the migrants' taste for life in rural France was not comparable to that of their French neighbours.

The ongoing search for an authentic life

As an ongoing characteristic of my respondents' lives, the quest for a better way of life cannot be explained, unlike in the literature on tourism, as something that takes place outside of everyday life; on the contrary, it was a central component of the way that my respondents understood and experienced these lives. The examination of how my respondents articulated this ongoing quest, the intersection of this with their identity-making processes, and the process by which their understandings of authentic living became more nuanced over time (impacting on their lived experiences), make the pursuit of a better way of life a particularly interesting topic for analysis.

I have argued that anthropological discussions of authenticity, derived largely from the literature on tourism, can be useful in explaining the persistence of this quest in everyday life. In particular, I have highlighted the value of the current literature on tourism in explaining migrant aspirations and expectations, and the role of these in subsequent lived experience. Indeed, although studies of lifestyle migration have often started from an interrogation of the cultural dimensions of migration, in more general research on migration this influence on migration practices has largely been overlooked. This is the result of the policy and problem-oriented focus that dominate contemporary migration research. Similarly, while migration is often explained in terms of pragmatic and rational economic models, much lifestyle migration research presents more individualized and emotivist accounts of migration and can therefore contribute to a renewed understanding of the complexity of the contemporary migrant experience.

The search for a better way of life is undoubtedly a cultural process, which, for my respondents, had a distinct taste framed by their rhetoric of the constraints that they experienced in their lives back in Britain. Life in the Lot, the rural idyll, clearly emerged as the antithesis of the lives they led in Britain. And although this better life required constant work to achieve, the migrants believed that after migration, their lives were more fulfilling and meaningful, even if they still had quite a distance to travel to fully realize their dreams. In this respect, not only was the quest for a better way of life intimately tied to the desire for difference and the reproduction of distinction: it was inherently connected to the migrants' self-realization projects. Indeed, migration often provided my respondents with access to new forms of self-expression that had not been available to them before. In their own perception, through migration to rural France they escaped the constraints that characterized their lives before migration and gained control over the future direction of their lives.

For my colleagues working with more bohemian respondents, lifestyle migration can be considered to be part of a spiritual quest as they seek new forms of spiritual engagement (D'Andrea 2007; Bousiou 2008; Korpela 2009a & b). The lives of such lifestyle migrants are characterized by their experimentation with new subjectivities and identities and their desire for expressive individualism (D'Andrea 2007). But it is the rhetoric behind these spiritualized quests that is more broadly applicable to my respondents and many other lifestyle migrants. Korpela (2009b) describes how her respondents – Westerners living part-time in Varanasi, India – define life in the 'Big Bad West(ern)' world as artificial, clearly opposed to their perceptions of life in Varanasi as authentic and natural. The spiritual, a key feature of their migration, therefore epitomizes their desire to overcome the inauthenticity of modern life, reflecting MacCannell's (1976) seminal argument about tourism. While the transformative potential of tourism has been questioned (Harrison 2003; Lindholm 2008), it is undeniable that the quest for authenticity underwrites many forms of tourism today.

As Bruner (2005) argues, such explanations of the tourist encounter rely on static understandings of culture and the meaning of objects and do not allow for the social processes through which authenticity is claimed. Furthermore, he stresses that relying on essentialized accounts of culture and authenticity, these explanations ignore the dynamic nature of authenticity, which, as culturally constructed, may shift and change over time. This leads me to question the value of such explanations for the lives of my respondents in the Lot beyond the basic reflections on the modern condition upon which they rest.

In previous research on the British living in rural France, scholars stressed that migration could be considered as the search for a better way of life (Buller and Hoggart 1994a; Barou and Prado 1995), but they did not examine the persistence of this quest in life following migration. It is therefore clear that the process of getting authenticity needs to be interrogated, both in terms of what the ongoing quest for a better way of life does for my respondents and what it reveals about their post-migration lives.

The role of authenticity

The migrants thus sought the authentic through their migration and through their everyday practices as they came to terms with their lives in the Lot. Their lives following migration can be characterized to a greater or lesser degree as engagement in forms of authentic consumption. They predominantly favoured homemade and locally produced foods and wines (*produits de terroir*), and getting their hands dirty by growing fruit and vegetables, which they then used in the preparation of preserves, chutneys, stews and frozen vegetables. And they demonstrated their extensive knowledge of local produce, another key component of authentic consumption (Lindholm 2008). In this manner, they appeared as connoisseurs of traditional and local foods. This is just one example of the way that authenticity manifested itself in their daily lives following migration, which demonstrates a cultural construction of authenticity that is recognizably romantic in origin, favouring purity and originality.

The flavour of authenticity

The individualized nature of the migrants' quest demonstrates a desire for an authentic self. In many ways, this is reflected in the migrants' rhetoric of self-realization, but it also reveals that the quest for a better way of life is a challenge through which they test their personal limits. Charles Lindholm, in a discussion of tourists, captures this duality, where personal authenticity is something to be discovered but which also challenges the individual:

> Adventurous, spiritually motivated tourists also want to get off the beaten track and venture deep into dangerous territory where they can test their physical and psychological limits and gain a heightened sense of who they really are. (2008: 39)

In the same manner, through their migration and their subsequent lifestyle choices, my respondents in the Lot put themselves to the test. This was, understandably, a risky strategy, but the end result was that they gained a feeling of personal self-worth. It was thus through lifestyle migration that the migrants gained an idea of who they could be; following migration they had the freedom to discover and experiment with their real selves as they moved closer towards the 'real' dream. Reflecting on the authenticity of their ways of living, they therefore contemplated their efforts to find themselves.

The migrants' beliefs about the appropriate way to live after migration, and their expectations about what they would discover about themselves, reflect romanticized and undeconstructed ideas about authenticity. Their persistent efforts to participate in local life significantly demonstrate an ideology of rediscovery made possible by an adherence to the mores and values of the authentic rurality that they have found in the Lot. In this manner, they believe that eventually they will be able to reach a level of authentic existence. In this respect, the question of what authenticity means to the migrants cannot be fully explained without recourse to the significance of rurality.

The concept of the rural idyll is the dominant discourse of rurality that inspires British migration to rural France (Buller and Hoggart 1994a; Barou and Prado 1995). This is equally a notion that has long influenced romantic renderings of authenticity in the Western world (Cohen 1988; Bruner 2005; Lindholm 2008). The coherence of rural society and the idea of untouched cultural traditions, as well as proximity to nature, are particularly significant to this understanding of authenticity. These themes are central to the migrants' ideas about how to live following migration. Authenticity and understandings of the rural idyll thus emerge as the markers by which the migrants are able to judge the relative success of their own lives against those of their compatriots.

Authenticity and distinction

Understood in this light, authenticity is intertwined with the processes of status discrimination in which my respondents engage and through which they gauge their individual process *en route* to a better way of life. Claims to authenticity are thus tied to claims for distinctiveness. It is this understanding of authenticity as a social process tied to the political economy of taste that lies at the core of discussions linking authenticity and consumption (see for example Bourdieu 1984; Appadurai 1986). In this rendering, it becomes possible to gain the authentic; Bourdieu (1984) argues that this goal is attained through the cultural acquisition of the authentic object, while Appadurai (1986) stresses that the end-point is achieved when the connoisseur learns how to claim the authentic. This allows for the possibility that my respondents might get to the better way of life that they seek if they are able to overcome all the obstacles in their way. Nevertheless, and as the ethnography presented in this book demonstrate, after migration, my respondents remained caught up in the quest for a more authentic way of living.

Bruner (2005) argues that the role of authenticity in processes of social distinction should be further developed, arguing that discussions of authenticity should shift to the question of who has the authority to authenticate (see also Bourdieu 1984). In this rendering, '[n]o longer is authenticity a property inherent in an object, forever fixed in time; instead it is a social process, a struggle in which competing interests argue for their own interpretations of history' (*ibid.* 2005: 163). The authentic or, in the case of my respondents, authentic living thus emerges as the site of struggles over social distinction. This interpretation allows for an understanding of the quest for authenticity as taking place, not in another time and place – as the literature on tourism often presents (see for example MacCannell 1976; Handler and Saxon 1988) – but within everyday life.

With authenticity understood in terms of its role within the political economy of taste, I question what the migrants gain from their continued engagement in the process of getting to the authentic. It seems that through migration my respondents gained increased control over the right to authenticate, providing 'expert testimony' (Lindholm 2008: 45) for their own lives. Nevertheless, this power was not absolute, as their continued efforts at getting to a better way of life demonstrated. As the migrants refined their ideas and knowledge of life in the Lot, hoping to gain an edge over their compatriots also living locally, they engaged 'in a never-ending cycle of enthusiasm, appropriation, imitation, and exhaustion' (*ibid.*: 62). The quest for authenticity was thus a meaningful process through which the migrants continually redefined their understandings of what constituted the better way of life that they sought.

Seeking authentication

Although my respondents gained some power to authenticate their lives through the process of migration, in order to maintain this, they had to convince others that they had the knowledge and skills to achieve authentic living, thus laying further claim to the authenticity of their lives. As Bourdieu (2000) argues, seeking authentication is an inherently risky process, particularly given that the real battleground for distinction lies in the question of who has the power to authenticate and legitimate perceptions of what is and is not authentic (see also Bourdieu 1984; Appadurai 1986; Bruner 2005).

The migrants' strategies for claiming authentication rested on their rhetoric of integration into local community life, demonstrating the continued influence of imagination on their actions and ambitions. In many ways, the reception given to them by their French neighbours played a key role in determining their success at getting to a better way of life. It was therefore common for migrants to stress that members of the local community received them positively. The migrants recalled neighbours who presented them in favourable terms, with comments such as: 'not like other Britons living in the Lot' and 'more French than British'. These recollections both served as claims to authenticity and drew attention to the fact that their new French friends recognized their post-migration lifestyles and efforts to become integrated. In this respect, the migrants valued these statements not only because they authenticated their experiences but also within the context of social distinction. The statements of their French neighbours witnessed to their efforts and successes at becoming local, a component of the post-migration lifestyle that was meaningful to a British middle-class audience.

My respondents who had not managed to bridge the cultural gap between themselves and the local French expressed their regret that this had not been possible. They listed a variety of reasons for this shortcoming, which ranged from statements about how unwelcoming the locals had been to their recognition that French social relations were often restricted to family. It was clear, however, that their inability to establish sustainable relationships with members of the local community adversely flavoured their experiences of life in the Lot. Some stressed that they might be tempted to leave – moving further south as they explained – while others insisted that they planned to keep trying.

It was predominantly through their relationships with their compatriots – friends and family in Britain, those living locally and those living in other destinations – that the migrants engaged in the struggle to authenticate their new lives. Through dialogue and interaction they once more engaged in processes of distinction, seeking recognition of and justification for their lives in the Lot. For the most part, they narrated their lives to an audience of their friends and families by drawing on a range of communicative technologies such as email, fax, telephone calls and face-to-face interaction. They demonstrated how they had actively changed their lifestyles to achieve a more fulfilling way of living, and while there were still improvements to make, they felt that they were continuing to make progress in this direction.

While they could not control fully the process of authentication, they influenced it through their awareness of the audience. In this rendering, the manner in which the better way of life was packaged became meaningful. Beyond its role in social distinction, authenticity, particularly as manifest in the rural idyll, appears to have made a double contribution to the migrants' search for a better way of life. It is evident that it influenced and directed beliefs about post-migration lifestyles, pre-ordaining the essential and desired components of these. By presenting their own efforts towards realizing rurality and locality, the migrants staged a convincing argument for the authentication of the decision to migrate and of their subsequent life experiences. Indeed, against the backdrop of the inauthenticity of social relations in modern society, the recourse to the perceived values of pre-modern society – the integration of community – demonstrated their resistance to the encroaching impersonality of life in Britain. While Lindholm argues that within the modern setting, 'individuals struggle to find satisfying and convincing ways to authenticate themselves' (2008: 66), my respondents drew on the trope of the rural idyll to present their lifestyle narratives to an audience of their compatriots. They thus expressed, in a persuasive and credible manner and to the best of their abilities, their 'real' selves, seeking authentication of their actions and lifestyles.

There is, however, an underlying paradox to such claims for authenticity and to the process of authentication more generally. On the one hand, Lindholm (2008) argues that authentication becomes possible through popularity and expert testimony. Indeed, for my respondents in the Lot, it was the popularity of rural France as a lifestyle migration destination and its recognizability within the middle-class cultural canon that made authentication of their lives there a more likely prospect. This was confirmed both in the expert testimony of local French actors and in the raft of travel-writing books dedicated to life in rural France (see for example Mayle 1989, 1990; Drinkwater 2001, 2003, 2004).

On the other hand, however, the migrants warned against overcrowding, stressing that they did not want the Lot to become overrun, as had happened in the Dordogne, and claiming that this threat might lead them to consider moving elsewhere. Through a conceptual lens focused on authenticity, it emerges that what the migrants feared was the possibility that their own lives would be perceived as less authentic as more people discovered the potential authenticity of the Lot. In this respect, the diminution of authenticity through overcrowding (MacCannell 1976; Lindholm 2008) was a perpetual concern for the migrants. In reality, I came across no examples of people having had to move on. Most of my respondents had come directly from Britain to the Lot; this was a primary migration. I argue that it was the momentous (emotional and economic) investment made in their new lifestyles and the recognition that transformation was a gradual process that kept my respondents in the Lot.

Authenticity and ambivalence

While migration was an attempt to escape their uncertainties about and dissatisfaction with life in Britain, the ethnography presented throughout this book has
demonstrated that for my respondents, post-migration life was equally characterized by ambivalence. Despite their attempts to mask this, an action that further
reinforced their rhetoric about migration, it soon became clear that their post-
migration ambivalence had a slightly different flavour from that which initially
motivated their migration. They were reminded of their outsider status – and the
degree to which they had been socially integrated into life back in Britain – as
they dealt with the more practical aspects of living in rural France and strived to
integrate into a new cultural context.

The persistence of ambivalence can nevertheless be understood as reflecting the more general ambivalence of individuals in the (late) modern world (see
for example Geertz 1975; Bauman 1991; Giddens 1990). In this rendering, the
migrants' efforts towards achieving distinction can be read as claims to ontological security, and thus as attempts to displace ambivalence. As the ethnography
demonstrates, they continued to make subtle changes in their lifestyles. Through
these actions they hoped to achieve the sense of uniqueness that lay at the core
of their quest. Their presentations of others as indistinct, and on occasion destructive, were one way in which they strived to displace their own feelings of
ambivalence.

Following Geertz (1975), I argue that the shifting boundaries of what the
migrants believe to be an authentic and different way of life revealed their continued efforts to become the authors of their own lives, augment their agency
and define the world in their own terms. As Geertz (1975) and Bauman (1991)
highlight, it is impossible to fully resolve the ambiguities of daily life; they are
symptomatic of the modern world. In this rendering, through the constant
re-assertion of their agency, the migrants could, at best, strive to keep their uncertainty and ambivalence at bay. It was therefore the case that my respondents
in the Lot developed various mechanisms to deal with the persistence of ambivalence in their lives, often incorporating ambivalence into their understanding
of the world through the redefinition of their aims and goals.

The complexity of the lifestyle migrant experience

My exploration of the everyday lives of the British residents of the Lot has
demonstrated that the decision to migrate is just one choice in a lifestyle trajectory that aims for a more fulfilling and meaningful way of living. Through the
pages of this book, it has become clear that the decision to migrate emerged from
a particular cultural framework that promoted rural France as the geographical
emplacement of the Arcadian dream. Furthermore, recognition of the cultural
logic behind migration aids in understanding the migrants' post-migration experiences as they struggled to reconcile their ambitions and expectations with
the realities of life in the Lot. As a result, life after migration was complex and
nuanced.

For my respondents living in the Lot, the end-point to their quest for a better way of life was articulated as a form of authentic living. They believed that this was uniquely available in their own particular corner of the Lot, manifest in local community life. In this respect, it became clear that their efforts to integrate into local populations were part of the process through which they believed they could achieve a better and more authentic way of life. This benchmark of social integration was a remnant of my respondents' British middle-class worldview – particularly the middle-class valorization of rural living – that nevertheless bounded their ideas about life following migration.

While they privileged a discourse of social integration into the local community and underplayed their transnational ties, it became clear that their relationships with their compatriots back in Britain and living locally remained an important source of emotional support. Their relationships with their compatriots did not, however, preclude the possibility of meaningful engagements with their French neighbours. They pursued these relationships with the local French in their desire to acquire certain elements of the local way of life, with varying degrees of success. In this respect, it became clear that the quest for authentic living, although articulated as the desire for local belonging, was in fact an existential statement. By distancing themselves from their compatriots and aligning themselves with local French actors, the migrants claimed that their lives were uniquely distinctive and that they were in the process of discovering their true selves.

While migration was an act through which the migrants were able to augment their individual agency, it emerged that the transformative potential of migration had been misconstrued in their individual migration narratives; the 'real' transformative potential of migration was not innate to migration but lay within the individuals themselves. Their ability to migrate had been made possible by their relatively high levels of capital and can in part be understood as a consumption choice. However, it also became evident that there was something about my respondents – an individual drive behind their migration – which meant that they took the initiative to act upon their ambitions to change their lives. Their self-presentations as 'pioneers', 'adventurers' and 'trailblazers' drew attention to the role that agency had played within their migration. Indeed, they highlighted the fate of many of their friends and family who were equally dissatisfied with their lives in Britain, but who had not done anything to improve their lot in life.

Lifestyle migration thus became an action through which my respondents authenticated their own ideas about themselves. Furthermore, as members of the British middle class, they continued to distinguish themselves from their compatriots, a process through which they were able to further authenticate and justify their unique lifestyle trajectories. In turn, the recognition of their post-migration lives, despite the fact that these remained in process, strengthened and reinforced their agency. In this respect, the act of migration plays a significant role within the transformation of individual lives as a result of how it is presented and how audiences respond to it.

Over time, it became evident that the quest for a better way of life was a process that continued until long after migration, as the migrants learned more about living in the Lot and settled into a new life. Their statements about their progress in this direction revealed their unique position *en route* to more authentic living. In this respect, their ambitions for life following migration were revealing of their subjectivities; seeking a different way of life, my respondents sought to transform their own lives and identities, a goal that reflected their ambivalence about life in the modern world.

For the British of the Lot, migration is not as transformative as was originally imagined. Instead it should be understood as one step in the (ongoing) process of getting to a better way of life. This is a lifelong endeavour that is intrinsically linked to the migrants' understandings of themselves and others and to their self-realization projects. The nature of the quest reflects particular ideologies of living, namely the desire to live within the rural idyll. However, the persistence of this quest is also telling, highlighting the extent to which the migrants continue to act on the basis of a middle-class culture. For now, it seems that only time will tell whether they will eventually escape from these structural constraints or whether they will forever continue to be haunted by the spectre of class.

Bibliography

Abram, S., and Waldren, J. (1997) 'Introduction: Tourists and Tourism – Identifying with People and Places', in S. Abram, J. Waldren and D. Macleod (eds) *Tourists and Tourism: Identifying with People and Places*, pp. 1–12 (Oxford: Berghahn).

Abramson, A. (2000) 'Mythical Lands, Legal Boundaries: Wondering about Landscape and Other Tracts', in A. Abramson and D. Theodossopoulos (eds) *Land, Law and Environment: Mythical Land, Legal Boundaries*, pp. 1–30 (London: Pluto Press).

Ackers, L., and Dwyer, P. (2004). 'Fixed Laws, Fluid Lives: The Citizenship Status of Post-retirement Migrants in the European Union', *Ageing and Society* 24, 451–475.

Agyeman, J., and Spooner, R. (1997) 'Ethnicity and the Rural Environment', in P. Cloke and J. Little (eds) *Contested Countryside Cultures*, pp. 190–210 (London: Routledge).

Ahmed, S., Castañeda, C., Fortier, A., and Sheller, M. (2003) *Uprootings/Regroudings: Questions of Home and Migration* (Oxford: Berg).

Amit, V. (2007) 'Structures and Dispositions of Travel and Movement', in V. Amit (ed.) *Going First Class? New Approaches to Privileged Travel and Movement*, pp. 1–14 (Oxford: Berghahn Books).

Anderson, B. (1983) *Imagined Communities: Reflections on the Origin and Spread of Nationalism* (London: Verso).

Anonymous (2004) 'Editorial', *Etnofoor* 17:1–2, 5–6.

Appadurai, A. (ed.) (1986) *The Social Life of Things: Commodities in Cultural Perspective* (New York: Cambridge University Press).

— (1996) *Modernity at Large: Cultural Dimensions of Globalization* (Minneapolis, MN: University of Minnesota Press).

— (2000) 'Grassroots Globalization and the Research Imagination', *Public Culture* 12:1, 1–19.

Ardagh, J. (2000) *France in the New Century: Portrait of a Changing Society* (London: Penguin).

Atkinson, W. (2008) 'Not All That Was Solid Has Melted into Air (or Liquid): A Critique of Bauman on Individualization and Class in Liquid Modernity', *Sociological Review* 56:1, 1–17.

Attan, C. (2006) 'Hidden Objects in the World of Cultural Migrants: Significant Objects Used by European Migrants to Layer Thoughts and Memories', in K. Burrell and P. Panayi (eds) *Histories and Memories: Migrants and their History in Britain*, pp. 171–188 (London: I.B. Tauris).

Aull Davies, C. (1999) *Reflexive Ethnography: A Guide to Researching Selves and Others* (London: Routledge).

Bailey, R. (2002) *Life in a Postcard: Escape to the French Pyrenees* (London: Bantam Books).

Bakalaki, A. (1997) 'Students, Natives, Colleagues: Encounters in Academia and in the Field', *Current Anthropology* 12:4, 502–526.

Barou, J., and Prado, P. (1995) *Les Anglais dans nos Campagnes* (Paris: L'Harmattan).

Bauman, Z. (1991) *Modernity and Ambivalence* (Cambridge: Polity Press).

— (1995) *Life in Fragments: Essays in Postmodern Morality* (Oxford: Blackwell).

— (1998) *Globalization: The Human Consequences* (Cambridge: Polity Press).

— (2000) *Liquid Modernity* (Cambridge: Polity Press).

— (2007) *Liquid Times: Living in an Age of Uncertainty* (Cambridge: Polity Press).

— (2008) *The Art of Life* (Cambridge: Polity Press).

Becker, G. (1997) *Disrupted Lives: How People Create Meaning in a Chaotic World* (Berkeley, CA: University of California Press).

Bell, M., and Ward, G. (2000) 'Comparing Temporary Mobility with Permanent Migration', *Tourism Geographies* 2:1, pp. 97–107.

Bell, P. (2004) 'The Narrowing Channel', in R. Mayne, D. Johnson and R. Tombs (eds) *Cross Channel Currents: 100 Years of the Entente Cordiale*, pp. 245–255 (London: Routledge).

Bender, B. (1993) 'Introduction: Landscape – Meaning and Action', in B. Bender (ed.) *Landscape: Politics and Perspectives*, pp. 1–18 (Oxford: Berg).

— (1998) *Stonehenge: Making Space* (Oxford: Berg).

Bendix, R. (1997) *In Search of Authenticity: The Formation of Folklore Studies*. Madison (Madison, WI: University of Wisconsin Press).

Bennett, T., Savage, M., Silva, E., Warde, A., Gayo-Cal, M., and Wright, D. (2009) *Culture, Class, Distinction* (London: Routledge).

Benson, M. (2009) 'A Desire for Difference: British Lifestyle Migration to Southwest France', in M. Benson and K. O'Reilly (eds) *Lifestyle Migration: Expectations, Aspirations and Experiences*, pp. 121–136 (Farnham: Ashgate).

— (2010a) 'The Context and Trajectory of Lifestyle Migration: The Case of the British Residents of Southwest France', *European Societies* forthcoming.

— (2010b) 'We're Not Expats; We Are Not Migrants; We Are Sauliaçoise': Laying Claim to Belonging in Rural France', in B. Bonisch-Brednich and C. Trundle (eds) *Local Lives: Migration and the Micro-politics of Place* (Farnham: Ashgate).

Benson, M., and O'Reilly, K. (2009) 'Migration and the Search for a Better Way of Life: A Critical Exploration of Lifestyle Migration', *Sociological Review* 57:4, 608–625.

Bésingrand, D. (2004) 'Les Maires Face à la Mobilité Résidentielle de Retraite sur la Façade Atlantique Française : Variations entre Bienveillance, Indifférence et Dédain', Unpublished conference paper presented at UMR Espaces Géographiques et Sociétés, Rennes, 21 and 22 October.

Betty, C., and Cahill, M. (1999) 'British Expatriates' Experience of Health and Social Services on the Costa del Sol', in F. Anthias and G. Lazaridis (eds) *Into the Margins: Migration and Social Exclusion in Southern Europe*, pp. 83–113 (Aldershot: Avebury).

Boissevain, J. (1996) 'Introduction', in J. Boissevain (ed.) *Coping with Tourists: European Responses to Mass Tourism*, pp. 1–26 (Oxford: Berghahn).

Bottero, W. (2004) 'Class Identities and the Identity of Class', *Sociology* 38:5, 985–1003.

Bourdieu, P. (1962) 'Célibat et Condition Paysanne', *Etudes Rurales* 5–6, 32–135.

— (1977) *Outline of a Theory of Practice* (Cambridge: Cambridge University Press (R. Nice trans.)).

— (1980) 'L'Identité et la Représentation: Eléments pour une Réflexion Critique sur l'Idée de Région', *Actes de la Recherche en Sciences Sociales* 35, 63–72.

— (1984) *Distinction: A Social Critique of the Judgement of Taste* (London: Routledge and Kegan Paul (R. Nice trans.)).

— (1990) *The Logic of Practice* (Cambridge: Polity (R. Nice trans.)).

— (2000) *Pascalian Meditations* (Cambridge: Polity Press (R. Nice trans.)).

— (2002) *Le Bal des Célibataires: Crise de la Société Paysanne en Béarn* (Paris: Editions du Seuil).

Bousiou, P. (2008) *The Nomads of Mykonos: Performing Liminalities in a 'Queer' Space* (Oxford: Berghahn).

Brewer, J. (1997) *The Pleasures of the Imagination* (London: Harper Collins).

Brooks, D. (2000) *Bobos in Paradise: The New Upper Middle Class and How They Got There* (New York: Simon and Schuster).

Brown, K., and Theodossopoulos, D. (2004) 'Others' Others: Talking About Stereotypes and Constructions of Otherness in Southeast Europe', *History and Anthropology* 15:1, 3–14.

Bruillon, M. (2007) 'A Peculiarly British Sense of Adventure? The Discourse of Emigrants', in C. Geoffrey and R. Sibley (eds) *Going Abroad: Travel, Tourism and Migration*, pp. 132–143 (Cambridge: Cambridge Scholars Publishing).

Bruner, E. (1991) 'Transformation of Self in Tourism', *Annals of Tourism Research* 18, 238–250.

— (2005) *Culture on Tour: Ethnographies of Travel* (Chicago, IL, and London: University of Chicago Press).

Bruner, J. (1990) *Acts of Meaning* (Cambridge, MA: Harvard University Press).

Bruter, M. (2005) *Citizens of Europe? The Emergence of Mass European Identity* (Basingstoke: Palgrave).

Buller, H. (2008) 'Du Côté de Chez Smith: Reflections on an Enduring Research Object', in J-P. Diry (ed.) *Les Etrangers dans les Campagnes* (Clermont-Ferrand: Presses Universitaires Blaise Pascal).

Buller, H., and Hoggart, K. (1994a) *International Counterurbanization* (Aldershot: Avebury).

— (1994b) 'British Home Owners in Rural France: Property Selection and Characteristics' (King's College, London: Department of Geography Occasional Paper 36).

— (1994c) 'The Social Integration of British Home Owners into French Rural Communities', *Journal of Rural Studies* 10:2, 197–210.

Burkitt, I. (2005) 'Situating Auto/Biography: Biography and Narrative in the Times and Places of Everyday Life', *Auto/Biography* 13, 93–110.

Burrell, K. (2008) 'Managing, Learning and Sending: The Material Lives and Journeys of Polish Women in Britain', *Journal of Material Culture* 13:1, 63–83.

Carrier, J. (1995) *Gifts and Commodities: Exchange and Western Capitalism Since 1700* (London: Routledge).

— (2003) 'Mind, Gaze and Engagement: Understanding the Environment', *Journal of Material Culture* 8:1, 5–23.

Casado-Díaz, M. Á. (2006) 'Retiring to Spain: An Analysis of Difference Among North European Nationals', *Journal of Ethnic and Migration Studies* 32:8, 1321–1339.

Casado-Díaz, M., Kaiser, C., and Warnes, A. (2004) 'Northern European Retired Residents in Nine Southern European Areas: Characteristics, Motivations and Adjustment', *Ageing and Society* 24:3, 353–381.

Castles, S., and Miller, M. (2003) *The Age of Migration: International Population Movements in the Modern World* (London: Macmillan).

Castoriadis, C. (1987) *The Imaginary Institution of Society* (Cambridge, MA: MIT Press (K. Blamey trans.)).

Chevalier, S. (1998) 'From Woollen Carpet to Grass Carpet: Bridging House and Garden in an English Suburb', in Miller D. (ed.) *Material Cultures: Why Some Things Matter*, pp. 47–72 (Chicago, IL: University of Chicago Press).

Cieraad, I. (1999) 'Introduction: Anthropology at Home', in I. Cieraad (ed.) *At Home: An Anthropology of Domestic Space*, pp. 1–12 (Syracuse, NY: Syracuse University Press).

Clarke, A. (2001) 'The Aesthetics of Social Aspiration', in D. Miller (ed.) *Home Possessions: Material Culture Behind Closed Doors*, pp. 23–46 (Oxford and New York: Berg).

— (2002) 'Taste Wars and Design Dilemmas: Aesthetic Practice in the Home', in C. Painter (ed.) *Contemporary Art and the Home*, pp. 131–152 (Oxford: Berg).

Cloke, P. (2006) 'Rurality and Racialized Others: Out of Place in the Countryside', in P. Cloke, T. Marsden, and P. Mooney (eds) *Handbook of Rural Studies*, pp. 379–387 (London: SAGE).

Cloke, P., and Jones, O. (2001) 'Dwelling, Place, and Landscape: An Orchard in Somerset', *Environment and Planning A* 33:4, 649–666.

Cohen, A. (1982) 'Belonging: the Experience of Culture', in A. Cohen (ed.) *Belonging: Identity and Social Organisation in British Rural Communities*, pp. 1–18 (Manchester: Manchester University Press).

— (1985) *The Symbolic Construction of Community* (London and New York: Routledge).

Cohen, E. (1988) 'Authenticity and Commoditization in Tourism', *Annals of Tourism Research* 15, 371–386.

Coleman, S., and Collins, P. (2006) 'Introduction: "Being…Where?" Performing Fields on Shifting Grounds', in S. Coleman and P. Collins (eds) *Locating the Field: Space, Place and Context in Anthropology*, pp. 1–22 (Oxford: Berg).

Coleman, S., and Crang, M. (2002) 'Grounded Tourists, Travelling Theory', in S. Coleman and M. Crang (eds) *Tourism: Between Place and Performance*, pp. 1–20 (Oxford: Berghahn).

Cosgrove, D. (2006) 'Modernity, Community and the Landscape Idea', *Journal of Material Culture* 11:1–2, 49–66.

Crang, M. (1996) 'Living History: Magic Kingdoms or a Quixotic Quest for Authenticity? *Annals of Tourism Research* 23:2, 415–431.

D'Andrea, A. (2007) *Global Nomads: Techno and New Age as Transnational Counterculture in Ibiza and Goa* (London: Routledge).

Dant, T. (1999) *Material Culture in the Social World* (Buckingham and Philadelphia, PA: Open University Press).

Depierre, F., and Guitard, F. (2006) *L'Accueil et l'Installation des Nord-Europeens en Limousin, l'Exemple des Britanniques: Quel Poids, Quels Effets, Quelles Perspectives?* (Rapport de Stage, Conseil Régional du Limousin et Université de Limoges).

Dittmar, H. (1992) *The Social Psychology of Material Possessions* (Hemel Hempstead: Harvester Wheatsheaf).

Dodd, J. (2007) *The Rough Guide to the Dordogne and the Lot* (London: Rough Guides).

Douglas, M. (1966) *Purity and Danger: An Analysis of Concepts of Pollution and Taboo* (London: Routledge and Kegan Paul).

— (1987) *Constructive Drinking: Perspectives on Drink from Anthropology* (Cambridge: Cambridge University Press).

Douglas, M., and Isherwood, B. (1978) *The World of Goods* (London: Allen Lane).

Drake, H., and Collard, S. (2008) 'A Case Study of Intra-EU migration. 20 Years of "Brits" in the *Pays d'Auge*, Normandy, France', *French Politics* 6:3, 214–233.

Drinkwater, C. (2001) *The Olive Farm: A Memoir of Life, Love and Olive Oil in the South of France* (London: Abacus).

— (2003) *The Olive Season: Amour, A New Life and Olives Too* (London: Abacus).

— (2004) *The Olive Harvest: A Memoir of Love, Life and Olives in the South of France* (London: Weidenfeld and Nicolson).

Fabricant, C. (1998) 'Riding the Waves of Postcolonial Migrancy: Are We Really in the Same Boat?' *Diaspora* 7:1, 25–52.

Faist, T. (2000) *The Volume and Dynamics of International Migration and Transnational Social Spaces* (Oxford: Oxford University Press).

Fassin, D. (2001) 'The Biopolitics of Otherness: Undocumented Foreigners and Racial Discrimination in French Public Debate', *Anthropology Today* 17:1, 3–7.

Favell, A. (2008) *Eurostars and Eurocities* (Oxford: Blackwell).

Featherstone, M. (1991) *Consumer Culture and Postmodernism* (London: SAGE).

Feld, S., and Basso, K. (1996) *Senses of Place* (Santa Fe, NM: School of American Research Press).

Findlay, A. and Rogerson, R. (1993) 'Migration, Places and Quality of Life: Voting with their Feet', in A. Champion (ed.) *Population Matters*, pp. 33–49 (London: Paul Chapman).

Fine, G. (2003) 'Crafting Authenticity: The Validation of Self-taught Art', *Theory and Society* 32:2, 153–180.

Frank, A. (2002) 'Why Study People's Stories? The Dialogical Ethics of Narrative Analysis', *International Journal of Qualitative Methods* 1:1, 1–20.

Frankenberg, R. (1966) *Communities in Britain: Social Life in Town and Country* (Harmondsworth: Penguin Books).

Franklin, A. (2003) *Tourism: An Introduction* (London: SAGE).

Garriaud-Maylam, J. (2004) 'The French in Britain', in R. Mayne, D. Johnson, and R. Tombs (eds) *Cross Channel Currents: 100 Years of the Entente Cordiale*, pp. 271–274 (London: Routledge).

Geertz, C. (1975) *The Interpretation of Cultures: Selected Essays* (London: Hutchinson).

Gergen, K., and Gergen, M. (1988) 'Narrative and the Self as Relationship', in L. Berkowitz (ed.) *Advances in Experimental Social Psychology*, pp. 211–244 (New York: Academic).

Gervais-Aguer, M. (2004) *Les Fondements de l'Attractivité Territoriale Résidentielle: Les Enseignements d'une Recherche Portant sur les Résidents Britanniques en Aquitaine (France)* (Cahiers du GRES 2004-25).

— (2006) *Prospective Analysis, Residential Choice and Territorial Attractiveness* (Cahiers du GRES 2006-30).

— (2008) 'Les Britanniques et l'Installation en France: Une Attractivité Territoriale à Approfondir', in J-P. Diry (ed.) *Les Étrangers dans les Campagnes* (Clermont-Ferrand: Presses Universitaires Blaise Pascal).

Giddens, A. (1990) *The Consequences of Modernity* (Cambridge: Polity Press).

— (1991) *Modernity and Self-Identity: Self and Society in the Late Modern Age* (Cambridge: Polity Press).

Glover, W. (2004) '"A Feeling of Absence from Old England:" The Colonial Bungalow', *Home Cultures* 1:1, 61–82.

Graburn, N. (1989) 'Tourism: the Sacred Journey', in V. Smith (eds) *Hosts and Guests: The Anthropology of Tourism* (2nd edn), pp. 21–36 (Philadelphia, PA: University of Pennsylvania Press).

Greenwood, D. (1989) 'Culture by the Pound: An Anthropological Perspective on Tourism as Cultural Commoditization', in V. Smith (ed.) *Hosts and Guests: The Anthropology of Tourism*, pp. 171–186 (Philadelphia, PA: University of Pennsylvania Press).

Greverus, I-M., and Römhild, R. (2000) 'The Politics of Anthropology at Home: Some Final Reflections', in C. Giordano, I-M. Greverus and R. Römhild (eds) *The Politics of Anthropology at Home II*, pp. 191–198 (Berlin, Hamburg, Münster: LIT Verlag).

Grundy, S., and Jamieson, L. (2007) 'European Identities: From Absent-Minded Citizens to Passionate Europeans', *Sociology* 41:4, 663–680.

Gunn, S. (2005) 'Translating Bourdieu: Cultural Capital and the English Middle Class in Historical Perspective', *British Journal of Sociology* 56:1, 49–64.

Gupta, A., and Ferguson, J. (1992) 'Beyond "Culture": Space, Identity and the Politics of Difference', *Cultural Anthropology* 7:1, 6–23.

Gustafson, P. (2001) 'Retirement Migration and Transnational Lifestyles', *Ageing and Society* 21:4, 371–394.

— (2002) 'Tourism and Seasonal Retirement Migration', *Annals of Tourism Research* 29:4, 899–918.

Halfacree, K. (1994) 'The Importance of "the Rural" in the Constitution of Counter-urbanization: Evidence from England in the 1980s', *Sociologia Ruralis* 34:2–3, 164–189.

Halfacree, K., and Boyle, P. (1993) 'The Challenge Facing Migration Research: The Case for a Biographical Approach', *Progress in Human Geography* 17:3, 333–348.

Hall, C.M., and Müller, D. (2004) 'Introduction: Second Homes, Curse of Blessing? Revisited', in C. Hall and D. Müller (eds) *Tourism, Mobility and Second Homes: Between Elite Landscape and Common Ground*, pp. 3–14 (Clevedon: Channel View Publications).

Hammersley, M., and Atkinson, P. (1995) *Ethnography: Principles in Practice* (London: Routledge).

Hampshire, D. (2003) (5th Edt.) *Living and Working in France* (London: Survival Books).

Handler, R. (1986) 'Authenticity', *Anthropology Today* 2:1, 2–4.

Handler, R., and Saxton, W. (1988) 'Dyssimulation: Reflexivity, Narrative and the Quest for Authenticity in "Living"', *Cultural Anthropology* 3:3, 242–60.

Hannerz, U. (2006) 'Studying Down, Up, Sideways, Through, Backwards, Forwards, Away and at Home: Reflections on the Field Worries of an Expansive Discipline', in S. Coleman and P. Collins (eds) *Locating the Field: Space, Place and Context in Anthropology*, pp. 23–42 (Oxford: Berg).

Hargreaves, A. (1995) *Immigration, 'Race' and Ethnicity in Contemporary France* (London: Routledge).

Harrison, J. (2003) *Being a Tourist: Finding Meaning in Pleasure Travel* (Vancouver and Toronto: UBC Press).

Harvey, D. (1989) *The Condition of Postmodernity: An Enquiry into the Origins of Cultural Change* (Oxford: Basil Blackwell).

Hastrup, K., and Fog Olwig, K. (1997) 'Introduction', in K. Hastrup and K. Fog Olwig, (eds). *Siting Culture: The Shifting Anthropological Object*, pp. 1–16 (London: Routledge).

Hecht, A., 'Home Sweet Home: Tangible Memories of an Uprooted Childhood', in D. Miller, *Home Possessions: Material Culture Behind Closed Doors*, pp. 123–145.

Herzfeld, M. (1992) *The Social Problem of Indifference: Exploring the Symbolic Roots of Western Bureaucracy* (Chicago, IL: University of Chicago Press).

— (1997) *Cultural Intimacy: Social Poetics in the Nation-State* (London and New York: Routledge).

Hirsch, E. (1995) 'Introduction. Landscape: Between Place and Space', in E. Hirsch and M. O'Hanlon (eds) *The Anthropology of Landscape*, pp. 1–30 (Oxford: Clarendon Press).

Hoey, B. (2005) 'From Pi to Pie: Moral Narratives of Noneconomic Migration and Starting Over in the Postindustrial Midwest', *Journal of Contemporary Ethnography* 34:5, 586–624.

— (2006) 'Grey Suit or Brown Carhartt: Narrative Transition, Relocation and Reorientation in the Lives of Corporate Refugees', *Journal of Anthropological Research*, 62:3, 347–371.

Howes, D. (2005) 'Introduction', in D. Howes (ed.) *Empire of the Senses: The Sensory Culture Reader*, pp. 1–17 (Oxford: Berg).

Hurdley, R. (2006) 'Dismantling Mantelpieces: Narrating Identities and Materializing Culture in the Home', *Sociology* 40:4, 717–733.

Ingold, T. (1993) 'The Temporality of Landscape', *World Archaeology* 25:2, 152–174.

— (1995) 'Building, Dwelling, Living: How Animals and People Make Themselves at Home in the World', in M. Strathern (ed.) *Shifting Contexts: Transformations in Anthropological Knowledge*, pp. 57–80 (London and New York: Routledge).

Ingold, T., and Lee Vergunst, J. (2008) *Ways of Walking: Anthropology and Practice on Foot* (Aldershot: Ashgate).

INSEE (2005) *Les Immigrés en France* (Paris: INSEE).

— (n.d.) *The Population Census*, Online at: www.insee.fr/en/bases-de-donnees/default.asp?page=recensements.htm [Accessed 22 November 2009].

Jackson, A. (1987) 'Reflections on Ethnography at Home and the ASA', in A. Jackson (ed.) *Anthropology at Home*, pp. 1–15 (London: Tavistock).

Jackson, M. (2002) *The Politics of Storytelling: Violence, Transgression and Intersubjectivity* (Copenhagen: Museum Tusculanum Press).

Johnson, M., and Clisby, S. (2008) 'Both "One" and "Other": Environmental Cosmopolitanism and the Politics of Hybridity in Costa Rica', *Nature and Culture* 3:1, 63–81.

Kidd, A., and Nicholls, D. (1999) (eds) *Gender, Civic Culture and Consumerism* (Manchester: Manchester University Press).

King, R., and Patterson, G. (1998) 'Diverse Paths: The Elderly British in Tuscany', *International Journal of Population Geography* 4:2, 157–182.

King, R., Warnes, A., and Williams, A. (2000) *Sunset Lives: British Retirement Migration to the Mediterranean* (Oxford: Berg).

Korpela, M. (2009a) *More Vibes in India* (Tampere, Finland: University of Tampere Press).

— (2009b) 'When a Trip to Adulthood becomes a Lifestyle: Western Lifestyle Migrants in Varanasi, India', in M. Benson and K. O'Reilly (eds) *Lifestyle Migration: Expectations, Aspirations and Experiences*, pp. 15–30 (Farnham: Ashgate).

Langellier, K. M., and Peterson, E. E. (2004) *Storytelling in Daily Life: Performing Narrative* (Philadelphia, PA: Temple University).

Lee, J., and Ingold, T. (2006) 'Fieldwork on Foot: Perceiving, Routing, Socialising', in S. Coleman and P. Collins (eds) *Locating the Field: Space, Place and Context in Anthropology*, pp. 67–86 (Oxford: Berg Publishers).

Levitt, P., and Glick Schiller, N. (2004) 'Conceptualizing Simultaneity: A Transnational Social Field Perspective on Society', *International Migration Review* 38:3, 1002–1039.

Lindholm, C. (2002) 'Authenticity, Anthropology, and the Sacred', *Anthropological Quarterly* 75:2, 331–338.

— (2008) *Culture and Authenticity* (Oxford: Blackwell Publishing).

MacCannell, D. (1976) *The Tourist: A New Theory of the Leisure Class* (London: Macmillan).

— (1992) *Empty Meeting Grounds: The Tourist Papers* (London: Routledge).

MacDonald, S. (1997) 'A People's Story: Heritage, Identity and Authenticity', in C. Rojek and J. Urry (eds) *Touring Cultures: Transformations of Travel and Theory*, pp. 155–175 (London: Routledge).

Macnaghten, P., and Urry, J. (1998) *Contested Natures* (London: SAGE).

Maines, D. (1993) 'Narrative's Moment and Sociology's Phenomena: Toward a Narrative Sociology', *Sociological Quarterly* 34:1, 17–38.

Mallett, S. (2004) 'Understanding Home: A Critical Review of the Literature', *Sociological Review* 52:1, 62–89.

Massey, D. (1994) *Space, Place and Gender* (Cambridge: Polity Press).

— (2006) 'Landscape as a Provocation: Reflections on Moving Mountains', *Journal of Material Culture* 11:1–2, 33–48.

Mauss, M. (1954) *The Gift: Forms and Functions of Exchange in Archaic Societies* (London:

Cohen and West (I. Cunnison trans.)).

Mayle, P. (1989) *A Year in Provence* (London: Pan Books).

— (1990) *Toujours Provence* (London: Pan Books).

McDonald, M. (1993) 'An Anthropological Approach to Stereotypes', in S. Macdonald (eds) *Inside European Identities*, pp. 219–236 (Oxford: Berg).

McHugh, K. (2000) 'Inside, Outside, Upside Down, Backward, Forward, Round and Round: A Case for Ethnographic Studies in Migration', *Progress in Human Geography* 24:1, 71–89.

McWatters, M. (2008) *Residential Tourism: (De)Constructing Paradise* (Bristol: Channel View Publications).

Miller, D. (1987) *Material Culture and Mass Consumption* (Oxford: Basil Blackwell).

— (1998) 'Why Some Things Matter', D. Miller (ed.) *Material Cultures: Why Some Things Matter*, pp. 3–21 (Chicago, IL: The University of Chicago Press).

— (2001) 'Behind Closed Doors', in D. Miller (ed.) *Home Possessions: Material Culture Behind Closed Doors*, pp. 1–19 (Oxford and New York: Berg).

— (2002) 'Accommodating', in C. Painter (ed.) *Contemporary Art and the Home*, pp. 115–130 (Oxford: Berg).

Morgan, D. (2005) 'Revisiting "Communities in Britain"', *Sociological Review* 53:4, 641–657.

Moss, R. (2003) 'The Lure of the Lot', *Everything France* 16, 26–27.

Müller, D. (2002) 'German Second Home Development in Sweden', in C. Hall and A. Williams (eds) *Tourism and Migration: New Relations Between Production and Consumption*, pp. 169–186 (Dordrecht: Kluwer Academic Publishers).

Neal, S. (2002) 'Rural Landscapes, Representations and Racism: Examining Multicultural Citizenship and Policy-Making in the English Countryside', *Ethnic and Racial Studies* 25:3, 442–461.

Neame, M. (2004) 'Lot: The Place that Time Forgot', *French Times* 8, 13–19.

Noiriel, G. (1996) *The French Melting Pot: Immigration, Citizenship, and National Identity* (Minneapolis, MN: University of Minnesota Press (G. de Laforcade trans.)).

Nudrali, O., and O'Reilly, K. (2009) 'Taking the Risk: The Britons of Didim, Turkey', in M. Benson and K. O'Reilly (eds) *Lifestyle Migration: Expectations, Aspirations and Experiences*, pp. 137–152 (Farnham: Ashgate).

O'Reilly, K. (2000) *The British on the Costa del Sol: Transnational Identities and Local Communities* (London: Routledge).

— (2003) 'When Is a Tourist? The Articulation of Tourism and Migration in Spain's Costa del Sol', *Tourist Studies* 3:3, 301–317.

— (2007) 'Intra-European Migration and the Mobility-Enclosure Dialectic', *Sociology* 41:2, 277–293.

O'Reilly, K., and Benson, M. (2009) 'Lifestyle Migration: Escaping to the Good Life', in M. Benson and K. O'Reilly (eds) *Lifestyle Migration: Expectations, Aspirations and Experiences*, pp. 1–14 (Farnham: Ashgate).

Ochs, E., and Capp, L. (2001) *Living Narrative: Creating Lives in Everyday Storytelling* (Cambridge, MA, and London: Harvard University Press).

Okely, J. (1996) *Own or Other Culture* (London: Routledge).

Oliver, C. (2007) 'Imagined Communitas: Older Migrants and Aspirational Mobility', in V. Amit (ed.) *Going First Class? New Approaches Towards Privileged Movement and Travel*, pp. 126–143 (Oxford: Berghahn).

— (2008) *Retirement Migration: Paradoxes of Ageing* (London: Routledge).

Oliver, C., and O'Reilly, K. (2010) 'A Bourdieusian Analysis of Class and Migration: Habitus and the Individualising Process', *Sociology* 44:1, 49–66.

Olwig, K. (2007) 'Privileged Travelers? Migration Narratives in Families of Middle-Class

Caribbean Background', in V. Amit (ed.) *Going First Class? New Approaches Towards Privileged Movement and Travel*, pp. 87–102 (Oxford: Berghahn).

Ong, A. (1999) *Flexible Citizenship: The Cultural Logics of Transnationalism* (Durham and London: Duke University Press).

Pan Ké Shon, J-L. (2007) 'The New French Census and its Impact on Mobility Studies', *Population* 62:1, 119–137.

Papastergiadis, N. (2000) *The Turbulence of Migration: Globalization, Deterritorialization and Hybridity* (Cambridge: Polity Press).

Parkin, D. (1999) 'Mementoes as Transitional Objects in Human Displacement', *Journal of Material Culture* 4:3, 303–320.

Perry, R. (1986) *Counterurbanisation: International Case Studies of Socio-Economic Change in the Rural Areas* (Norwich: Geo Books).

Plummer, K. (2007) 'The Call of Life Stories in Ethnographic Research', in P. Atkinson et al. (eds) *Handbook of Ethnography*, pp. 395–306 (London: SAGE).

Polkinghorne, N. (1991) 'Narrative and the Self-Concept', *Journal of Narrative and Life History* 1, 135–153.

Putnam, T. (1993) 'Beyond the Modern Home: Shifting the Parameters of Residence', in J. Bird, B. Curtis, T. Putnam, G. Robertson and L. Tickner (eds) *Mapping the Futures: Local Cultures, Global Change*, pp. 150–165 (London: Routledge).

Rapport, N. (1993) *Diverse World-Views in an English Village* (Edinburgh: Edinburgh University Press).

Rapport, N., and Dawson, A. (1998) (eds) *Migrants of Identity: Perceptions of Home in a World of Movement* (Oxford: Berg).

Reay, D. (2008) 'Psychosocial Aspects of White Middle-Class Identities: Desiring and Defending against the Class and Ethnic "Other" in Urban Multi-Ethnic Schooling', *Sociology* 42:6, 1072–1088.

Reed-Danahay, D. (1996) *Education and Identity in Rural France: The Politics of Schooling* (Cambridge: Cambridge University Press).

Reimer, S., and Leslie, D. (2004) 'Identity, Consumption and the Home', *Home Cultures* 1:2, 187–208.

Robertson, R. (1992) *Globalization: Social Theory and Global Culture* (London: Sage).

Rodríguez, V. (2001) 'Tourism as a Recruiting Post for Retirement Migration', *Tourism Geographies* 3:1, 52–63.

Rodríguez, V., Fernández-Mayoralas, G., and Rojo, F. (1998) 'European Retirees on the Costa del Sol: A Cross-National Comparison', *International Journal of Population Geography* 4:2, 91–111.

Rogers, S. (1991) *Shaping Modern Times in Rural France* (Princeton, NJ: Princeton University Press).

Rosenwald, G. (1992) 'Conclusion: Reflections on Narrative Self-Understanding', in G. Rosenwald and R. Ochberg (eds) *Storied Lives. The Cultural Politics of Self-Understanding*, pp. 265–289 (New Haven, CT, and London: Yale University Press).

Rozenberg, D. (1995) 'International Tourism and Utopia: The Balearic Islands', in M. Lanfant, J. Allcock, and E. Bruner (eds) *International Tourism: Identity and Change* (London: SAGE).

Savage, M., Bagnall, G., and Longhurst, B. (2005) *Globalization and Belonging* (London: SAGE).

Savage, M., Barlow, J., Dickens, P., and Fielding, T. (1992) *Property, Bureaucracy and Culture: Middle-class Formation in Contemporary Britain* (London: Routledge).

Schmied, D. (2005) *Winning and Losing: The Changing Geography of Europe's Rural Areas*

(Aldershot: Ashgate).

Scott, J. (2002) 'Class and Stratification in Late Modernity', *Acta Sociologica* 45:1, 23–35.

Scott, S. (2004) 'Transnational Exchanges amongst Skilled British Migrants in Paris', *Population, Space and Place* 10:5, 391–410.

— (2006) 'The Social Morphology of Skilled Migration: The Case of the British Middle Class in Paris', *Journal of Ethnic and Migration Studies* 32:7, 1105–1129.

Segalen, M. (1983) *Love and Power in the Peasant Family: Rural France in the Nineteenth Century* (Oxford: Blackwell (S. Matthews trans.)).

Segalen, M. (1991) *Fifteen Generations of Bretons: Kinship and Society in Lower Brittany, 1720–1980* (Cambridge: Cambridge University Press (J. Underwood trans.)).

Selwyn, T. (1996) 'Introduction', in T. Selwyn (ed.) *The Tourist Images: Myths and Myth Making in Tourism*, pp. 1–32 (Chichester: John Wiley and Sons).

Sennett, R. (1998) *The Corrosion of Character: The Personal Consequences of Work in the New Capitalism* (New York: W. W. Norton).

Silverman, M. (1992) *Deconstructing the Nation: Immigration, Racism and Citizenship in Modern France* (London and New York: Routledge).

Smallwood, D. (2007) 'The Integration of British Migrants in Aquitaine', in C. Geoffrey and R. Sibley (eds) *Going Abroad: Travel, Tourism and Migration*, pp. 119–131 (Cambridge: Cambridge Scholars Publishing).

Smith, J. (1993) 'The Lie that Blinds: Destabilizing the Text of Landscape', in J. Duncan and D. Ley (eds) *Place/Culture/Representation*, pp. 78–92 (London: Routledge).

Sriskandarajah, D., and Drew, C. (2006) *Brits Abroad: Mapping the Scale and Nature of British Emigration* (London: Institute for Public Policy Research).

Stone, I., and Stubbs, C. (2007) 'Enterprising Expatriates: Lifestyle Migration and Entrepreneurship in Rural Southern Europe', *Entrepreneurship and Regional Development* 19:5, 433–450.

Strathern, M. (1982) 'The Village as an Idea: Constructs of Village-Ness in Elmdon, Essex', in A. Cohen (ed.) *Belonging, Identity and Social Organisation in British Rural Cultures*, pp. 247–277 (Manchester: Manchester University Press).

Theodossopoulos, D. (2003a) *Troubles with Turtles* (Oxford: Berghahn).

— (2003b) 'Degrading Others and Honouring Ourselves: Ethnic Stereotypes as Categories and as Explanations', *Journal of Mediterranean studies* 13:2, 177–188.

Thorbold, P. (2008) *The British in France: Visitors and Residents since the Revolution* (London: Continuum Books).

Tilley, C. (1994) *A Phenomenology of Landscape: Places, Paths and Monuments* (Oxford: Berg).

— (2006a) 'Introduction: Identity, Place, Landscape and Heritage', *Journal of Material Culture* 11:1, 7–32.

— (2006b) 'The Sensory Dimensions of Gardening', *The Senses and Society* 1:3, 311–330.

— (2008) 'From English Cottage Garden to the Swedish Allotment: Banal Nationalism and the Concept of the Garden', *Home Cultures* 5:2, 219–249.

Tombs, R., and Tombs, I. (2007) *That Sweet Enemy. Britain and France: The History of a Love–Hate Relationship* (London: Pimlico).

Torresan, A. (2007), 'How Privileged Are They? Middle-Class Brazilian Immigrants in Lisbon', in V. Amit (ed.) *Going First Class? New Approaches to Privileged Travel and Movement*, pp. 103–125 (Oxford: Berghahn).

Trundle, C. (2009) 'Romance Tourists, Foreign Wives or Retirement Migrants? Cross-cultural Marriage in Florence, Italy', in M. Benson and K. O'Reilly (eds) *Lifestyle Migration: Expectations, Aspirations and Experiences*, pp. 51–68 (Farnham: Ashgate).

Turner, V. (1969) *The Ritual Process: Structure and Anti-Structure* (London: Routledge and Kegan Paul).

— (1982) *From Ritual to Theatre: The Human Seriousness of Play* (New York: Performing Arts Journal Publications).

Urry, J. (1990) *The Tourist Gaze: Leisure and Travel in Contemporary Societies* (London: SAGE).

— (2007) *Mobilities* (Cambridge: Polity).

van de Port, M. (2004) 'Registers of Incontestability: The Quest for Authenticity in Academia and Beyond', *Etnofoor* 17:1–2, 7–22.

van Ginkel, R. (2004) 'The Makah Whale Hunt and Leviathan's Death: Reinventing Tradition and Disputing Authenticity in the Age of Modernity', *Etnofoor* 17:1–2, 58–89.

Veblen, T. (1953[1899]) *The Theory of the Leisure Class* (New York: Mentor).

Waldren, J. (1996) *Insiders and Outsiders: Paradise and Reality in Mallorca* (Oxford: Berghahn Books).

— (1997) 'We Are Not Tourists – We Live Here', in S. Abram, J. Waldren, and D. Macleod (eds) *Tourists and Tourism: Identifying with People and Places*, pp. 51–70 (Oxford: Berg).

Walsh, K. (2006) 'British Expatriate Belongings: Mobile Homes and Transnational Homing', *Home Cultures* 3:2, 123–144.

Williams, A., and Baláž, Z. (2009) 'Low-Cost Carriers, Economies of Flows and Regional Externalities', *Regional Studies* 43:5, 677–691.

Williams, A., and Hall, C.M. (2000) 'Tourism and Migration: New Relationships between Production and Consumption', *Tourism Geographies* 2:1, 5–27.

— (2002) 'Tourism, Migration, Circulation and Mobility: the Contingencies of Time and Place', in C.M. Hall and A. Williams (eds) *Tourism and Migration: New Relationships between Production and Consumption*, pp. 1–52 (Dordrecht: Kluwer Academic Publishers).

Williams, R. (1973) *The Country and the City* (London: Paladin).

Zonabend, F. (1984) *The Enduring Memory: Time and History in a French Village* (Manchester: Manchester University Press (A. Forster trans.)).

Index